ROYAL AIR FORCE
AT WAR

ROYAL AIR FORCE

AT WAR

Edited by Air Chief Marshal Sir Christopher Foxley-Norris GCB, DSO, OBE, MA, CBIM, FRSA

Photo research and captioning by CHAZ BOWYER

Produced in conjunction with and on behalf of the
ROYAL AIR FORCE BENEVOLENT FUND

BOOK CLUB ASSOCIATES LONDON

Foreword

Air Chief Marshal Sir Alasdair Steedman
GCB, CBE, DFC, FRAeS, CBIM
Controller, Royal Air Force Benevolent Fund

This book is by and about aircrew in the Royal Air Force. It is people who have made the RAF what it is today — people of all ranks and trades — and it is essentially the teamwork of that wide range of professionals which has created the success of any flying service. It is membership of that team at all levels which establishes the wonderful comradeship which all of us who have had the privilege of spending our working lives in the RAF cherish.

We are a special family and owe each other and our predecessors, and our dependants, special family care. The Royal Air Force Benevolent Fund is the prime means by which the Royal Air Force looks after its own.

As I write this in December 1982, we are approaching the end of yet another record year in which we shall have disbursed about £4,000,000 to some 9,000 cases, most of which probably involve a family. There are only two criteria considered by our independent Grants Committees when a case comes before them — eligibility and the existence of distress. Where these exist, help is given.

In buying this book you will be helping us help those in need. Thank you from the Fund and from those you will be aiding.

First published 1983

This edition published 1984 by
Book Club Associates,
by arrangement with Ian Allan Ltd

All rights reserved. No part of this book may be reproduced or transmitted in any form or by any means, electronic or mechanical, including photocopying, recording or by any information storage and retrieval system, without permission from the Publisher in writing.

© Royal Air Force Benevolent Fund 1983

Printed in the United Kingdom by
Ian Allan Printing Ltd

Contents

Introduction

Air Chief Marshal Sir Christopher Foxley-Norris

I was very pleased to be invited by the Controller of the RAF Benevolent Fund to edit this book, and my pleasure has increased as the work has proceeded, because the contributions received have each had their especial interest and in many cases recount stories previously untold and unpublished.

It is quite appropriate, although the genesis of the book is for a peaceful and eminently worthy cause, that its subject-matter should be the 'RAF at War', because but for the threat or fact of warfare there would be no requirement for air forces or any other military forces. Apart from the inherent interest of the various stories told, we find ourselves with a fascinating account of the development of war in the air. In spite of the 40 or so years of experience that is covered there is a single thread running through the whole book; a thread of courage, endurance and indeed often of humour, which is perhaps the key to the successes and accomplishments recorded.

The period covered is from 1918 (not previously because the Royal Air Force as such did not come into being until that year) until the end of World War 2. Consequently it may be regarded as now incomplete because the RAF has been 'at war' only too often since then, in Korea, at Suez, in Malaysia and, most recently of all, in the South Atlantic. Among the many operations undertaken by the RAF in that campaign the bombing of the Port Stanley runway has certainly been underrated. The Task Force Commander, Admiral 'Sandy' Woodward, has publicly and generously acknowledged that without that bombing the Argentinian high-performance aircraft could have operated from that runway after refuelling, and his major warships would have been put dangerously, perhaps unacceptably, at risk.

The personal stories in this book derive predominantly but not exclusively from World War 2 for the good reason that few people now have personal memories of fighting in World War 1, with the honourable and distinguished exception of Marshal of the Royal Air Force Sir William Dickson and Air Commodore Freddie West. I also particularly welcome the contributions from French, Belgian and Rhodesian authors. The RAF was by no means manned solely by the British in World War 2 and it is appropriate that this fact should be recognised in this book.

Each story is different but they have one thing in common. They describe ordinary men performing extraordinary deeds when submitting to extraordinary pressures and demands. Probably no one could be found who would describe warfare as something to be desired or advocated. Nevertheless, once embarked on, it does produce some admirable results. The lines describing the Battle of Britain come to mind:

> '. . . a common, unconsidered man, who, for a moment of eternity, held the whole future of mankind in his two sweating hands. And did not let it go.'

Our stories tell of men of that mould and that calibre.

In closing I would like to express my thanks to all the authors who, often at considerable trouble to themselves, enthusiastically and willingly made their contributions (and even on occasion accepted revision and amendment to them), to Alan Hollingsworth and Chaz Bowyer whose professional advice on the text and illustrations was so readily given; and last but not least to Sue Eveleigh who did most of the typing and, almost alone in the world today, can read my handwriting.

C. N. Foxley-Norris

A Truly Historic Development

Marshal of the RAF Sir William Dickson GCB, KBE, DSO, AFC

Marshal of the Royal Air Force Sir William Dickson was originally commissioned in the Royal Navy, and made a considerable name in the testing and development of all forms of the embryo Royal Naval Air Arm, its machines, capabilities and potential; being three times mentioned in despatches. In 1918 he transferred to the RAF and performed with equal distinction on operations.

During the period between the wars he played an active and effective part in the organisation and indeed the battle for survival of the RAF, being a trusted and valuable supporter of Viscount Trenchard. When war came again he commanded groups in Fighter Command and the Tactical Air Force, and later the Desert Air Force.

After World War 2 he eventually became Chief of Air Staff and even more notably, as Chairman of the Chiefs of Staff, became in 1956 the first holder of the newly created appointment of Chief of Defence Staff.

Right: The author.

This first story concerns a particular and less familiar development of air power for which the Royal Air Force became responsible in World War 1.

It starts with some background. Strictly the history of the 'Royal Air Force at War' should commence on 1 April 1918, but its real beginning lies in the activities of both the Royal Naval Air Service and the Royal Flying Corps from the outset of the war. To understand these activities one has to remember that man's so-called 'Conquest of the Air' had only just happened. So both we and the Germans were striving to use this new element and dimension in warfare in every way we could to gain advantage in the main struggle. The Navy and the Army both started the war with small air arms, but so crucial did ascendancy in the air become that by the date of their amalgamation they had each grown into self-contained flying services with their own esprit de corps. The operations of the RFC are better known because of the air battles over France but those of the RNAS were none the less remarkable. Although the smaller of the two it reached a strength of some 2,500 aircraft and in addition to its maritime operations it had fighter squadrons on the Western Front; responsibilities for air defence at home; it carried out bombing raids on German targets and it operated airships. It also played a leading part in the development of the aircraft industry.

My service started in the RNAS when I was commissioned as a pilot in October 1916 at the age of 18. The experiences which form this story commenced a little later when I joined a squadron forming to provide the fighter complement of HMS *Furious*, then being converted into an aircraft carrier.

The *Furious* was a fast unarmoured battle-cruiser. She had been chosen for conversion to deal with the German Zeppelin airships and to give air support to the Fleet. The

Zeppelins were thwarting our primary object of bringing the German Fleet to action because they had our Fleet's movements under constant observation. The *Furious* with her high speed and heavy armament would be able to operate independently on the German side of the North Sea where she would have a better chance of intercepting the Zeppelins. She carried seven Sopwith Pup fighters (later Camels) and two seaplanes for reconnaissance housed in a hangar which had been built over the forward part of the ship. The roof of this hangar had been extended to the stem of the ship to provide the long flying-off deck needed for the seaplanes to take-off on trolleys. In the stern was an enormous 18in gun.

We 'Commissioned' the *Furious* in June 1917 and joined the Grand Fleet in Scapa Flow the same month. The pilots of the squadron were all temporary officers from civil life except our commanding officer who was a regular. It did not take long to find our sea legs and we fell in with the ship's routine under the firm supervision of the ship's officers. We knew little about ships but they knew nothing about aircraft, so there was mutual respect and we soon became a united ship and anxious to show what we could do. To fulfil our mission we had to be almost

continuously at sea patrolling near the Danish and German coasts where we hoped to intercept the Zeppelins operating from their forward base in Schleswig Holstein. Though we failed to make any interceptions our patrols much restricted their reconnaissances because they were alive to our presence and to the vulnerability of the airship to fighter attack. Nevertheless we were very conscious of our limitations. The number of sorties we could make was limited to the number of fighters we carried. After each sortie we would have to ditch our aircraft in the sea and return to harbour in a destroyer. We could not be returned to our ship because of the risk of submarine attack. It is not surprising, therefore, that the pilots should be the first to see what might be a better way of operating landplanes at sea.

And it happened like this. When we were at Scapa Flow we carried out our flying practice from an airfield called Smoogroo. We would often end our flights with a run past the ship and a wave to our sailor friends. With the ship lying head to wind a slow run alongside made the 228ft flying-off deck look an inviting platform. So we began to practise approaches to the deck and to run our wheels along it. Our CO, Squadron Commander Dunning, became so impressed with the

Below: Sqn Cdr E. H. Dunning making his first historic landing in a Sopwith 9901 aboard HMS *Furious* on 2 August 1917.
courtesy OC 201 Sqn RAF

landing possibilities that he persuaded our captain to propose landing trials with the ship under way in the Flow. The proposal was approved by the C-in-C and the Admiralty.

Making a landing on a deck, the approaches to which are obstructed by the central structure of the ship, was not as difficult as might be thought for two reasons. The landing speed of the Pup was very low and the wind speed into which it landed could be increased by steaming the ship into the wind. In a wind of 20knots with the ship steaming at 25 knots, the wind speed over the deck approximated the landing speed of the Pup so by careful flying and use of the engine one could momentarily hover over the deck before touching down. The two difficulties to be overcome were getting the aircraft lined up properly over the deck and securing it after the touch down. The first was dealt with by painting white lines on the deck, and the second by having a landing crew of pilots to run under the aircraft as it hovered and to bear it down and secure it the moment it landed.

The technique of landing was to approach along the port side of the ship keeping the aircraft under control on a flat approach by the use of the engine ('blipping' it). When clear of the structure the aircraft was gently yawed over the centre line of the deck, then straightened up and the wheels eased down on to the deck before cutting the engine.

The first landing was made on 2 August 1917 with Dunning as the pilot. The conditions were good and the landing brought off as planned. We were of course delighted but the result of the trial had a much more important effect in the Admiralty because it opened their eyes to the idea of the deck landing

carrier. In the *Furious* this one successful landing was not enough. We all had to make a landing before landings could be made on operations. We started on this six days later.

Dunning decided to do one more landing before sending off the rest of us. This time he landed safely but due to a gusty wind we could not prevent the aircraft moving backwards and damaging its elevator. Dunning was not happy about this landing and insisted on doing one more. We thought it was going to be all right but, either because he decided he was a bit too high or that he felt he was losing control, he opened up his engine to go round again. It choked, and the aircraft stalled and came down heavily on the starboard wheel. The tyre burst and the Pup cartwheeled over the side into the sea. We expected to see Dunning emerge but something prevented him and he was drowned. We expected the landings to continue but the tragedy of Dunning's death stopped all further landings on the flying-off deck of the *Furious*.

The discussions which led to this decision took place above our heads but we were told that the *Furious* would soon be going in for alterations which would make deck landings easier. So we resumed operating as before. The second conversion of the *Furious* started in November 1917 and was completed in March 1918. When we rejoined her one look at the ship was enough to tell us that this was not the answer. They had taken out the big gun in the stern and built a landing deck in its place with a hangar beneath, but the mast, funnel and all the central structure were still there. It was plain to see that they would cause severe turbulence over the new deck.

In the intervals when we were not at sea we carried out landing trials on the after

Below: Dunning, safely down after his first landing, surrounded by personnel of HMS *Furious*, 2 August 1917. *G. S. Leslie*

This page: After a successful second landing aboard HMS *Furious* on 7 August, Dunning tried for a third landing that same day, this time in a different Sopwith, No N6452. These three views show his third, fatal attempt, and the retrieved wreckage of N6452 with the body of Dunning still in its cockpit. *G. S. Leslie*

Above: An alternative experiment in 'landing on'. Skid-type undercarriage fitted to Sopwith Type 9901A, N6438 aboard HMS *Furious* on 15 April 1918.
MRAF Sir W. Dickson

deck. Everything was tried to make landings possible. Arrester wires were laid along the deck and hooks fitted to the undercarriages. A ramp was built at the end of the deck and a barricade of rope hawsers erected to prevent us hitting the funnel. Skids were tried in place of wheels. But it was no good; the turbulence behind the funnel was too great. We only made three landings without crashing. By sheer luck I think I was the first to pull off a successful landing. I remember it earned me a dinner with the Admiral.

And so these trials were abandoned. The second conversion had not given us a landing deck but the trials had concentrated minds on the deck landing problem and identified the solution which was a deck clear of obstructions. The amalgamation of the RNAS and the RFC had come about just after we rejoined the ship in March. Our first reactions were unfavourable. Our bond with the Navy was a close one, we were proud of the RNAS and we disliked changing our ranks and uniform. But the more we thought about it the more the idea of a single flying service appealed to us. The thrill of flying and of being airmen made us feel more akin to the RFC, for whom we had high respect, than to the Navy. We had a high respect for them too but in a different way. The general Naval reaction was bound to be one of strong disapproval. They were proud of their Naval Air Service and did not like the idea of the Air Force being part of the Fleet. But in the

Furious they took it very well and it made no difference. We were the same people, carrying out the same mission and we carried on as before. On our return to the *Furious* in March we found we had become a Flagship. The C-in-C had appointed an Admiral Commanding Aircraft with an air staff, which included a senior RNAS officer, to direct Fleet air operations. We viewed this with approval. It added to our importance and strengthened our link with the Fleet Flagship which had no airman on its staff.

The amalgamation had incidentally brought an immediate benefit to myself for in May 1918 I was sent on a Flying Instruction Course. This was a system of training pioneered by Lt-Col Smith Barry of the RFC which revolutionised flying training. It taught the pilot to be the complete master of his aircraft in every situation and attitude. To crash on a forced landing was inexcusable. It gave flying a new thrill.

On my return I found the ACA and his staff had recommended a more positive way of dealing with the Zeppelins. It was to destroy them at their base. And so began the planning of the first seaborne landplane bombing operation; the attack of the Zeppelin base at Tondern. It needed careful planning and preparation. The naval operation itself was both complicated and dangerous. The *Furious* and its supporting force had to maintain a position from which our short range Sopwith Camels could reach Tondern and return to the destroyers, but she must not go too close to the enemy coast because of the risk of being cut off by the enemy battle-cruisers. The area was also heavily mined. The Main Fleet was involved in the operation because the vulnerability of the *Furious* might itself serve as a bait to bring out a part or the whole of the enemy Fleet. The plan had therefore to allow for the Fleet to be in the right position during the critical period.

For the air operation special bombs were designed for the Camels and we practised dive-bombing attacks on targets laid out to resemble the shape of a Zeppelin hangar. The operation took place on 19 July 1918. The attack was made by one flight of three Camels followed up by another of four Camels. I was in the first flight. The attack went according to plan. A dawn start and low visibility gave our approach protection from the enemy fighters on Sylt and once we had fixed our position on the main coastline, we broke up to search for the base. We soon spotted the giant airship sheds to the north of the town and converged to make our attacks. We took the northernmost shed and there was no doubt about the result of the attack for a huge cloud of smoke and flame rose up to a great height. We had been told not to

Left: The author taking off from HMS *Ramilles* in a Sopwith 2F.1 Camel from a wood-board 'runway' fitted to the ship's main guns. *MRAF Sir W. Dickson*

Below: A view of a Sopwith 2F.1 Camel on a typically improvised 'runway' aboard ship, 1918. *C. Bowyer*

waste fuel in reforming after the attack and to proceed independently up the coast to a position from which we were to steer a course out to sea to make the rendezvous with the destroyers. If in doubt about our fuel supply we were to land in Denmark. There seemed just enough petrol in my tank for the odd 40 miles so I decided to risk it and turned out to sea. I remember the relief in picking up the wakes of the destroyers in the hazy visibility. I ditched and was picked up by the leading destroyer and we returned to Rosyth. The leader of the second flight, Captain Smart, also was able to make the rendezvous. The others, too low in fuel, wisely landed in Denmark. Lest that decision to turn out to sea be thought to savour of heroics I have to say that it came from an impulsive homing instinct and not from good judgement or sense of duty. But the effect of our return to the destroyers was sensational and far-reaching. Our signalled reports gave the Fleet and the Admiralty the first news that this carefully planned Fleet operation had achieved its object. The Admiralty decided to allow the Press unusual freedom to publicise it and they took full advantage. It was hailed as a triumph of the Fleet over the Germans and there were colourful and exaggerated accounts of the exploits of the Air Force pilots. These gave the public its first news of the Air Force working with the Fleet.

This publicity flared up again a few days later when King George V paid a visit to the Fleet at Rosyth, and Smart and I were made the heroes of the Fleet's success when the King decorated us on the quarter-deck of the Fleet Flagship. I know I felt acutely embarrassed. I did not like to think what my fellow pilots would feel when they got back from Denmark, and I knew that our single raid could not compare with all that had been happening in France. But that was unimportant. What was important was the credit the Fleet gave to the *Furious* and to its Air Force component. It made the Air Force an accepted part of the Fleet.

After Tondern the position of the Air Force in the Fleet became firmly established under the control of the Admiral Commanding Aircraft in the *Furious* and its strength was increased with the arrival of a new carrier, the *Argus*, and the mounting of aircraft on more capital ships of the Fleet. An Air Force Group was formed in Edinburgh to support the Air Force afloat and to co-operate with the ACA. But then came the dramatic surrender of the German Fleet to the Grand Fleet at Rosyth on 21 November 1918 and the end of hostilities. That should end this story of one personal experience of the RAF at war in World War 1 but the story needs a postscript because that eventful commission of the *Furious* was to have historic consequences.

Below: Another view of a Sopwith 2F.1 Camel aboard a RN vessel in 1918. *C. Bowyer*

The end of the war left the Navy and the Air Force in a situation which was both urgent and delicate. The Navy had to reshape itself to carry out its traditional role but it was seriously concerned about its weakness in the air. The Admiralty was therefore giving high priority to the development of deck landing carriers. The situation was delicate because the war had left the Navy with no air service or airmen of its own and it was completely dependent on another Service for its air support; a prospect which the Admiralty viewed with concern and disapproval.

The Air Ministry had the task of establishing the regular Air Force and it knew that its future depended on it fulfilling its responsibilities to the Navy. The situation required most careful handling and the closest co-operation and fortunately for both Services the end of the war saw this off to a very good start in the Fleet. Peace saw no let-up in our activities. There was still everything to learn about deck landing and what was required in both ships and aircraft to make it a practical operation at sea, and during the post-war years and Navy and Air Force co-operated well in deck landing experiments and trials and in the development of Fleet aircraft. The carriers *Argus* and *Eagle*, with their Air Force components, became operational units of the Fleet and work was in hand for further development of the deck landing carrier. But then came the economic recession which cut the Defence Vote to the bone and there were demands for drastic cuts in expenditure. One of the heads for the axe was the Air Force itself which Prime Minister Bonar Law and some others began to regard as an expensive luxury; a view which was shared by the Admiralty and the War Office. In 1923 the Government started a high level Ministerial enquiry into Defence priorities. It sat for four months and visited the Fleet. It conclusions were that the country could not afford the duplication of resources which would result if the Government was to agree to the understandable desire of the Navy to repossess the Naval Air Service it lost in 1918; that the Air Force should remain a separate Service and concentrate on the development of air power over both sea and land, and that the existing system of Navy / Air Force co-operation should continue.

The Government endorsed these recommendations and this gave the Air Force time to establish itself. In later years modifications were introduced which led to a gradual transformation of the RAF units with the Fleet into Naval units and thus to the birth of the Fleet Air Arm as we know it today.

So that first commission of HMS *Furious* was historic in more ways than one.

Below: Seven Sopwith 2F.1 Camels aboard HMS *Furious* on 17 July 1918 — the aircraft used for the successful Tondern attack on 19 July, described in text. *C. Bowyer*

From Mud To Air

Air Commodore F. West VC, CBE, MC

Air Commodore West, whose given name is Ferdinand but who is universally known as Freddie, was commissioned in the Royal Munster Fusiliers in 1914, but spent the last two years of World War 1 with the RFC on flying duties. There he established an unsurpassed record of gallantry, being wounded three times, twice mentioned in despatches, and awarded, apart from a number of foreign decorations, the Military Cross and the Victoria Cross. The circumstances of the latter award disclosed a story of almost incredible courage; it is typical of him that he declined to describe them first-hand in the account of his experiences given below.

His personal characteristics led to much of his later Service life being spent in diplomatic surroundings and he held a number of critical Attache appointments before and during World War 2.

Since eventual retirement from the RAF in 1946 he has led an active and successful life in business, including becoming Managing Director of J. Arthur Rank Overseas Film Distributors.

Below: Lt F. M. F. West (rt) and his pilot Lt Golding, No 3 Sqn RFC, 1917. *C. Bowyer*

In 1914 I was 18 years old, a law student but secretly hoping for adventure and excitement. War broke out between Britain and Germany and I immediately volunteered for service in the Army. In November 1915, I arrived in France as a second-lieutenant in the Royal Munster Fusiliers. After a few days in the trenches my disillusion about warfare was complete — it wasn't the mud or the rats that upset me but the tedious routine duties which consisted in keeping a continuous watch on the few hundred yards which separated us from the German lines. All I could see was masses of barbed wire, shell holes and several corpses in various stages of decay — I was bored. But I was thrilled whenever I saw aircraft manoeuvring in the vastness of the sky and fascinated watching air combats. I felt that airmen went to war like gladiators — I wanted to be one of them — but how to achieve this?

Towards the end of 1916 the Royal Flying Corps, in France, suffered heavy casualties and the Army called for officers with war experience to volunteer to transfer to the Royal Flying Corps for duties as observers. This was my great chance and I immediately volunteered. After training in England I was posted on 22 April 1917 to No 3 Squadron in France, which co-operated with Army units of the 4th Army.

The Squadron was equipped with two-seater Morane Parasols. On my first flight in France my pilot, Lt Edgar Golding, taxied rather fast over a patch of rough ground, the aircraft turned over on its nose and I was catapulted to the ground. Lieutenant Golding scrambled out of the cockpit and having ascertained that I was not hurt told me 'Sorry about this, West. The Moranes are delicate on the ground but most manoeuvrable in the air. Have you heard that Lieutenant Warneford destroyed a German airship with a Morane Parasol and got the VC for it?' Golding tried again, this time successfully. My impression in the Morane Parasol was that I was sitting on the back of a bird and that any hit would cause the aircraft to go down with us in it — parachutes were known but not yet used in aircraft.

Golding gave me about four hours' flying experience over our own lines, during which he made me fire my Lewis gun several times; satisfied with my progress he flew me over the German lines. The Squadron duties consisted of artillery spotting, general photographic reconnaissance, bombing specific targets and firing in to enemy trenches.

I gained my baptism of enemy fire in the air a week later. Whilst Edgar Golding was trying unsuccessfully to destroy a German observation kite-balloon, I suddenly spotted two German aircraft flying above us — I distinctly recollect seeing the 'iron crosses' and yellow and green stripes on the fuselage. They split, one banking to the right and the other to the left of our aircraft. I estimated that they were almost 300 yards behind and about 100ft above us; Golding shouted to me 'I shall keep a steady straight course and you open fire before they do'. I did exactly what I was told to do — as the German fighters dived singly on our tail I opened fire before they did and both German pilots broke combat. This incident made a deep impression on me; I felt that observers should only observe for enemy fighters and at no time concentrate on observing activities on the ground. I must say, however, that there was no general agreement on this in our Squadron.

During the following weeks Golding attacked enemy troops and transport from low heights — our aircraft was often hit by rifle or machine gun fire but luckily not in vital spots. The Squadron suffered a considerable number of casualties and replacement pilots and observers arrived from England. The Commanding Officer split the experienced crews, placing experienced pilots and observers with new pilots and observers. As a result of this action, Golding and I were separated. A week later Golding was fatally wounded and crashed in enemy lines — we had become close friends and his death hit me hard. Fortunately, within a few days I was notified of my selection for training as a pilot in England.

I wanted to be a fighter pilot, but I was told that on the basis of my experience as a soldier in the trenches and as an air observer in the air, I would be more useful in an Army Co-op Squadron. My flying training commenced at Grantham on 1 October 1917 in No 15 Training Squadron commanded by Major Leigh-Mallory (whose brother had climbed Mount Everest). My first aircraft was a two-seater De Havilland 6 Trainer better known to pilots as the 'Sky Hook' or

the 'Clutching Hand'. I received my wings two months later, and found myself with an additional uniform, that of the Royal Flying Corps. It consisted of a double-breasted khaki tunic buttoned up to the throat — familiarly known as the 'Maternity Tunic' — and we wore a Sam Browne belt and khaki forage cap. Dressed in this uniform I was sent for by Leigh-Mallory who told me that he had just been posted to command No 8 Squadron in France and that he had arranged for my posting to this Squadron. I told him how grateful I was for this posting — I liked Leigh-Mallory very much and this was the beginning of a long friendship.

I arrived in France shortly after Christmas — No 8 Squadron was situated in the Amiens area which I knew so well as a soldier in the trenches and as an air observer; I felt quite at home! No 8 Squadron was equipped with Armstrong-Whitworth FK8 aircraft powered by a very reliable 160hp Beardmore engine. The aircraft was known colloquially as the 'Big Ack. It was a general purpose two-seater with a maximum operational speed of about 95mph. The armament comprised a fixed Vickers machine gun for the pilot, while in the rear cockpit the observer had one or occasionally two Lewis machine guns mounted on a movable Scarff Ring. Leigh-Mallory told me that he would

Below: Morane 'P', A6607, of 3 Sqn RFC. *G. S. Leslie*

Bottom: Morane 'P', B1604, of 3 Sqn RFC. *G. S. Leslie*

Right: Captain F. M. F. West standing by the Arc de Triomphe, Paris, 1918 while serving with No 8 Sqn.
C. Bowyer

place me in C Flight — my observers would be Wilkinson, an Australian, and Beaton, a South African. 'These chaps are very tough and independent,' he added, 'but propably very good in a scrap. Remember, West, that you are the pilot and in command of your aircraft — not them.'

For two days my flying was restricted to an area near the aerodrome — this to enable me to get accustomed to my new type of aircraft, especially its manoeuvrability. I did not have an observer with me but just a few sandbags securely strapped into the rear cockpit and as I taxied out ready to take off, I noticed the Australian and the South African observer sitting on the grass watching me. When I completed my test flying no comments were passed — I was told later by other pilots that this was a very good omen.

The routine of our Squadron was two sorties daily — one in the morning and one in the afternoon. We were detailed for any of the following duties: photographic reconnaissance, spotting for artillery batteries, bombing and machine-gunning enemy troops and transport. Of these various duties photographic reconnaissance was most unpopular; flying at about 6,000ft on a steady course we were an ideal target for anti-aircraft gun fire — hardly a photographic sortie was accomplished without damage to our planes. The most popular job was the machine-gunning of enemy troops from a low height. Throughout the month of March No 8 Squadron had been very active. The informa-

tion brought back by all the pilots was of increasing enemy activity. Photographs taken by us clearly showed many more batteries in the Amiens-Bapaume battle zone — we were junior officers, our knowledge and experience was confined to our particular front area, but all of us were convinced that the Germans were 'up to something', probably an early offensive. We repeatedly told this to Leigh-Mallory who agreed and kept 4th Army HQ informed of our reports. On 21 March 1918 the German offensive in the Amiens area was set in motion with considerable initial success. Several other squadrons were then moved into our area — the Germans also brought in air units, amongst them the well-advertised 'Richthofen Circus'. We were told that the circus consisted of their most experienced pilots. Leigh-Mallory concentrated his Squadron effort in ground stafing from low heights. During the period of the relatively short German offensive, the weather was foggy and misty and this in one way protected us from the German fighters. Ground fire, however, was intense and practically every aircraft of our Squadron was hit by either rifle or machine-gun fire. The German offensive was halted by our Army — activity on our front greatly diminished and the Squadron returned to normal sorties.

On 21 April, whilst flying behind our lines in the Amiens sector, I saw a considerable number of flashes from our batteries indicating that German fighters were in our area. I then saw, a few miles east of Amiens, three red Fokkers diving through the smoke of shells bursting around them. I saw one of them diving on what I thought was one of our machines and then to my astonishment the German continued to dive, crashing into the ground near Corby village. There was a rather large field in that locality and after reconnoitering from about 50ft I landed on it. It took Lieutenant Grice, who was with me on this occasion, and myself almost an hour to reach the spot of the crash. We were greeted by a large number of cheerful, enthusiastic Australian artillery officers and men who told us that they had shot down the famous Baron Richthofen. Before leaving I was given by the Australians, as a souvenir, a small piece of Richthofen's cowling roughly cut in the shape of Australia (this is now in the Torbay Aircraft Museum).

Leigh-Mallory told me a few days later that there was much controversy about who shot down Richthofen. His death in any case was a psychological blow to German pride and morale. Later a staff officer at Corps HQ told Leigh-Mallory that a Canadian pilot shot down Richthofen. Although this was not what I had seen, I was not surprised with the news as situations in the air arise and often end in a matter of seconds and of course I

was a few miles away, concentrating on my
work and flying at heights of not much more
than 3,000ft. (60 years later a very large
painting of Manfred FreiHerr Von Richthofen and a small one of me, painted by
the same artist, Mr Henry Campbell, were
unveiled in the RAF Museum in London.
The same day Kommodore E. Willing, Commanding *Jagdgeschwader 71 Richthofen*,
telephoned me at Sunningdale inviting me to
attend the 60th Richthofen anniversary
dinner at their Station in Wittmund,
Germany. My friend, the later Air Marshal
Sir John Stacey at the Allied Forces Central
Europe, also telephoned me to say that the
Germans were most anxious to have as their
guest a British RAF Officer who was actually
flying in the Amiens area when Richthofen
was shot down and who saw his body, and
apparently I was the only ex-RAF Officer
available to attend the dinner.)

The Germans and the French gave much
publicity in their radio and press to the
exploits and victories of their fighter aces —
we in No 8 Squadron were told the names of
Richthofen, Göring (German), Guynemer
and Fonck (French) but we were not told the
names of our own aces. I do not know if this
was a deliberate policy or, as I suspect, just
bad staff work. It is only after the war that I
have read with pride the feats and air
victories of McCudden, Bishop, Barker,
Proctor and Mannock.

In April 1918 the Royal Flying Corps was
renamed Royal Air Force, having
amalgamated with the Royal Naval Air
Service. The reaction in our Squadron was
wonderful — it was a joy and an inspiration
to us to belong to a new arm of the Forces. It
was up to us flying crews to win spurs and
build up the reputation of the new Force.
Leigh-Mallory, about this time, informed me
that I was to take over command of B Flight
and that my promotion to captain would be
published in due course in the *London
Gazette*. As I was leaving his office he asked
me to get hold of J. Haslam, an outstanding
and brilliant artillery officer who was my
observer in the majority of my sorties during
the month of April. When I returned to the
office with Haslam, Leigh-Mallory said 'It is
with great pleasure that I inform you that
you have both been awarded the Military
Cross — well done — thank you'. It is
difficult to explain my feelings that day; to be
in a new Force, in the rank of Captain with
an MC! I felt I could walk on clouds until I
came across the Australian boys who greeted
me with 'Feel important?' That brought me
down to earth. On 2 June Leigh-Mallory
informed me that No 8 Squadron had been
attached to the Tank Corps for specific co-
operation duties, and that my flight would
undertake this task. He added that Captain
Inglis and Captain Tappet of the Tank Corps
would join me the following day. These two
officers explained to us that visibility in tanks
was rather restricted and they thought that
we could be their eyes. We carried out many
experiments but were soon confronted with

many snags. The main difficulty was how to establish a means of communication between aircraft and moving tanks. The tank crews tried to use various coloured flags, but these often were covered with grease and dirt and could not be easily identified from the air. We thought W/T would probably be the answer but if the rumours of a summer offensive were true we would not have the time to try this out. Then the best temporary solution was for pilots to fire Verey lights above or near enemy gun emplacements. The tank officers agreed with our suggestions and we trained on these lines.

On 9 July our Squadron was at Auxi-le-Chateau; at about 6pm on that day one of our fighter aircraft landed, probably for refuelling. After about ten minutes the pilot took off again — when he climbed to about 100ft he turned steeply to the left and in so doing, stalled and crashed. The pilot was killed. Our medical officer told us that the dead pilot was wearing the purple ribbon of the Victoria Cross. The following day we were told that he was Major McCudden — he was buried with full military honours in the small British cemetery at Wavans a couple of miles north of Auxi-le-Chateau.

On 7 August General Sir John Salmond, the head of the Air Force in France, visited our Squadron, now situated at Vignacourt in the Amiens area. We were not told beforehand of his visit. I was so busy detailing crews for various duties and showing on a board the latest air photographs, pinpointing location of enemy batteries, that I did not notice the various visitors in our marquee. Apparently Major General Sir John Salmond, two Army Staff Officers and Leigh-Mallory had been listening in the background

for several minutes — Leigh-Mallory then called us to attention and Sir John came forward, saying 'I have some important news for you — tomorrow the Army are launching the biggest and probably the last offensive of the war. They expect the Germans to throw in their considerable reserves. The Army C-in-C needs the earliest possible information of where these reserves are massing or moving to — I ask every one of you to do all you can to get this information — Good Luck'. The morale of the Squadron was marvellous. On the following day, my observer Lieutenant J. Haslam and I took off at dawn. There was a thick mist on the ground but at about 1,000ft the sky was blue and cloudless. Hundreds and hundreds of gun flashes and hundreds of lights of various colours were piercing the mist and creating a kind of red glow. It was a beautiful sight — the whole front, on the ground and in the air, was alive but unfortunately the movement of German troops and transport was taking place under a blanket of mist. On 8 and 9 August we had narrow escapes both from the ground and from enemy fighters. On the 10th however, weather conditions changed and whilst flying low at about 1,500ft we saw a large concentration of German troops around vehicles and lorries. This I knew was what the Army needed to know so I decided to return immediately to our aerodrome to pass on this information.

The sky was full of enemy fighters and on that day the RAF suffered heavy casualties, Haslam and I amongst them. A German fighter of the Richthofen Squadron shot us down. On the same day I suffered the amputation of my left leg, well above the knee, in a disused monastery situated a few

Below: Armstrong Whitworth FK8 — nicknamed 'Big Ack' by its crew. *C. Bowyer*

miles behind our lines and which had been converted into a casualty field post, and Haslam, who was wounded in the legs and wrists, was sent to a hospital further down the lines.*

Towards the end of September my name was removed from the 'Dangerous List'. I was then transported to the London Hospital in Whitechapel; whilst in that hospital, awaiting to be invalided out of the RAF, I resigned myself to resuming my law studies. My hopes and dreams of a flying career had suddenly vanished. Life, however, is to a

*It was for this action that Captain West was awarded the Victoria Cross. The most effective way to perform the essential task of locating major enemy formations proved to be to fly low and attract their fire. This Captain West and his observer did for three consecutive days. On the third day he came under sudden and heavy fire from a wood, clearly indicating the unsuspected presence of a large concealed enemy force. Having flown over his target three times to confirm this fact, he set course for base to bring back this vital information. But enemy fighters were also well aware of its importance and he came under heavy and continuous attack from them, during which he was shot through the right foot and his left leg was almost completely severed by explosive bullets. He suffered enormous loss of blood but managed to improvise a tourniquet with his underwear and eventually contrived to make a safe landing behind our lines, where his machine continued to be strafed by enemy fighters in an unsuccessful attempt to silence him. After being rescued by Canadian troops, he insisted on transmitting an accurate and detailed account of his reconnaissance before allowing himself to be taken to hospital for treatment.

Sir John Salmond, then Major-General Commanding the RAF in France, later Marshal of the Royal Air Force, has justifiably described his conduct as 'of superb gallantry'.

certain extent like a roulette game — you never know in which slot the ball of destiny will fall. Shortly after Armistice Day I met a Mr Desoutter, a Swiss Engineer, maker of precision instruments. He told me that he had lost a leg in a car accident, after which he designed for himself an aluminium leg which enabled him to climb mountains and fly an aircraft. He then told me that he had recently fitted an English actor, Herbert Marshall, with one of his aluminium legs. This actor was very happy with it and had resumed his acting on the stage. If you can spare about £80, he added, I will fit you with one. Fortunately I accepted the offer. General Sir John Salmond and Sir Hugh Trenchard, I don't know how, heard that I could walk reasonably well with my new artificial limb. Sir Hugh Trenchard sent for me at the Air Ministry and in his very deep voice straight to the point told me 'Do you think that you could fly with that tin leg of yours?' I replied 'Certainly, Sir'. He then said 'Good'. 'Sir John Salmond,' he added, 'told me about your work in France. I want you in my new Force — I shall have problems with the medics but I will see that you will get a permanent commission in the RAF.' My name was in the first list issued to the *London Gazette* in 1920 and to my delight also Leigh-Mallory and Haslam's names were also on the list.

I began flying again at Northholt. I didn't visualise it then, but in September 1939, as a group captain, I would fly to France in command of No 50 Wing, consisting of Nos 4-13 and 5 Squadrons, flying a Blenheim, in the very same area which I had seen war service both on the ground and in the air.

Below: Capt F. M. F. West MC, with Italian Lt Delagard, 8 Sqn, 1918. The AWFK8 is C8594 in which West earned his VC on 10 August 1918.
C. Bowyer

Cocks O' the North

Air Vice Marshal A. Johnstone CB, DFC, DL

'Sandy' Johnstone made his name as a fighter-pilot, particularly as a squadron member of 602 Auxiliary Air Force (the native squadron of Glasgow whence he hails) and in the epic battle for Malta.

After the war he served several times in the Far East, being the first Chief of Air Staff of the Royal Malayan Air Force, and also Forward Air Commander in Borneo during 'Confrontation' with the Indonesians. His last appointments before retirement in 1968 were with Coastal Command.

He has a considerable reputation, particularly in Scotland, as a radio and TV broadcaster, to which his friendly outgoing personality is well suited. He wrote and recounted the TV series *Where No Angels Dwell* and his books include *Enemy in the Sky* and *Adventure in the Sky*. His is an active member of the Battle of Britain Fighter Association.

Below: The author.

No 602 (City of Glasgow) Squadron AAF Drem October 1939-August 1940

As soon as the boundary fence disappeared under the port wing I knew I was travelling too fast and started swish-tailing the aircraft from side to side in a desperate attempt to lose speed. But it was no good; the Spitfire bounced merrily into the air again whenever its wheels touched the ground and went on bucketing and leaping down the hill like a hen on a hot griddle. I knew I should have opened up and gone round again, but it would have been such a blow to my pride. After all, I was a senior flight lieutenant in 602 Squadron!

We seemed to be gathering speed, not losing it, as the Spitfire continued its mad career down the slope — a slope much steeper than I had been led to expect — and the boundary hedge was coming closer at an alarming rate. Then there was a wonderful moment when we began to slow down, but the hint of relief quickly turned to one of acute alarm on realising it was only because the wheels were sinking into a stretch of soft ground, with the aeroplane squelching noisily into the middle of a bog, sending a spray of mud in all directions. The Spitfire finally came to rest with its nose buried in the quagmire and its tail sticking in the air like a grotesque old totem pole long since abandoned by the Indians.

I got down from the elevated cockpit by sliding down the sloping mainplane, reflecting ruefully that it was the 13th — Friday the 13th of October 1939, to be exact. What a way to turn up at our war deployment base! The only consolation was that the pupils of the Flying Training School had already left Drem or I would have never heard the end of it.

A fire engine was rapidly approaching and I watched with increasing alarm as its crew leapt off and unrolled a length of hose which was pointing in my direction. I dodged quickly out of the line of fire. 'There's no need for that, Sergeant,' I shouted. 'I've switched everything off and it's not going to blow up!'

I was saved a soaking in the nick of time. That would have been altogether too much. The NCO in charge turned to his men. 'Leave the flippin' foam, Murphy, and roll up the hose . . .' then he turned to me and saluted. ' . . . You know, sir, we've never had one down here before!'

I could well believe it as I watched some of our comparatively inexperienced pilots coming in with no trouble at all. Granted it was my first flight in a Spitfire since recovering from the concussion received when crashing into a hillside at the beginning of the month, but I had nevertheless underestimated the degree of the slope at the bottom of the airfield and should have known better than make the approach at such unseemly speed. Now there was nothing for it but to swallow my pride and accept a lift to the flights in the fire tender. Rupert Watson was there to greet me. 'Irvine warned me you would be coming,' he grinned, 'but he didn't say you'd be arriving on a fire engine! Never mind, toddle over to the house for a drink this evening if you haven't been put in jail before then!'

Rupert's brother, Irvine, and I had been instructors at the flying training school at Prestwick until I was called up in late August, when he had stayed on at Prestwick to help churn out more pilots. In the meantime, his elder brother had continued to run the family farm at Fenton Barns, part of which comprised the airfield at Drem.

This Watson property seemed destined for disruption, for a large part of it had been commandeered in 1915 as an aerodrome for the RNAS during World War 1. Nevertheless it had borne fruit, for Dr Chalmers Watson had then only recently developed a vaccine for ridding dairy cattle of tubercular diseases, and had subsequently bred the only TT-tested herd in the country. The financial compensation had been considerable. The family re-possessed their property at the end of that war and the famous herd continued to thrive so, when the place was requisitioned for the second time in 1938, the Exchequer was again faced with a hefty bill by way of recompense. In fact Irvine once confided that it was all a darn sight more profitable than having to face the caprices of weather and marketing — the normal bugbears of Scottish farmers.

Fortunately my Spitfire had only sustained minor damage so, after fitting a new prop and receiving a sharp dressing down from my commanding officer, we were back in business the following day, thanks to the sterling efforts of the servicing crews who worked late into the night to get 'Q' back on the line. And it was as well they did, for we had no sooner settled into our new surroundings when the entire Squadron was ordered off to tackle a formation of enemy bombers which ventured up the Forth estuary to attack a number of naval units moored off the dockyards at Rosyth. This was the first occasion when British fighter squadrons had gone into action over the United Kingdom after which, having broken the ice, the Luftwaffe began paying frequent visits to our local shores, thenceforth keeping us on our toes — morning, noon and night.

Sensing better pickings at Drem than from fighter bases further south, a few regular squadrons talked their way into being sent there, after which the permanent staff of the

21

one-time flying training school, long indoctrinated in the spit and polish associated with ab initio training establishments, suddenly found themselves faced with the slap-happy, casual ways of fighter pilots, to say nothing of the Auxiliaries' well-known tendency to interpret King's Regulations in their own fashion. A certain tension soon became noticeable and it was not long before the staff realised that the station was now running them instead of the other way round. This was a situation the Station Commander was clearly unwilling to tolerate.

Charles Keary was one of the old school; a man of stern principles who himself set high standards and expected the same from those serving under him. Although never admitting it, Charles Keary must have been disappointed when he posted to No 13 Flying Training School, for Drem was a rough sort of place, having only a scattering of wooden buildings and two or three small hangars, and lacking many of the trappings of an up-to-

date flying training establishment. Besides, the surroundings were drab and frequently muddy, so it was not easy for him to impose his high standards of dress and discipline.

Nevertheless he had ruled his command with a rod of iron from its inception and had just managed to get things into some sort of order when the war started and he was told that his training school would be moving out to make way for at least one fighter squadron. His heart must have sunk at the news, for he had heard plenty about those extroverts who paid scant regard to protocol and even less to barrack square disciplines.

No 602 Squadron must have been a particular thorn in Keary's side during these first few months at Drem, for the weather was at its worst and most of us took to wearing hand-knitted mufflers and other non-regulation items of apparel to combat the extreme cold. Douglas Farquhar, our CO, was frequently summoned to the Station Commander's office. '... Farquhar...,' the air of grievance was more marked than usual on this occasion, '... your officers cause me nothing but worry. They must be smartened up or there will be trouble, and I mean to do something about it. I am calling a station parade and inspection for ten o'clock on Saturday morning when all personnel not on duty will attend. Best blues will be the order of the day!'

Douglas pointed out that some of his pilots would be resting after maintaining the readiness state throughout the night and might they be excused. He also drew his attention to the 10 inches of snow lying everywhere around, so where was the parade to be held? 'Between numbers one and two hangars, of course, and there are to be no absentees. Those on night duty can turn in after the parade.'

Saturday was a crisp clear day, a sub-zero temperature making the snow sparkle in the early light while parties of disgruntled airmen toiled with picks and shovels to clear an area large enough to accommodate the personnel of two squadrons as well as the unfortunates from the station headquarters staff. Eventually all was set for the parade to begin.

Officers and airmen alike were stamping feet and swinging their arms vigorously across their chests in an effort to keep the circulation going. It was cold — bitterly cold — and all were hoping the Old Man would take pity and shorten the proceedings accordingly. The order to 'stand properly at ease' rang across the parade ground when the adjutant spotted the highly polished staff car edging its way slowly towards the cleared area, the noise of its tyres crunching on the frozen snow clearly audible to those on parade. The car skidded to a standstill in front of the small saluting dais and I watched

Below: Sqn Ldr Andrew Douglas Farquhar OC 602 Sqn AAF, receiving a DFC from HM King George VI, 26 February 1940.
via N. L. R. Franks

an orderly step forward to hold the rear door open as the Group Captain climbed out. We braced ourselves for the next words of command. They were not long in coming.

'Pa - rade . . . !' The precautionary word of command sounded very loud in the icy stillness. 'Parade, A - TEN - SHUN!'

The echo of 600ft stamping the ground had barely died away when there was a muffled oath from out front. This was followed by a heavy thud. All eyes were now riveted on the Station Commander who, caught unawares by the icy conditions, had come an almighty cropper and was arriving on the parade ground flat on his back, leaving us with nothing more to salute than a pair of immaculately polished size eights sticking up in the air. The parade was abandoned there and then.

January 1940 wore on into February, the snows finally melted and we were able to concentrate on the more orthodox tasks of keeping watch over our shores or carrying out protective patrols over convoys of small ships creeping up and down the neighbouring coastline. And, as time went on, Charles Keary began to appreciate that we were not always as bad as he had first thought, although he was reported to have heaved an enormous sigh of relief when 602 Squadron moved to Aberdeenshire in early March to help cover the withdrawal of the British forces who had been battling it out with the Germans in occupied Norway. But his period of solace was short-lived as we were ordered back to his station after only six weeks in the chilly north. But Drem had taken on a new look in our absence.

Sandbags had been piled round most buildings on the operational site whilst windows had been heavily taped to stop glass from splintering in the event of a bombing raid. The hangars had been covered in camouflage paint and the aircraft dispersed along the eastern perimeter of the airfield: a battery of anti-aircraft guns poked muzzles over the tops of their emplacements and a number of Army officers were sharing our mess. Drem at least *looked* ready for war.

A great many patrols were flown during this period although few brought us into contact with the enemy. Nevertheless, by the end of May, the Squadron had been credited with the destruction of eight German aeroplanes, with others probably destroyed or badly damaged, although we ourselves had also suffered damage to a number of our own aircraft, mostly in the course of training new pilots. Several youngsters were experiencing difficulty in seeing over the long noses of the Spitfires when making their approaches in the dark and the profusion of flames spurting from the short exhaust stubs only made matters worse. However one learned in time

to devise one's own best way of creeping round a circuit at night.

Everything appeared to be running smoothly and we were settling into a comfortable groove. Most were getting a fair whack of time off and perhaps were not fully alive to the fact that the German hordes were steam-rollering across Western Europe and even then driving hard for the Channel ports. Suddenly the whole scene changed. Charles Keary was posted from Drem in the middle of June.

There were few in the Royal Air Force of 1940 who had not heard of the Atcherley brothers, Richard and David. Identical twins, their exploits were legion long before the outbreak of hostilities and there can be few officers in any of the Services who managed to survive so many official raps over the knuckles, as did Richard, and still go on to attain air rank. As a member of the winning Schneider Trophy team in 1932, for example, he executed a perfect slow roll in the SRN.6 at the end of the course after most experts predicted that the seaplane would almost certainly break into a thousand pieces if subjected to more than a gentle rate one turn. Nor did his propensity for knocking off policemen's helmets endear him to members of that force either, particularly as his father, Sir Llewellyn Atcherley, was then the Chief Constable of Yorkshire.

Nonetheless, whatever else could be said of him, Dick Atcherley took up the reins at Drem with an unrivalled reputation for getting things done — albeit not necessarily things of which his superiors always approved — and we had looked forward with great interest to the arrival of this legendary character who had been described to me on one occasion as the nearest thing to an unguided missile. Having myself only recently assumed command of the Squadron, it was not long before I was working hand in glove with the new boss and finding out that the old order was in for a might big shock.

The dispersal of our aircraft was the first item to attract his attention: 'The present arrangements are lousy — worse than useless!'

Walter Churchill and I watched Batchy pacing the floor of his office. Churchill was CO of 605 Squadron.

'Go and take a look if you don't believe me. All lined up in neat rows just asking to be strafed! You'll need to do better than that! Find somewhere else to park them and let me know when you've come up with a sensible answer.' Walter pointed out that we had already tried everything we could think of, including flying our spare aircraft to another airfield. 'Besides, sir,' we added, 'There aren't enough starter batteries to go round and it would play havoc with scrambling times if

we had to run the equipment from one side of the aerodrome to the other every time we were called on.'

Batchy took the point and sat down. 'Then we must find somewhere to hide the aircraft,' he went on, '... somewhere protected and near the ground crews, eh? Come on you two, it shouldn't be beyond your meagre intelligence to solve a small problem like that!'

The Station Commander joined us when we went on to the airfield to size up the situation. Batchy was right. 602's aircraft were stretched out in a vulnerable straight line along the eastern perimeter whilst those of 605 Squadron were in equal jeopardy to the north. But everywhere else looked just as exposed — nothing but open ground for miles around except for a small wood beyond the southern boundary.

'What about those trees?' Atcherley was pointing in the direction of the distant copse. 'Let's walk there and take a look!'

In spite of muttered protests about lots of paper work waiting for us in our orderly rooms, we found ourselves striding in the wake of our energetic station master towards the trees. We came upon the fuselage of a wrecked transport aircraft half way down the slope. Walter spotted it first.

'What's this? It looks like the remains of an airliner!'

Of course, neither Batchy nor Walter had been at Drem when *Scylla* came to grief. They stopped to examine the wreckage while I explained how it happened.

Most civilian transport aircraft had been pressed into service by the RAF at the outbreak of hostilites and the larger machines were often used to ferry essential personnel and equipment of fighter squadrons when they were being deployed from one airfield to another. The well-tried HP42's of Imperial Airways were particularly suitable for this task and *Scylla* had landed at Drem one evening in April on just such a mission. It had been a windy day — so much so that our aircraft had already been picketed down before the giant transport landed — and we realised it would be no easy job to tether such a large aeroplane. So, when the call went out for more picketing screws and men to handle her, we gathered outside the crew room to watch the monster being secured for the night.

It was clearly going to be quite a problem. Every gust snatched at the huge biplane and shook it like an angry parent scolding a naughty child. Its massive fabric-covered wings fluttered alarmingly. Yet the picket ropes held and several petrol bowsers were run alongside to begin the task of refuelling the large tanks fitted high on the upper mainplanes. We could see the navigator and flight engineer sitting inside the spacious cabin, presumably working out their flight plan for the following day.

The wind increased in strength. It also began to veer to the north, when there was a sudden scurry as hats were blow off by a particularly fierce gust which sent their owners scampering in hot pursuit. Then someone shouted above the noise.

'Look! Look!' Everyone was pointing excitedly towards the giant aeroplane as it slowly began to tilt. It continued to heel over — quite gently at first — plucking picketing screws from the ground as if they had been hatpins stuck into a slab of butter.

We stared in awe while the cumbersome craft went on rolling until her starboard wingtip was about to touch the ground. Surely she must now right herself. But no, poor old *Scylla* continued her gyration with a fiendish screeching of tearing metal and twanging of snapping wires until she finally came to rest upside down with a loud thump, her cabin now high in the air. Then, as if glad to be rid of the intolerable weight resting upon them, the two large landing wheels began to turn round in the howling wind.

As soon as the aircraft began to heel over the two unfortunate crew members realised they were trapped and were forced to walk up the walls and on to the ceiling as *Scylla* came to her undignified resting place. However they were not unduly worried, for someone would surely fetch a ladder and get them down. But they had failed to make allowances for the quick-wittedness of the troops who, as soon as quantities of aviation spirit began pouring from the inverted tanks, disappeared to a man to fetch anything that would contain this manna from heaven.

They quickly reappeared, whooping with delight and bearing a motley collection of pots, pans, tins, jugs, teapots — anything watertight — and raced towards the hapless machine like a horde of Red Indians on the warpath to gather beneath the wings whilst trying desperately to catch a few pints of the precious fluid to eke out their own meagre rations. That most of it was being blown away by the wind was no deterrent; they chased the flying spray far and wide until the last vestige had gone and then, and not until then, did someone suggest it would be a kindness to fetch a ladder and release the stranded crew. The derelict fuselage had been dragged from the scene soon after and had remained abandoned on the edge of the perimeter ever since.

'We could use it as a dispersal!' Batchy was quick to appreciate the potential of our find. 'Dammit, it's even got a galley — and a loo!'

We had not gone far into the wood before Batchy stopped and looked around. 'This will do famously . . . !' Walter and I stole a look at each other as Batchy went on ' . . . Don't you see, if we clear away a few trees we could bring the aircraft in here. It'll make a first class dispersal! Come along, we'll fetch some paint and start marking the trees we want taken out.'

Thus a gang of us, armed with pots of paint and billhooks, spent many tiring hours splashing blobs of paint on trees and tough pieces of briar, to say nothing of ourselves, as a guide for a number of bulldozers conjured up by the amazing Atcherley. Not only had he come by these mechanical monsters with apparent ease, but he had paid a visit to nearby Fettes College in Edinburgh to persuade the Head of that splendid establishment that a few days in the freshness of the Drem woods would do his boys infinitely more good than swotting over musty desks in pursuit of less demanding academic matters. So a fleet of double-deckers arrived on the airfield and decanted several hundred youngsters ready and willing to come to grips with the toughest parts of Batchy's wood. Recompense? Nothing more than a couple of square meals and the promise of a flight in an RAF aeroplane at a later date.

To meet the latter commitment, a fleet of multi-seater aircraft was got together by the Station Flight — Harvards, Battles, Tiger Moths were all pressed into service — whilst Batchy himself managed to borrow a visiting Blenheim bomber into which he packed the lads four or five at a time, usually subjecting them to a programme of aerobatics or, as happened at the end of one trip, to a final screaming approach across the airfield upside down, at the same time raising the undercarriage just in time to roll the aircraft the right way up and land off the subsequent turn. That the boys said they enjoyed these flights spoke wonders for the quality of tact they were being taught at Fettes College. Thanks largely to their sterling efforts, however, the strange dispersal was completed in record time and remained in use for many years to come.

Having dealt successfully with the wellbeing of our aeroplanes, Batchy then turned his attention to that of the fellows who flew them — particularly the senior pilots who, because their added experience made them the regular choices to carry out the night patrolling, had been finding it difficult to get adequate rest amid the hurly burly of normal daylight station routine.

'We'll look for somewhere quiet where they can get a decent rest away from the noise of aircraft.' he pronounced one day.

'Somewhere out in the country. Hand me that survey map, Sandy.'

Walter and I again found ourselves being sidetracked from our normal duties while we toured the countryside in search of suitable premises with Batchy. Charles Keary's pride and joy, the highly polished staff car, was now unrecognisable under a livery of mud-coloured camouflage paint and, as Batchy always drove it himself, it rapidly showed signs of wear and tear, probably because he only seemed to know two speeds — flat out and stop! Not surprisingly, too, his passengers quickly showed signs of early distress when driving with the gallant wing commander, for it was his policy never to slow down at a cross-road, believing that the faster it was crossed the less chance there was of anything else hitting him. Indeed it wasn't long before we were behaving like two jibbering idiots and reduced to such a state of funk that we were prepared to recommend the very first property to come into sight, irrespective of its suitability or location.

Batchy must have cottoned on to this for we found ourselves replaced by our wives who, he said, would have a much better understanding of what was required. But we had to put a stop to that ploy too after discovering the girls drinking doubles in their attempt to anaesthetise themselves against the nerve-wracking rides ahead.

A few nights after we had been relieved of the house-hunting chore, an intruder suddenly appeared from nowhere and flashed low across the airfield, disappearing westwards at a rate of knots. We could only assume that the crew of the Ju 88 had not spotted Drem in passing for he neither dropped any bombs nor opened fire. Being the stand-by pilot, I was airborne and after him in a matter of seconds, of course, but never managed to catch up with him in the dark. Apparently the wretched fellow merely climbed to a few thousand feet and dropped a number of small bombs on the outskirts of Leith before stuffing his nose down and scooting back to base on the other side of the North Sea. However, returning later to the vicinity of the airfield, I found it impossible to pick out the flarepath through a steady drizzle, even when I switched off the cockpit lighting completely. For some reason, too, the exhaust flames seemed to be more intrusive than usual that night.

Unbeknown to me, however, Batchy had been so infuriated at the impudence of the German raider that he had ordered all airfield lighting to be extinguished, including the goosenecks on the flarepath. 'Johnstone . . .' he was heard to mutter, ' . . . knows enough about Spitfires to find his own way down without having the place lit up like a Chinese fairground!'

But it was not as easy as all that. Granted, I had been able to position myself on the downwind leg by the headlights of a couple of cars approaching the main gate, but was baffled to see no flarepath ahead and had to open up and go round again. Having no radio contact with the airfield itself I was unaware that the flares had been dowsed in my absence, so had another shot at coming in, thinking I had perhaps flown too far to one side. Fortunately Batchy was still at our dispersal and ordered the first two flares to be lit after which I could make the usual curved approach on to the path itself. He waited in the crewroom until I came in.

'Getting scared in your old age?' he greeted me with a wide grin. 'Never mind, I think I've got the answer and we'll try it out tomorrow. I'll have them put a radio set in my car, then I can talk to you. What's your operating frequency?' I told him and asked what was on his mind.

'I'll lay a semi-circle of glim lamps round the circuit which should lead the chaps on to the correct approach path. I'll load the car with glims tomorrow night and you can tell me by radio where to position them.'

It surprised me that no one had thought of this simple solution before. We put it to the test the following evening. Fortunately the weather was dark and clear and I was easily able to pick out each glim lamp as Batchy put it in position.

'Hello Villa Leader,' his voice was indistinct on the makeshift radio link.

'How's that for size?'

After adjusting an odd position here and there we hit on a pattern which just fitted the normal circuit of a Spitfire, thus leading the pilot accurately to a position whence he could easily pick up the leading flares over the side of his cockpit. Batchy was delighted with his handiwork.

'We'll call it Drem Lighting, eh? I'll get the electricians to wire up the circuit so that it can be switched on and off from the Watch Office, then it needn't be used until an aircraft comes into the circuit.'

He was also angry at the anti-aircraft gunners for failing to respond to the recent intrusion.

'Dozy lot! They'd probably have missed in any case for I doubt whether they've mastered even the most elementary principles of deflection shooting!'

So our worthy colleagues in the Royal Artillery became next in line for the Atcherley corrective treatment.

Thenceforth frequent practice attacks were laid on to keep the gunners on their toes, whilst camera attachments were fitted to the guns themselves to help assess the results. Regretfully they were not encouraging. The young detachment commander was naturally apprehensive on being summoned to Batchy's office. He was well aware of his men's shortcomings — they stuck out a mile — but, as he was at pains to point out, most were young conscripts who had received very little training before being sent to join his battery. '...besides, Sir...', he added, '...few have a natural aptitude for it and appear incapable of understanding the reason for laying off for deflection. I'm doing all I can to teach them but seem to be getting nowhere. Can you do anything to help me?'

Batchy thought for a moment before replying. 'Leave it with me for a day or two, Taylor, and I hope I'll find a solution. Carry on with normal training for the time being.'

I was passing one of the gun sites a few days later when a familiar voice hailed me from behind the sandbagged emplacement. 'Hey Sandy, come and see my new toy!'

Rupert Watson and one of his farm hands were inside, alongside a couple of regular soldiers. All were wrapped up against the chilly wind. And, judging by the way Rupert was bossing everyone around, he seemed to be the man in charge. 'Did Batchy not tell you? He's asked us to man the guns for a while as he believes we country folk, including our poacher friends, are better natural shots than these young townies. He wants us to take over as soon as we can master the gubbins, but I hear Taylor's not very happy about the arrangement. I don't think he likes the idea of his guns being taken over by a bunch of scruffy civilians!'

I was not surprised. In fact Lieutenant Taylor was most put out by Batchy's latest ploy and reported to his bosses in Edinburgh who bore down on Drem in a fleet of staff cars to restore the status quo without more ado, when the lads in khaki retrieved their weapons and things returned to normal.

No one at Drem escaped the dynamism of Batchy's presence, even if they did not set eyes on him from one week to the next. Even if they failed to see him, they certainly heard him.

The wing commander often chose to sleep in a camp bed in his office rather than waste time travelling to and from the Officer's Mess. He had also instructed his signals staff to install a public address system throughout the station and he used this on every conceivable occasion to ensure all personnel were kept in the picture. Alas he had a habit of waking early when his first act of the day was to press down all switches together and subject the entire station to an exhortation to pull its collective finger out and get on with the tasks of the day. But Drem was a happy station under his dynamic leadership.

When Batchy and I happened to be walking across to the mess one evening we pased one of the orderly room clerks who was coming from the airmen's dining hall. The young lad's face lit up on sighting his popular Station Commander. 'It's a fine evening, Sir!' he called in passing. Batchy stopped.

'Come here, young man,' he called after the airman, 'What I want from you is a salute, not a ruddy weather report!'

Even then one felt instinctively that no policemen's helmets would be sacrosanct so long as Batchy was alive.

Nor were they.

Below: Re-arming and refuelling a 602 Sqn Spitfire, 1940. *C. Bowyer*

Two Escapes at Tangmere

Marshal of the RAF Sir Thomas Pike GCB, CBE, DFC

The late Marshal of the Air Force Sir Thomas Pike joined the RAF through Cranwell. Much of his wartime services was in Fighter Command and in the Desert Air Force. He established a considerable personal reputation as a night fighter pilot and played an important part in the development of its early techniques.

His postwar career included senior appointments in NATO, in which he played an important part in the establishment both of the military navigation of the Alliance and of the influence and participation of the United Kingdom in it. His last three Service appointments were as Commander-in-Chief Fighter Command; as Chief of the Air Staff (he was the first Cranwell graduate to hold the latter office); and as Deputy Supreme Allied Commander, Europe.

After leaving the active list he played a major part in the activities of the Royal Air Force Association. He died in June 1983.

In January 1941 I left the Air Ministry and went to the night fighter OTU at Church Fenton near York for a short refresher course and conversion to the Blenheim. There were not enough Beaufighters to spare for training and so all our flying was done in the Blenheim. After one month I was judged proficient and went straight to Tangmere as CO of No 219 Beaufighter Squadron. Here I did a little more flying in their one and only Blenheim and then on to the Beaufighter. This was a good aeroplane which I liked very much. It was strong and very well-armed, with four cannons and six machine guns, but it was slow. It was equipped with Radar (or RDF as it was then called) but this was of a very rudimentary kind — unreliable and difficult for the operator to understand and to use. However, it was vastly better than nothing and without it the interception rate was almost zero.

The night of the first of these stories, in early 1941, was a moonlit night with quite a lot of cloud about and there was every reason to suppose that German bombers would be over as soon as it became dark. So we went to have an early supper in the mess as usual. This was a peacetime building which consisted of a central area with dining room and recreation rooms and a wing on either side for the bedrooms. Solidly built it was very comfortable, but too small, of course, for the large wartime influx of officers. However, we all enjoyed the spirit that pervaded everywhere (mostly led I may say by Douglas Bader) and it was good to be among the Spitfire pilots from the other squadrons on the station.

After an indifferent supper on wartime rations, I went off to the Squadron dispersal hut which was the other side of the airfield about a mile away, I suppose. By this time it was dusk and the Beaufighters were parked on both sides of the taxi track and near, to the hut. After a word with the flight sergeant and the two ground crew to make sure all was OK with my aircraft, I went into the hut — put on my dark glasses and sat on one of the beds. All the night fighter aircrew wore these glasses before take-off and it tookabout 20 minutes before one's eyes got completely acclimatised to the dark. The glasses were dark blue and although it was possible to recognise people and see where you were going it was not possible to read through them. We always took off singly and we had a roster for the order of take-off. We flew the same aircraft (unless, of course, it was unserviceable) and we flew as a crew of two. My crew-man or radar operator was Sergeant Austin, a quiet and imperturbable type and we got on very well together. He was not a man to grumble about anything, which was just as well!

We were second off on this night and were told to patrol Beachy Head at angels 20 (20,000ft). Soon we were above the cloud, with no chance at all of seeing Beachy Head

and so we could only guess that we were more or less in the right place. Nothing happened for about half an hour as we went slowly round and round, when suddenly I saw an aircraft pass directly under us. It was going north and just slid by underneath at right angles. It was a simple matter to turn right, drop down 500ft and soon we were on its tail. We were quite close and could see it quite clearly but I simply could not recognise what it was. I asked Austin what he thought it was and got the unhelpful reply 'No idea'.

At this point I recollected that a few nights previously someone had shot down a Wellington by mistake. My gun sight was on the target, the safety catch was off and my finger, or rather my thumb, was on the firing button, but I hesistated. Better to call ground control and be sure I thought. So I called up ground control and asked if there were any friendly aircraft near me, which was a silly question really because they had no more idea than we did where we were and so back

Above left: Boulton Paul Defiant 'nightfighter' — an early makeshift. *C. Bowyer*

Left: Beaufighter X7583 in black 'soot' livery, which served with No 68 Sqn later.

Above: Sqn Ldr George McLannahan of 604 Sqn AAF in his Beaufighter at Middle Wallop. *G. McLannahan*

ground control and told that there was trouble at base — change to Channel C on the radio and call 'Vanguard'. This I knew was Middle Wallop about 50 miles away where 604 Squadron — another Beaufighter Squadron — were based. So we diverted to Middle Wallop and spent the night there, swapping experiences with some of the pilots of 604. At dawn we started up again and flew back to Tangmere where we saw last night's 'trouble' — a few bomb holes on the airfield and very close to the runway was a sandbag castle which turned out to be an unexploded bomb which the army had surrounded by sandbags. I thought to myself — every man to his trade and how glad I am that I am not required to put sandbags round unexploded bombs!

Having landed, I went over to the mess to get some breakfast and as I approached I could see more trouble. First I saw a thin wisp of blue smoke and as I rounded the corner I could see that the right hand wing had received a direct hit. The front half of the roof had collapsed and the whole place was in a mess with soldiers and a bulldozer trying to straighten it up. Then, as I came up to it, I could see that the bomb had acutally entered my room and there was nothing left but a large hole in the ground now being filled up by the bulldozer. I got the driver to stop for a few minutes whilst I searched for some of my belongings but there was nothing left at all. No money, no clothes, no razor — it was a strange feeling, but a lucky escape for me although sadly not so for two of my friends sleeping nearby — I could so easily have been the third.

Now to come to the second 'Tangmere escape'. Some 25 years later, I found myself serving at the NATO Headquarters of SHAPE just outside Versailles. This was an international headquarters and of course there was quite a large German element of navy, army and air force. Once a year we would leave our desks for a week and disappear into the forest for an exercise. We all enjoyed this interesting experience and after the day's work was over we would sit around and gossip not only about the exercise and life at SHAPE, but what was really more interesting — we would swap experiences of the last war.

On one of these occasions I was talking to a German friend who by this time was a brigadier general in the German Air Force. He told me this story. 'In 1941', he said, 'I was a second lieutenant stationed at Lille. I was the pilot of a Ju 88 and one night we set off to bomb Liverpool. It was a moonlit night and we flew along the north coast of France in order to avoid any British night fighters. In due course we turned right and headed for Liverpool. We attacked our target and then

came the reply 'Transmit for fix'. This was always rather a laborious business in those days: it involved three D/F stations each about 20 miles apart listening to your transmission, rotating the aerial until the transmission reached maximum volume and then noting the angle of the aerial. This, they would then telephone to the operations room where three people would place a string across the map table and where the strings intersected, this is where you were — more or less.

I gave the usual transmission for a fix with plenty of words to tell them to hurry up — but alas in my haste I cut it too short and the reply came back 'Transmit again'. This I did and after what seemed like hours back came the reply 'No friendlies in your area'.

Unfortunately, with all this fooling about, I had throttled back too far and the target was now out of sight. I pushed the throttles full open, but it was too late, we never saw it again. Where it was going I don't know, somewhere in the Midlands, because there was no attack on London that night.

After this very amateurish and shameful episode I continued on patrol for a further hour without event and was then called by

turned for home along the same route that we had come. The weather was clear and all seemed well. When we reached what I thought to be the north coast of France I turned left on a heading that would take me to Lille. (It is interesting to note here that the distance between the southern tip of Wales and the north coast of Cornwall is much the same as the distance across the English Channel at that point.)

After flying for an hour or so I began to realise that something was wrong. I had seen no navigation beacons which I should have recognised and in fact I was completely lost. However, I continued on course because there wasn't anything else I could do and after a while I saw runway lights ahead and thought to myself 'home at last'. The lights seemed quite familiar and I came down and landed along the runway. At the end I turned off along the taxi track which I could see partly in the moonlight and partly with the aid of my landing lamp. After a short while I made out the shape of a hangar and to my dismay I saw an aircraft and vehicles which were certainly not German.

I realised at once that I had landed somewhere in England and immediately swung the aircraft off the taxi track and on to the grass, opened the throttles and took off at right angles to the runway. The aircraft was lightly loaded and we soon cleared the airfield and climbed away. I headed south-east as I thought this must certainly take us over France or Germany and flew on this course

Above: Beau crew. Sqn Ldr G. McLannahan (rt) and Flt Lt R. C. Wright, with Beaufighter T4637, NG-O, 604 Sqn.
G. McLannahan

Left: Beaufighter VI, MM856, NG-C, of 604 Sqn.
J. Wilkinson

for two hours. By this time the weather had clouded over and since we had no idea where we were, I slowly descended through the clouds. Soon we were under the cloud and to our consternation the anti-aircraft guns opened up — the aircraft was hit and set on fire. At this point we all baled out and landed in our parachutes on the edge of Frankfurt airfield.'

This is the story which he related to me and I only asked him one question because it never crossed my mind that I should ever try to write it down. 'Where was it you landed in England', I asked? 'I'm not sure', was the exact reply, 'but taking everything into account, it must have been Tangmere'.

Now the funny thing is that I was stationed at Tangmere for almost the whole of 1941 and if a German aircraft had landed at night and then taken off again I should certainly have known about it. Or should I? We normally only operated two or three aircraft at a time and after having departed on patrol there would be little activity for about two hours. We had no flying control in those days — only one chap on top of the watch tower with a red or green lamp. He was usually asleep! The operations room was in Chichester and could neither see nor hear anything that was happening on the airfield.

No one with any sense was sleeping on the airfield unless he had to and so there were very few people about. This may sound hard to believe, but it is well illustrated by another experience I had at about the same time. I was on patrol minding my own business when suddenly one engine stopped. Since a Beaufighter did not like flying on only one engine, I called the operations room and told them the problem and then landed back at Tangmere. At the end of the landing run I tried to taxi back to my dispersal point, only to find that it was impossible to taxi anywhere other than in a circle and a small circle at that. So, Sergeant Ausin and I climbed out and walked back the half mile or so to our dispersal hut. When we got there, everyone seemed to be a bit surprised to see us and someone said 'you're back early — what happened?' 'We walked home', I replied, and no one thought it the least bit funny — least of all myself.

Perhaps if these stories tell us anything, it is how casual and amateurish everything operational was in the early days of the war, in comparison with the later stages and of course the state of affairs today. But at least they show how one could be lucky enough to get away with things nevertheless — and at least justice was done since the first escape was British and the second German!

Right: More Teeth. R2274, a Beaufighter V fitted with a four-gun BP turret and test-flown by 29 Sqn. It later served with 406 Sqn, RCAF. *Imperial War Museum, MH.4563*

Below: Beau VIF (NF) 'K' taxying. *Imperial War Museum, CM.15213*

The Munsterland Business

Pierre Clostermann DFC and bar

Pierre Closterman was one of the small but select band of French pilots who refused to accept the national surrender in 1940 and followed General de Gaulle to England to renew and continue the fight against Germany. A number of the finest pilots, Monchotte, Martell, Remlinger and Closterman formed the first Free French unit, No 341 'Alsace' Squadron. Later with increasing experience and with natural gifts of leadership, they were dispersed among regular RAF and Commonwealth fighter squadrons.

Closterman himself established a reputation second to none among his compatriots. For three years he was continuously and hectically engaged on fighter operations in the European theatre. He was awarded the DFC and bar; he has graphically described his experiences in his book *The Big Show*.

Since the war he has had a distinguished career in two fields, politics and civil aviation. He was elected as a Deputy to the French parliament; and he has been a leading figure in the Marcel Dassault organisation.

The Germans, in war-time, raised obstinacy to the level of a national virtue. When Providence adds luck to this attribute, certain situations arise which defy logic. The *Munsterland* will certainly go down to posterity as a symbol of Teutonic stubbornness, and of British obstinacy too, if it comes to that.

The *Munsterland* was a fast ultra-modern cargo ship of 10,000 tons equipped with oil-burning turbine engines. She had been surprised in a Central American port by the Pearl Harbor attack and had made for Japan. There in due course she had loaded a precious cargo of rubber and rare metals and had then calmly sailed for Germany again. Fortune favours the brave, and, by a series of incredible circumstances, she had succeeded in slipping through the air and naval patrols and making Brest. She was immediately photographed and dive-bombed three hours later by 24 Typhoons. Towards 6pm on the same day, 32 strongly escorted Mitchells attacked her, still without appreciable results. In the course of the night she made for Cherbourg at full speed and was again photographed as soon as she made port. A study of the prints showed that everything was ready for her to be discharged. Three flak ships from Havre and two from Saint-Malo had anchored off the Pelée at dawn and sizeable light and heavy flak units were in position. Extremely unfavourable meteorological conditions led to the failure of a raid laid on at about eight in the morning.

Without medium bombers it was difficult to cope with a problem of this magnitude. The Beaufighters could not intervene as the layout-out Cherbourg harbour did not lend itself to a torpedo attack. The Bostons might at a pinch have tried a low-level bombing attack, but the powers that be could really not send them in to be slaughtered at 250mph.

Left: Pierre Clostermann congratulating Flt Lt Ken Charney DFC when serving with 602 Sqn AAF (Spitfires).
Imperial War Museum, CL.552

The weather was getting worse — rain, fog, low cloud.

At 0845 the flying personnel of the Spitfire Wing, in which I was a pilot, were urgently summoned to the Intelligence Room. Nos 602 and 132 squadrons were put at immediate readiness.

First Willie Hickson, in a speech improvised for the occasion, reminded us that the *Munsterland's* cargo was of vital importance to German industry. The thousands of tons of latex she carried, suitably mixed with the synthetic leuna product, would enable no fewer than 22 armoured divisions to be equipped and maintained for two years. The special metals would be precious for German metallurgists producing jet engines. In addition the Kriegsmarine must not be allowed to get away with the moral fillip of such a flagrant breach of the blockade. Thirty-six Typhoons equipped with 1,000lb delayed action bombs were to force an entry into the bay and try to sink the *Munsterland* or set her on fire. A special dispensation of Command had bestowed the delightful task of escorting them on 602 and 132 Squadrons. Our rôle would consist in neutralising the flak ships with cannon and machine-gun fire and then covering the operation against the important German fighter forces massed in the Contentin peninsula in case of need. To increase our radius of action the Wing would put down at Ford, where the refuelling of the aircraft had been arranged, and from there we would take off again for the rendezvous with the Typhoons, over Brighton at zero feet.

Wing Commander Yule, prospective leader of the operation, reminded us briefly that flak ships were normally armed with four quadruple automatic 20mm mountings, and with four or eight 37mm guns, also automatic. The last Photographic Reconnaissance Unit photos had revealed, along the mole linking the six forts of the roadstead, at least 190 light flak guns, probably reinforced and very active since our client's arrival.

In principle the two squadrons would split up into six sections of four which would each look after a flak ship, in order to reduce them to silence for the few seconds necessary for the passage of the Typhoons. After that, they were free to take such offensive action against any fighter formations as might be necessary. Obliging to the end, Command had decided to lay on a special air-sea rescue service, the fast launches of which would be strung out between Cherbourg and the British coast along our track. Even for the most enthusiastic among us, this last arrangement looked suspiciously like belated remorse on the part of Command and had a sinister implication which considerably chilled the atmosphere. The last preparations before we took off were carried out in silence. Only Joe Kestruck made a disillusioned remark to the effect that every time the Navy made a balls of a job, the poor bloody RAF had to clear up the mess. At Ford there was the usual panic about tyrebursts and flat starter-batteries. Luckily Yule's long experience of advanced airfields had led to the provision of three reserve aircraft per squadron and at 0950hours 602 and 132

Squadrons took off at full strength. I was flying as Blue 4, next to Jacques who was Blue 3, in Ken Charney's section.

On our way to the rendezvous we passed three Bostons whose task was to scatter, over a stretch of 20 miles towards Cape de la Hague, strips of tinfoil designed to jam the German radar. Thanks to this, and to the mist, we would probably reach the entry to Cherbourg without being picked up. We joined up with the Typhoons at house-top level over Brighton, and set off obliquely for Cherbourg, skimming the grey sea. I loathe flying so low as that with all the paraphernalia of supplementary tanks and cocks. Somewhere or other there is always liable to be an airlock, enough to make the engine cut out for just the fraction of a second necessary to send you slap into the drink at 300mph.

We flew through belts of opaque mist which forced us to do some very tricky instrument flying a few feet above the sea, which of course we could not see. The Typhoons, in spite of the two 1,000-lb bombs under their wings, were setting a cracking pace and we had a job to keep up with them. Obsessed by the idea of seeing the red light on the instrument panel going on (indicating a drop in the flow of petrol to my carburettor), I began to sweat from head to foot. What would it be like when the flak started?

1015hours. The fog thickened and its started to pelt with rain. Instinctively the sections closed up to preserve visual contact. Suddenly Yule's calm voice broke the strict RT silence: 'All Bob aircraft drop your babies, open up flat out, target straight ahead in sixty seconds!'

Freed of its tank and drawn by the 1,600hp of its engine, my Spitfire leapt forward and I took up my position 50 yards on Jacques' left and slightly behind him, straining my eyes to see anything in the blasted fog.

'Look out, Yellow section, flak ship, 1 o'clock!'

And immediately after Frank Wooley, it was Ken Charney who saw a flak ship, straight in front of us!

'Max Blue attacking 12 o'clock!'

A grey mass rolling in the mist, a squat funnel, raised platforms, a mast bristling with radar aerials — then rapid staccato flashes all along the superstructure. Christ! I released the safety catch, lowered my head and nestled down to be protected by my armour plating. Clusters of green and red tracer bullets started up in every direction. Following Jacques, I went slap through the spray of a 37mm charge which only just missed me — the salt water blurred my windshield. I was 50 yards from the flak ship. Jacques in front of me was firing; I could see the flashes from his guns and his empties cascading from his wings.

I aimed at the bridge, between the damaged funnel and the mast, and fired a long, furious continuous burst, my finger hard on the button. My shells exploded in the water, rose, towards the water line, exploded on the grey black-striped hull, rose higher to the handrails, the sandbags. A windscoop crashed down, a jet of steam spurted from somewhere. Twenty yards — two men in navy-blue jerseys hurled themselves flat on their faces — 10 yards — the four barrels of a multiple pom-pom were pointing straight between my eyes — quick — my shells exploded all round it. A loader carrying two full clips capsized into the sea, his legs mown from under him, then the four barrels fired; I could feel the vibration as I passed a bare yard above — then the smack of the steel wire of the aerial wrenched off by my wing as I passed. My wing tip had just about scraped the mast!

Phew! Passed him.

My limbs were shaken by a terrible nervous tremor, my teeth were chattering. Jacques was zigzagging between the spouts raised by the shells. The sea was seething. Half a dozen belated Typhoons passed to my right like a school of porpoises, bearing down on the hell going on behind the long granite wall of the breakwater. I skimmed over a fort whose very walls seemed to be belching fire — a curious mixture of crenellated towers, modern concrete casements and Thirty Years' War glacis.

We were now in the middle of the roadstead — an inextricable jumble of trawler masts and rusty wrecks sticking out between the battered quays. The weather seemed to have cleared a little — look out for Jerry fighters! The air was criss-crossed with tracers, lit up by flashes, dotted with black and white puffs of smoke.

The *Munsterland* was there, surrounded by explosions, flames and debris. Her four masts bristling with derricks and her squat funnel well aft emerging from the smoke. The Typhoon attack was in full swing, bombs exploding all the time with colossal bursts of fire and black clouds of smoke, thickening as they drifted away. A Typhoon vanished into thin air in the explosion of a bomb dropped by one in front. One of the enormous harbour cranes came crashing down like a house of cards.

'Hullo, Bob leader, Kenway calling — there are Hun fighters about, look out!'

Want an inferno! I was close to Jacques, who was gaining height in spirals, making for the layer of clouds. Two Typhoons emerged from a cumulus, a few yards from us, and I just stopped myself in time from firing at them. With their massive noses and clipped wings they looked uncannily like Fock-Wulfs.

'Break, Blue Four!'

Jacques broke away violently and his Spitfire flashed past a few yards under my nose, a white plume at each wing tip. To avoid a collision I waited for a fraction of a second and a Focke-Wulf — a real one this time — flashed past, firing with all four cannon. A shell ricocheted off my hood. As I went over on my back to get him in my sights, a second Focke-Wulf loomed up in my windshield, head-on, at less than a hundred yards. Its big yellow engine and its apparently slowly turning propeller seemed to fling themselves at me and its wings lit up with the firing of its guns. Bang! Stars appeared all over my splintering windshield which became an opaque wall before my eyes. Thunderstruck, I dared not move for fear of a collision. He passed just above me. A stream of oil began to spread all over my hood.

The sky was now alive with aircraft and full of flak bursts. I let fly at another Focke-Wulf and missed. Luckily!... it was a Typhoon. Robson was circling with a German fighter. I saw his shells explode in the black cross on the fuselage. The Focke-Wulf slowly turned over, showing its yellow belly, and dived, coughing smoke and flames.

'Good show, Robbie! You got him!'

My oil presure was disquietingly down. The rain began again and within a few seconds my hood was covered with a soapy film. I slipped into the clouds and set course north on instrument flying, first warning Jacques and Yule over the radio.

I reached Tangmere as best I could, with my oil pressure at zero and my engine red hot and ready to explode. I had to jettison my hood to see to land.

In this business we had lost two pilots, as did 132. Seven Typhoons were destroyed, plus two which came down off Cherbourg and whose pilots were picked up by the launches.

As for the *Munsterland*, although seriously damaged and with part of her cargo on fire, she succeeded two nights later in sneaking as far as Dieppe. She finally got herself sunk off the coast of Holland by a strike of Beaufighters.

Ops Tonight

Wing Commander E. W. Anderson OBE, DFC, AFC

'Andy' Anderson was a schoolmaster in peacetime and joined the RAF in 1940 as a Pilot Officer in administration. The death of an air crew friend led him to volunteer for flying and, despite 'advancing age' and a suspect right eye, he managed to pass on to training in Canada and then on to bomber operations. He soon discovered another inherent 'weakness' — he was air-sick every time he flew. That he overcame all obstacles and continued on operations is evidenced by the fact that he left the Royal Air Force in 1954 as a Wing Commander OBE, DFC, AFC.

He joined the Path Finder Force as the senior navigation officer on the headquarters staff and stayed for two years, often going on operations to test new ideas. His navigation logs were later used by postwar bomber crew instructors as model examples and became known as the RAF's foremost navigator.

Anderson's story is taken from *Path Finders at War* by Chaz Bowyer (Ian Allan).

The most striking thing about operations is the unreality. You wake up in the morning, warm, safe, and comfortable, roll out of bed, wash, shave, and stroll through the fields to the mess for breakfast. The sun is shining and the little white clouds are chasing each other across the sky. Everything is quiet and peaceful. Only — curious thought — you may be shot at tonight.

At about 10 o'clock the word comes round, 'Ops tonight, briefing at 1800 — six o'clock'. The routine work goes on, a training flight with a new navigator, a visit to the gen-men who look after the 'magic eye' on the aircraft to discuss a mysterious fault that developed the night before last; or a browse in the intelligence library reading reports of past raids and looking at photographs of the results.

The navigators' briefing begins half an hour earlier than the main briefing. The room is a long, low Nissen hut with 15 or 20 tables and a 100 or so chairs all facing an array of maps and blackboards. There is a large wall map of Europe covered with red and blue patches to show the Hun defences. The route is marked out with coloured tape, and by the target a collection of brightly-coloured pins indicate the colours of the markers that will be dropped. On the blackboard to one side is a large drawing of the target; on the other side is another blackboard with a list of skippers who are 'on', together with times of take-off, bomb loads, and so on. Above is a third blackboard, long and thin, with a cross-section of the weather and the clouds to be expected on the journey.

Out of the satchel comes the chart — pink. The route to be followed must first be drawn, and then a flight plan calculated. This is a forecast for the flight, complete with the times for the various stages or 'legs', and the directions in which the aircraft must be flown to offset the drifting caused by the wind. The work is done very carefully and precisely, and

Left: The author.

the mind escapes gratefully into a maze of intricate little niceties. The height that we shall cross the enemy coast is at the moment just an academic problem.

The rest of the crew come in and chatter and are helpful and distracting, but by six o'clock the work is nearly finished. Then the squadron commander walks over towards the map of Europe, and the talking dies away as we settle back in our chairs to listen. Even the briefing itself is curiously remote and unreal, full of drab technicalities. First, weather; cloud heights, freezing levels, icing indexes — 'moderate icing in the layers of stratocumulus cloud'. Then the route; 'turning point, 52.17 north 00 00 west, then on a track of one-four-two true . . .' — we note it all down. Next, the exact instructions for the target; 'If there's more than seven-tenths of cloud below, primary flare-droppers will revert to the role of blind markers dropping sky-markers yellow with green stars' — and so on. The details of the run-in; '. . . . come in at 17,000, air speed 170 indicated, release first bundle 27 seconds after coincidence' — cold, impartial, and precise. England expects that every man will have his stop-watch working accurately. One last word, 'There's four pounds eleven on it tonight, and the photos before zero don't

count'. For we each put a shilling into the pool every trip, and the crew that gets the best aiming point photo, scoops the lot. And we turn and grin at the crew who were disqualified for cheating the other night. On the last operation that crew had deliberately gone into the target two minutes early, all alone with no protection, just to get a picture before the smoke of battle spoilt it — the cads!

Briefing is over. The gunners, wireless operators and flight engineers drift away, and the pilots, navigators and bomb aimers are left to make the final arrangements and to complete the flight plan. Soon everything is ready, and we go down to the Mess for supper. The operational 'supper' is a curious business. For some extraordinary reason it must consist of bacon and eggs, which is just about the worst thing possible on which to fly. For the fried food makes gas inside, and as you fly up into the rarer air four miles up, you swell a little and feel the more uncomfortable. Yet cries of rage and disappointment would rend the air if for this traditional dish a more digestible titbit was substituted. So we eat our bacon and eggs and think how lucky we are and how the poor types in civvy street must envy us with their one or two eggs a month. Afterwards, we sip

Below: The last moments — crew ready to leave.

our coffee and then the word comes round that transport has arrived to carry us up to the airfield.

From now until we are off the ground the tension will grow. The mind slips away to a safe distance, and sits somewhere far off, watching the hands pull on flying boots and tie the knots on the tapes of the Mae West. It listens, detached, to the last instructions from the skipper. Suddenly stops and catches itself in the curious feeling that exactly this has happened somewhere before. Looks at the sunset and counts the rooks going home, and then contemplates the body climbing into the lorry. Is suddenly grateful for the cheerfulness of the gunner sitting on the tailboard. Climbs into the aircraft and watches while the chart is pinned down. Smiles ironically at the grin and the thumbs-up sign that you give the skipper as he clambers by, and notices how effeminate he looks in his helmet, like a bathing cap. Then sits and waits. Knowing that in three hours' time the body will be over the target. And that once there, some twisted pride will drive it to do the job almost against the will of the mind itself.

Then comes the loneliness and a longing for the waiting to be over. The operation, that will be a cold impersonal routine once it has begun, seems awful as the huge, black shapes of childhood's dreams. A message. 'Operations scrubbed. Weather over target is hopeless.' Flat, cold and deflated, like the shrivelled toy balloons of yesterday's Christmas party we climb heavily out of the aircraft and go back to the changing room, the mess, and to bed. Safe, warm, comfortable again. Only — there will be tomorrow night.

Climax

'Oxygen full on'. In six minutes' time we shall be over Berlin amongst the first wave of Path Finders. But our 'magic eye' has broken down, and so I am lying down in the bomb-aimer's position glaring through a sheet of glass at the ground four miles below. We shall not drop our fireworks, for eyes are liable to mislead, wishful seeing is all too easy, and there are only two places for our markers, the exact aiming point or the bomb bays. Yet our journey will not have been wasted. We shall go in with the first wave and that will help to swamp the defences. If we do get 'picked on', well, someone else will get a free run-in. And, incidentally, we have in addition to our markers several tons of bombs on board which will do the target just a little bit of no good. So at the moment we

Below: Karlsruhe under fire — note T1s cascading at top left.

are all eyes and perhaps that little extra oxygen may help. For we must find out where we are so that we don't blunder along all on our own.

The defences are waking up. Ahead, slightly to port, are great, menacing cones of searchlights that divide and come together and divide again, like sinister but stately folk dancers. Flashes of light in the sky are appearing to starboard, flak bursts, looking somehow surprised like asterisks. 'Three minutes to go' from the navigator. 'Can you see anything?' from the skipper. 'Searchlight coming up behind to port' from the tail gunner, and one of the points of light at the bottom of a pale beam becomes dazzling and light up the bomb sight and the frost on the window, and then fades and passes on. No sign yet of the early flare-droppers. They ought to be on target by now. And in spite of the voice of past experience, the present doubt comes stealing in, are we alone? Are the others with us? Why is everything so horribly quiet?

Quite gently, a little ball of golden light appears far below and to starboard, and then another and another. Beside them little patches of houses begin to grow, and reflections of water and roads. The first Path Finder flares are down. More golden balls appear, silently and mysteriously, and these little patches piece slowly together. Quite suddenly, there is that bend of the river, there the railway station, there the great wide avenues run together, there is the Templehof! Berlin is spready out ahead and to starboard. The skipper swings the aircraft over and I am pressed hard down on to the floor. Slowly, very slowly, the world tilts, and the lights of those flares swing round ahead. Then we level out for the final bombing run. Time stands still. The target lies quietly before us with the little golden balls floating just above it. More searchlights spring into life and flashes appear on the ground, either guns or bombs from the flare-dropping Path Finders. A bump tells us that we have flown through a slip-stream. Ahead and below the black shape of a Lancaster, tilted slightly, slides across in front and disappears to port. Puffs of smoke, black against the searchlight below, run by. Then just ahead a little worm of pale green fire appears abruptly in the sky and sprays forward like shining drops of water from the rose of a watering can, then splashes suddenly alongside the railway station. 'Bomb doors open'.

After that there is nothing but those green markers and the cross of light on the bombsight, like the handle of a sword. Those bright flashes are photographs being taken, those big, dull, slow splashes of light are

'cookies' those quick spurts are guns firing or 500-pounders bursting. Two more green markers go down and make a rough triangle, and then right in the middle falls a red so that the aim is shifted a little. For tonight, specially picked crews are carrying red markers which will be dropped only if they are absolutely sure of their aim. Very slowly the red marker creeps up underneath the aircraft. The whole world is concentrated in your two eyes. A word and the markers are twitched a little to the right, and now they are just touching the sword blade itself. There is no Berlin, there is no bomber, just a red mark and a sword handle. Slowly the mark slides up the hilt, and for a second the sword handle is poised above it, and then with all my might I squeeze the tit, my right thumb forcing the button down into its socket, as I drive those bombs out of the bomb bays down on to the target below. 'Bombs going' — the little light by the bomb switches goes out — 'Bombs gone'. I peer forward and watch them go, black and shiny in the searchlights.

It is hopeless to try to tell where those bombs actually hit. Sticks are dancing continuously across the target. Deep, angry, red pools are lighting up below the smoke. Intense white flashes and slower yellow gleams, waving searchlights and red flak bursts. The navigator's voice comes over the intercomm, 'Course out two-nine-one, two-nine-one', and I realise that I am still squeezing the bomb tit desperately. I climb up and stand beside the pilot. Slowly, so slowly, the aircraft banks over and dips one wing into the smoke and fire that is Berlin. Suddenly a red dotted line of tracer shells goes streaming by our wing tip, not aimed at us, but there must be fighters about. Over the target something is burning in the sky, an aircraft is on fire, and the green lights are falling from it. She blows up with a slow red flash and pieces go flaming down while the searchlights hold for a few moments on to the cloud of black smoke.

The aircraft levels off and we set out on our long struggle home. Flying blindly on calculations, helped a little by the line of searchlights by Magdeburg, and the cones at Bremen and Wilhelmshaven, we cross the German coast at last and head out across the North Sea for England and bacon and eggs. Soon the searchlights are left behind, and everything seems quiet and still. Then, far below on the water, a little light starts blinking faintly. And the mind sees there or four men huddled in a dinghy, cold and wet. There is just nothing we can do. We circle once and then carry on. When we get back we shall be able to estimate the position and let the rescue boys know. So we leave the light winking desperately behind until finally it is lost to sight. And we are silent for a little while.

The rings of lights round base twinkle cheerfully up at us and we learn that our 'turn to land is number three. Fly at 4,000 feet'. Then follows a code word to tell us that there are no intruders about. Intruders are Hun night fighters who sneak across with the returning bombers hoping to shoot them down as they come in to land. We circle the airfield, seeing every now and then the green and red wing-tip lights of other aircraft stooging round waiting their turn to land. Below is the flarepath, a double row of lights, with a red and green pin-prick crawling along between them as a Lancaster lands on the runway.

A few minutes later and we are bumping along between those two rows of lights, and taxying round to Dispersal between lines of faint blue glow-worms, waved on by ground crew with torches. 'Are they all back?' is the first question. 'All but one have either landed or are overhead.' An hour later and the interrogation is over. 'Any news?' 'Still one not back yet.' And we remember the aircraft that blew up over the target, and the light on the water that we left winking behind us. We go back to the mess for food. And afterwards, 'Any news?' 'Afraid not'. In a few days' time seven new faces will be on the squadron — that's all...

Below: Hanover on 22 October 1943; note Salkstrasse illuminated.
Imperial War Museum, C.3898

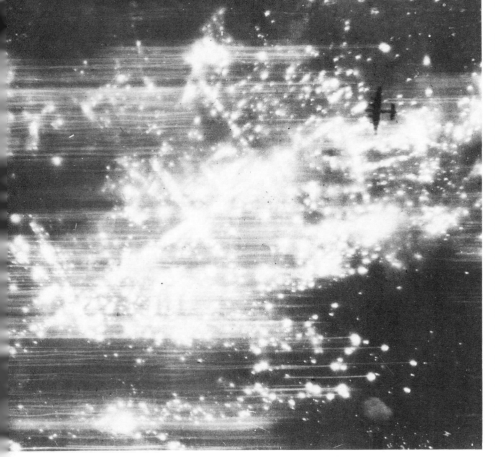

Below: Lancaster crew after
bombing Berlin at de-briefing
at Swinderby on
23 November 1943.
*Imperial War Museum,
CH.18658*

Left: Flg Off P. Ingleby at his
navigator's position in a
619 Squadron Lancaster on
14 February 1944.
*Imperial War Museum,
CH.12288*

Flying Secret Agents To and From Enemy Territory

Air Chief Marshal Sir Lewis Hodges KCB, CBE, DSO, DFC

Air Chief Marshal Sir Lewis Hodges entered the RAF through Cranwell shortly before the war. He served on operations throughout the first four years of the war specialising in and pioneering the techniques of flying agents into and out of occupied France. For his skill and courage in these particularly hazardous operations he not only received four British decorations but the French Legion d'Honneur and Croix de Guerre.

After the war he had a varied and highly successful Service career. His last two appointments were as Air Member for Personnel, and later Deputy Commander in Chief, Allied Forces, Central Europe.

Since retirement he has remained closely involved with the welfare of the RAF and its people, particularly through the RAF Benevolent Fund, the Royal Air Force Association and the Royal Air Force Club, for whose current thriving condition he has been largely responsible.

A bomber station in England, 1942. A Halifax four-engine bomber took off from Tempsford and flew south, towards the Channel and France. The night was clear and the moon just rising above the horizon. As the aircraft approached the French coast to the west of Le Havre, the observer took up his position in the nose, to be ready to get an accurate pin-point as they crossed into France. The pilot pushed the control column forward and the aircraft nosed down to gain speed and lose height ready for the low level journey into the interior of enemy-occupied territory. As the coast loomed up, clearly defined in the light of the moon, a searchlight beam could be seen sweeping the sky away to the left towards the port of Le Havre. The captain warned the crew to stand by for evasive action in the event of light flak from German anti-aircraft guns, and the dark sky was illuminated with what looked like 'fire-balls' spurting up from unseen gun emplacements.

A rapid jink to the right and the bomber was through and over the mainland of France, gaining speed and losing height down to an altitude of 500ft above the ground; the height at which it would speed on its way southwards towards its destination — a remote area in central France, where men of the Maquis were waiting to receive a load of arms and stores to be dropped to them by parachute. The task of the bomber crew was now to navigate to the particular spot where the 'reception committee', as they were called, would be waiting, and this was no easy job. At low level, map reading was the only aid, and with the French countryside flashing by at 200mph — villages, roads, rivers and railways — it required great concentration to keep the aircraft on track. In the moonlight, the undulating farm lands of northern France always looked so serene and peaceful and it was difficult to imagine that the country was under enemy occupation. As

Right: The author.

the ETA for the dropping zone approached, the crew of the aircraft scanned the horizon ahead, looking for the winking light which would guide them to the dropping area. Once the morse signal was seen and acknowledged by the crew, the DZ was illuminated by a triangle of torches and the pilot ordered 'stand by to drop'. The aircraft swept round for a run into the target area; the bomb doors were opened and the red light came on, followed by the green, and the dispatcher would let go his load from the hole in the floor and at the same time containers would be released from the bomb bay. The whole load of much-needed weapons and explosives would float gently by parachute into the hands of those gallant Frenchmen who fought in the resistance movements.

This was the pattern of the operations carried out by Nos 138 and 161 Squadrons, the special duties squadrons of Bomber Command, during World War 2. These squadrons had the job of supplying the French, Belgian, Dutch, Danish and Norwegian resistance movements, and guerilla forces in Poland and Czechoslovakia with men and materials they needed to carry on the task of harassing the Germans in every possible way. After the collapse of the Allied armies in France in 1940, and the evacuation from the Dunkirk beaches, we were cut off from the Continent, and we had left behind in France many of our men who had escaped or evaded capture and were in hiding or making their way south to Spain to

regain their freedom. In addition, many patriots on the Continent were forming themselves into resistance groups to oppose the German occupation.

It was very much in our own interests to foster these resistance groups and to build them up against the day when we would be able to land in France again. The best way of maintaining regular contact with our friends across the Channel was by radio and by aeroplane, and we set about making plans as quickly as possible. A special headquarters was established in London, known as the Special Operations Executive (SOE) and this headquarters was responsible for building up the resistance movements and for arranging for the supply of trained men and women and weapons which were flown out to the Continent almost nightly from 1941 to the end of the war.

The 1941 the only aircraft readily available and suitable for this parachuting work were the Whitleys of Bomber Command and therefore this Command was charged with the task of initiating these secret operations. In the early part of 1941 a special flight of Whitley aircraft was formed at Newmarket Heath, where the racecourse made a fine aerodrome, and training began. Frenchmen, Belgians, Dutchmen, Norwegians and others who had escaped to England after Dunkirk, and Englishmen and women who had been brought up on the continent and spoke of language, volunteered for training as agents. A special school was started by the SOE to

Below: Halifax II, NF-W, of 138 Sqn. *PRO, Air/27/1068*

train them for sabotage work, and in addition they had to complete a course of parachute jumping at the RAF school at Ringway, near Manchester. These agents were then available to be parachuted into the occupied countries at the right moment to establish themselves as respectable citizens, and to make contact with other patriots and set up active resistance organisations. The whole of France was zoned into areas and it was the aim of the SOE Headquarters in London to build up a comprehensive network of agents in each area, capable of conducting sabotage operations and providing assistance to allied airmen who were shot down over the continent of Europe and who had survived and were escaping through occupied territory.

In addition to parachuting people into the continent, it was also necessary to be able to bring people out of France — agents who had special information or were required for special training in England. For this purpose, a Lysander was added to the Flight at Newmarket and this made it possible to land at night in France, pick up agents, and return them to England. Fields having a minimum length of 500 yards were used as landing grounds and an improvised flarepath of torches served to guide the aircraft in to land.

The Lysander proved an ideal choice for this job with its excellent short landing and take-off performance. Its range was improved by fitting a special long-range tank under the fuselage between the undercarriage legs — a long black cylindrical object like a torpedo and provided an admirable cover story for the real work these aircraft were doing! A ladder was also mounted on the side of the fuselage to enable passengers to scramble in and out quickly, as the aircraft remained on the ground in enemy territory for a few moments only.

The first few Lysander operations carried out were rather hazardous, due to inadequate experience of the pilots and agents concerned. One incident in the early days, which I remember well, was when a Lysander was fired on just after landing. In this instance the Germans had arrived at the landing ground shortly before the aircraft was due and had caught the agents redhanded. At the point of the gun they were forced to flash the all-clear light signal and the aircraft duly landed. The pilot received a bullet through the neck, but fortunately in the fleshy part, and he opened the throttles immediately and took off again. Although weak from loss of blood, he was able to fly back to England and land safely at Tangmere. This was the only incident that I know of when the Germans actually interfered with a landing operation, and we carried out over 200 of them.

By early 1942 the intensity of these special operations went up by leaps and bounds and the special flight at Newmarket became No 138 Squadron, to be joined shortly afterwards by No 161 Squadron. These two squadrons were based at RAF Tempsford in Bedfordshire and carried out this special work until the end of the war. The Whitleys were replaced by Halifaxes for parachuting and the Lysanders were supplemented with Hudsons for 'pick-up' operations as they were called.

How did we train our people for this work? The pilots and crews for the parachuting operations presented no problems, and they were drawn from bomber squadrons and converted to parachute work after a few weeks at Tempsford. Many practice drops were carried out to ensure extreme accuracy as the DZ's on the continent were often very small and if containers or men fell outside the area it would be very difficult and dangerous and might compromise the whole operation.

The training of the pick-up pilots and the agents on the ground, who would supervise the landing arrangements, presented a more difficult problem. The job of flying and navigating a Lysander to France and back solo at night and locating a small field up to 400 miles from the base airfield was no mean task and required constant training and practice; map reading was only possible on moonlight nights and these operations were confined to the moon period, as were generally the parachuting operations. In addition, the pilots had to be capable of landing on an improvised L-shaped flarepath consisting of three torches — the length of the flarepath being 150 yards. Having navigated accurately to the area, the landing ground was identified by a flashing torch which was switched on by the agent as soon as he heard the aircraft. The aircraft would then give the correct code signal and the flarepath would be illuminated. A landing would then be made as quickly as possible, with the aid of the aircraft landing light and, provided the moon was reasonable, this presented no problem. The more difficult problem was that of navigation and map reading and, for this, good weather was essential.

For these pick-up operations we had to rely entirely on the efficiency and good judgment of the agent, who was responsible for finding a field suitable for a Lysander or Hudson to land in and for laying on the whole show. We had to train these agents most carefully for this work and 161 Squadron undertook this task. The training was entirely practical and the agents would be sent off from Tempsford by car with our pilots and SOE instructors to find suitable landing grounds. Their choice would then be criticised with regard to surface, obstructions, approaches and landing run. We practised them continuously in the technique of laying out the lights at night and in landing aircraft and embarking passengers in the minimum of time. When the agents were regarded as proficient, they were parachuted or sometimes landed by Lysander, in France, together with their wireless sets, and they set about selecting suitable landing grounds for future operations. The details of these fields were wirelessed back to London and photographic cover of the area was then arranged, to pinpoint the spot exactly and to check the dimensions which the agents had signalled to London. All 'pick-up' operations took place in France and most of the fields used were either in the Chateauroux district along the banks of the River Loire, near Dijon, or north of Lyon. The most interesting operation I personally took part in was a 'double' Hudson operation, when we landed two Hudsons near Dijon in quick succession and picked up 20 people, among whom was Vincent Auriol, later President of France. Shortly after this, in November 1943, I successfully carried out another Hudson operation landing in a field in the Loire Valley, near Angers. This time I took out five agents and brought back six — one of whom it transpired was Francois Mitterand. Unfortunately I was unable to complete the hat-trick!

The bulk of the work was, or course, parachuting, not only into France but also into Belgium, Holland, Denmark and Norway as well, and some very fine long-range missions were carried out, particularly those to Poland and Czechoslovakia, where the deep penetration of enemy territory in moonlight brought its toll of casualties. Nevertheless, it was the pick-up operations which always attracted the most glamour. This was natural as these were more specialised and personal. The Lysander pilots were based, during the moon period, at Tangmere on the south coast, so as to be as near as possible to the scene of operations. Due to the special nature of their work, they lived a separate life away from the main station in the 'Tangmere Cottage' and there they got to know the agents well and there was always a close bond of mutual understanding between them.

And so now 40 years on these activities of the war days seem a very long way off. They were testing and exciting times and dangerous too, both for our own people but more especially for the agents working in occupied Europe, many of whom were captured and suffered torture and death. But today we still maintain our contacts, meeting with our friends of the resistance to keep alive the spirit and comradeship and understanding which prevailed during the war years.

Colonel Maurice Buckmaster, who commanded the French section of the Special Operations Executive from 1941 to 1943, summed it up very well in a recent article: 'Is the Franco-British Entente Cordiale becoming less cordial? . . .

'Inevitably there are some people in Britain who have closer links with France than others — and the same applies to other countries. Why do we not do more to ensure that our businessmen and politicans have a closer understanding of the people across the Channel?

'Take the men and women who worked together in France during the Second World War under the clandestine banner of Special Operations Executive, for example. The experiences of the French resistance workers and their British partners bound them in indissoluble friendship . . . To do their job properly our men and women needed a deep and instinctive knowledge of the way French people thought. How invaluable that intuitive sense would be now to those who handle problems of Common Market differences of opinion . . . Why can we not do more to persuade those who served and worked in France and elsewhere, and forged close links with local people, to play an important part today? Their knowledge could be invaluable.'

An interesting thought. All I can say today is that from a personal point of view those of us who during the war years were closely involved with the French resistance believe that by maintaining our regular contacts with our friends across the Channel we are, if only in a very small way, contributing something to the fostering of better Anglo-French relations and that, I believe, is a very worthwhile objective.

Below: Westland Lysander, named 'Elaine' on engine cowling. *C. Bowyer*

Sand in My Shoes

Air Chief Marshal Sir Frederick Rosier GCB, CBE, DSO

Air Chief Marshal Rosier's early career in the Royal Air Force was largely as a fighter pilot and leader. Although wounded in 1940, he served with distinction in France and the UK and then perhaps most notably, in the Western Desert.

After the war much of his service continued to be with Fighter Command, including at the Central Fighter Establishment and as Group Captain Plans during the critical period of the development of the jet fighter; and he finally became C-in-C of the Command in 1966. He also saw overseas service in the Middle East, in CENTO, and in NATO as Deputy C-in-C Allied Forces Central Europe.

After retirement from the RAF in 1973 he maintained his connection with military aviation by becoming the senior representative of BAC in Saudi Arabia, where his experience and forceful and cheerful personality did much to modernise and develop that country's air force.

Right: The author when a wing commander with the Desert Air Force.
Imperial War Museum, CM.3335

When I look back on my life in the RAF during World War 2 my thoughts invariably return to the time I spent in the Western Desert. It is not that other periods in that long war were without interest — far from it. Indeed events up to that day in May 1941 when I embarked most of my squadron pilots and aircraft in the Aircraft Carrier HMS *Furious* en route to the desert probably had a great impact on me than any others during the war.

For example, there was my marriage at Henlow in September 1939. Incidentally, it was followed the very next morning by the unexpected but hoped for news in my immediate posting back to a flying appointment. The news, prefaced by the clatter of pebbles on our bedroom window, was brought by some of my friends on the same Specialist Engineering course. The next day I left for Aston Down, a Spitfire station. My wife was returned to her mother. Then, in the following May, came the unforgettable experience of thinking that my last moments had come as I sat trapped in the cockpit of a burning Hurricane over an airfield in France only to become aware perhaps a second or so later that I was falling free of the aircraft. After pulling the ripcord of my parachute I remember vaguely trying to stop my trousers burning and then nothing more until I woke up in an Army hospital in Arras.

My stay there was brief. That same evening it was decided to evacuate the hospital because of the proximity of the German army. Five days later, after a painful and tedious journey by road and rail, we left Cherbourg for Southampton. At first it was thought that I would not be able to see again but my sight soon came back, and, in the following September after spending most of the summer in the RN Hospital at Netley and the Cottage Hospital at Poole, I was passed fit to return to flying duties. Shortly afterwards I took command of my old

Above: Hurricanes aboard HMS *Furious*, bound for Malta. *via C. Bowyer*

Left: Hurricane V7803 leaving HMS *Furious* en route to Malta. *via C. Bowyer*

Below left: Hurricane I, V7892, 73 Sqn, with 'spaghetti' paint on its forward sections. *I. McConnell*

squadron, No 229, at Northolt in time for the last part of the Battle of Britain.

The years in the UK and Europe after my 'Desert Interlude' were also not without interest and excitement; but, for me there was something unique about life and operations in the desert. There were few diversions from duty. Conditions were always adverse but the underlying cheerfulness and the camaraderie amongst all ranks was tremendous. It was a hard fought war which, in the air, went on relentlessly day after day. It was a war that saw the beginning of real army/air co-operation and great improvements in the mechanics of providing timely air support for the Army. The Desert war was a war in which we gradually obtained ascendancy over the German and Italian air forces and were able to create the conditions which allowed our land and naval forces to operate relatively free of interference from the enemy air forces. Indeed air operations by the Desert Air Force contributed so much to ultimate victory in North Africa that it is surprising that so little has been written about this Force

The start of our voyage from the Clyde to the Mediterranean had its amusing side. Together with an old friend from the Fleet Air Arm and the CO of one of the other two Hurricane squadrons on board we were enjoying a drink with the captain of a destroyer which had just returned from the Lofoten raid when we were ordered to return to the *Furious*. A drink or two later came the news that the *Furious* was getting under way, and by the time we reached her, cold sober by then, she was actually moving. We were then faced with a long and somewhat ignominious climb up rope ladders to the flight deck where we were piped aboard much to the amusement of our pilots and many of the ship's company. We were now on our way to Gibraltar.

Soon after we arrived at Gibraltar the *Furious* went off to help hunt the *Bismarck* whilst we were left behind to enjoy nearly three glorious weeks of enforced holiday. On her return we rejoined the carrier which set off into the Mediterranean on the evening of 5 June 1941. The following morning, just after dawn, we took off on our flight to Malta.

The last thing we wanted on this long flight, during which our route took us close to enemy bases, was to be intercepted by enemy fighters. Any fighting en route would have prejudiced our chances of reaching the island. Furthermore, because the extra fuel tanks needed for these long flights had been installed at the expense of much of the aircraft's fire power, we would have been at a disadvantage in any dog fight. The emphasis therefore was on accurate navigation and

strict wireless silence; a Blenheim, which led us provided the first, whilst the absence of any emergencies ensured the second. We were fortunate in that both this flight and the next one from Malta to Mersa Matruh in Egypt were trouble free.

The first few weeks in Egypt were most frustrating. My squadron ground crews were still on their way by sea round the Cape; most of my pilots had been detached to other squadrons and I was left with nothing to do at Abu Suwair in the Canal Zone. However, one day, with the boldness and confidence of youth, I approached the C-in-C himself, Air Marshal Sir Arthur Tedder, who, after listening to my story, promised that my pilots would be returned and that we could then start operating as a squadron. This was done and shortly afterwards my squadron joined No 73 Sqn, over which I was given temporary command, on one of a clutch of airfields in the Desert near Mersa Matruh. When the CO of No 73 Sqn, Sqn Ldr P. Wykeham-Barnes eventually returned to resume command of his squadron he presented me with a silver tankard, inscribed 'in memory of 73/229'. The subsequent history of this tankard epitomises the vagaries of the Desert war.

One of the most uncomfortable and hazardous routine operations we carried out during the late summer and autumn of that year was the air patrolling over 'A' lighters en route to Tobruk. These slow craft carrying supplies by sea to Tobruk, where they were unloaded at night, were at their closest to the

Right: Wg Cdr (later, AM Sir) Peter Wykeham-Barnes.
Imperial War Museum, CM.1776

main Luftwaffe airfields at Gambut in the late afternoon. Invariably that was when the Stukas, sometimes with Me 110s and with Me 109s as top cover chose to strike, taking advantange of the setting sun on their approach. One evening I nearly 'bought it', as we used to say, during a fight over these ships. I was shooting at a Stuka, perhaps a hundred or so feet above the sea, when my Hurricane went into a violent roll to the right and nearly hit the sea. Fortunately I managed to regain control and was able to fly back to our advanced base at Sidi Barrani by keeping the speed low, holding the stick hard over to the left and by using a lot of rudder. On landing it was found that some of the skin of the starboard wing had peeled off and hit the tailplane.

In early September I was attached to Air HQ Western Desert for a short time prior to taking command of a newly formed wing, No 262, which, together with the established No 258 wing commanded by Gp Capt KBB Cross, would have operational control over the desert fighter squadrons. During this time information, somewhat fragmented, started coming through about a number of Stukas which had crashed or force landed close to 'the wire' which marked the border between Libya and Egypt and generally between hostile and friendly territory. Wg Cdr Bowman, a big, bluff, hearty, determined officer who was in charge of training and for whom I was working at the time began to take a great interest in these reports. It was not long before he and I decided to get per-

mission to investigate them and if possible to fly back a Stuka. The AOC Air Vice-Marshal 'Mary' Coningham readily agreed and preparations began. First we got hold of a captured Italian Stuka pilot so that he could check us out on the Stuka cockpit, and then we managed to obtain a Wapiti, big enough for the three of us. After correlating all the latest available information we set off. The first Stuka we found had somersaulted on landing, was lying on its back with bombs still attached, and was of no use to us. Further searches that day from the air and on the ground, where we received the willing co-operation of forward Army units, proved fruitless. However, we had come to two important conclusions: first, that because of the enemy air activity it would be safer to dispense with the Wapiti and carry out all our future reconnaissances on the ground; and second that because our Italian, very nervous by this time, had become more of a liability that a possible asset we should send him back in the returning Wapiti. When we told him he became a changed man.

That night we stayed close to Maddalena with a Hussar regiment. The officers were most friendly and having heard what we intended to do entered into the spirit of the adventure with enthusiasm.

The following morning with a couple of their trucks and as escort of an officer and several troopers we set off again on our search, this time going into an area where enemy patrols might be encountered. After a few hours of nothing but sand, we saw dust

Above left: Captured Italian Junkers Ju 87 in the desert.
C. Bowyer

Left: Another 'prize' of the air war over the desert. Junkers Ju 52, used by 216 Sqn and named 'Libyan Clipper'.
C. Bowyer

on the horizon, but were soon able to relax as a British patrol came in sight. The patrol carried the news we wanted, pinpointing the position of a Stuka which appeared to be in one piece and in good condition. On the way to it we saw, in the distance, two Italian CR42 biplanes circling round and deduced that they were probably above the Stuka. Hoping that we had not been seen we laid low until they flew away. After a few more miles we reached the aircraft which still had its bombs on and appeared undamaged.

By now it was late afternoon and we were anxious to get the Stuka refuelled and to fly it back whilst it was still light. We had several cans of petrol with us and whilst our army friends were pouring this in under the direction of the wing commander I was fiddling about in the cockpit. Suddenly there was a commotion and everyone started running away. I had mistakenly pressed a switch or moved a lever which had jettisoned the bombs. Reacting to their shouts, I was out of that cockpit in a flash, but it was not long before common sense prevailed: the bombs could not have become armed in a short distance they had fallen. So back to the Stuka we went to continue the preparations which seemed to be going well when two more CR42s came over at about 5,000ft. Convinced this time that we must have been spotted we decided to try to start the engine and to get away as quickly as possible. After a few attempts with the starter handle the engine fired and within a few minutes we took off and set course towards the east. The wing commander was at the controls and I was in the rear cockpit.

Although there was little daylight left we were reasonably confident that we would get back to one of our airfields. The plan was to fly east until we were well over friendly territory and then to change course to north east to reach the coast line. However, we had only been flying for about 20mins when the engine spluttered and stopped. After a perfect forced landing on quite scrubby desert and some tinkering with the fuel system we managed to get the engine started again and resumed our flight; but it was not to be our lucky day. Shortly afterwards we again had trouble. This time, although the touch-down was fine, the aircraft suffered a burst tyre and damage to its undercarriage as it ran into a shallow wadi — a dried up river bed — just at the end of the landing run. Although we consoled ourselves with the thought that if this had happened a little later we would have been faced with trying to land in darkness, there was no hiding the fact that we were in serious trouble. We were in the heart of the desert, many miles south of the coast, with the prospect of a long walk home. To make matters worse, in the excitement of preparing for take-off, we had failed to put aboard a reserve of water and had only our two water bottles.

That night we slept in the folds of our parachutes and at dawn, after leaving a message in stones stating that we were walking due north, we set off. Having concluded that we would probably have to walk for two days before there was much chance of sighting our own forces, we were surprised in the late morning to see two trucks in the distance. As they came closer and we became confident that they were friendly we streamed in the wind the parachute we had been carrying. To our great relief it was seen and we were picked up, none the worse for our walk in the desert.

For me that was the end of an interesting diversion from my normal life for I had to return to Air HQ. However, Wg Cdr Bowman, true to character, set off again to get the necessary bits and pieces to make 'ours' serviceable from the first crashed Stuka we had seen. A small RAF team was sent out to help and soon the wing-commander was in the air again this time accompanied by a red-headed RN lieutenant-commander who was spending some leave from his destroyer with the units in the Desert and who had expressed the wish to fly back in the Stuka. They got back safely to Mersa Matruh.

Preparations were going ahead at this time for a renewed offensive to be known as Operation Crusader. It got off to a good start on 18 November, and two days later I moved my wing HQ to Maddalena. On 22 November I was suddenly ordered to fly to Tobruk where I was to organise the airfield and facilities for the operation of fighters. Flying a Hurricane, and escorted by over 20 Tomahawks from No 3 RAAF and No 112 Squadrons, I set off that same afternoon. All went well until we were approaching El Adem when we were intercepted by a large number of Me 109s and a fight started. The official 3 Sqn Operatinal Record book writes of this battle '20 Me 109s were encountered south east of El Adem. The fight lasted over an hour and ended up with Tomahawks circling at 500ft with 109s above'. The fight certainly seemed to last an eternity but apart from some Tomahawks which had formed a defensive circle, I seem to remember that aircraft were scattered all over the sky — as invariably happened. Towards the end I saw one of the Tomahawks diving down with the tell-tale stream of glycol showing that it had been hit. As I followed it down the pilot lowered his undercarriage and landed. I suppose it was because he was deep inside enemy territory and the odds were that he would be captured that I decided to attempt to rescue him. I landed, and as I came to a stop not far from him he ran across to me. I

Above: 112 (Shark) Sqn personnel, LG 122, Fort Maddelena, 30 November 1941. L–R: Sgt Leu; Plt Off N. Duke; Flg Off Soden; Flg Off Humphreys; Sqn Ldr Morello; Flt Lt Ambrose; Fg Off Dickenson; Sgt Burney; Flg Off Westenra. Kneeling: Flg Off Sabourin; Flg Off Bowker; Flg Off Bartle; Sgt K. Carson.
Imperial War Museum, CM.1820

jumped out and discarded my parachute. He climbed into the cockpit; I sat on top of him and opened the throttle. Then came disaster. Just as the aircraft started moving a tyre burst; the wheel dug into the sand; and abruptly we came to a full stop. For the second time within two months I was faced with the prospect of a long walk because of a burst tyre. But unlike the previous one this walk would be through many miles of hostile territory. My companion, whom I came to admire greatly, was an Australian sergeant pilot, named Burney.

I had with me in my Hurricane all my worldly possessions — my wife's picture, the silver tankard I mentioned previously, clothes, sheets, blankets, some tinned food and a few cans of beer. Having lowered the bottom panel of the fuselage on which these were stowed we removed them and, with the exception of some food and beer which we kept, hid them under some brushwood. We then hurried off to the shelter of a nearby wadi as I was afraid that a motorised column which I had noticed during my landing approach would soon come to investigate.

My concern was justified for we had only just reached the wadi when a couple of lorries arrived. Whilst some of the Italian soldiers stood by the aircraft others started searching for us. I am certain it was the fading light which saved us, for two of them came within yards of where we were hiding behind some rocks. Before going away they found and took all my possessions.

Later, when we felt it was safe we started walking east, using the North Pole star for our direction. We were anxious to get as far away as possible from the scene of our landings: the search for us was bound to continue in the morning. We stumbled along for three or four hours before deciding to rest for the remaining hours of darkness. The following afternoon, having walked for several miles and beginning to suffer as a result, we spotted what we took to be an Italian camp ahead of us and were forced to make a long detour round it. As night fell we stopped; had a tin of fruit and some water, which we were strictly rationing, and lay back tired out.

Later that evening I decided that we must continue walking for I had a feeling that

unless we did so later on we would find ourselves getting weaker and weaker as we ran out of water. I was also getting worried about the state of the sergeant's feet. He was wearing ill fitting flying boots and in places his feet were raw. So, we pressed on until some time in the middle of the night we began to see various shapes on all sides of us. To our dismay, they proved to be a number of enemy tanks and trucks. We lay low for a time and then started to crawl away. At one stage we thought we had been spotted for there were shouts in German and the odd lights came on, but after again lying motionless for what appeared an age the lights went out and there was silence. We continued to crawl and then to walk crouched down until at last it started to get light. We found we had made little progress. We were still no more than a mile away from the enemy force. However, the fates were with us that morning, for close by was a ring of brushwood inside which we found a dried-up, shallow, abandoned well, into which we sank, completely exhausted.

Some time during the morning we heard the sound of gunfire with the shells passing over us and exploding amongst the enemy vehicles, which began to disperse and withdraw. I began to think of making a dash for it for we could see our guns firing in the distance and when we eventually heard orders being shouted in English my mind was made up. We ran.

I wish I could remember the identity of the gunner unit we reached. At first we were looked upon with suspicion but soon we were given food and drink before being sent on to an armoured brigade HQ not far away. There we were given a truck and driver and set off to the south-east towards Maddalena. However, even this journey was not uneventful. We had not gone far and were approaching a line of armoured cars manned by South Africans when shells started dropping around us. I remember when their commander plaintively told me that an enemy armoured force had broken through and that he was now the only defence before the wire how sorry I felt for them. Presumably this was the enemy force we had found ourselves mixed up with the previous night.

On arriving back at Maddalena, to a heart warming reception by Gp Capt Cross and others I found that my wing had already been taken over by another old friend, Wg Cdr Jimmy Fenton. His reign was shortlived for he returned immediately to his former post. For me there was no respite. I had come back to a scene of great activity. The German armour had really broken through our defences and our bases at Maddalena were threatened.

The following spring, just before the retreat to El Alamein, I took a weekend break in Cairo staying in my favourite hotel, the Continental. There I was paged and found that a South African major wished to meet

Above: Sidi Rezegh airfield, 1941. No 260 Sqn's Hurricanes parked among abandoned Italian Fiat G50s.

Left: Kittyhawk Ia, AK772, GA-Y of 112 Sqn at Gambut Main airfield, circa March 1942. On 30 May 1942 Plt Off Burney was shot down in this aircraft.
Imperial War Museum, CM.2895

me. He told me he had something in his room which he thought would be of interest to me. He was right: it was my silver tankard. He had been commanding a South African armoured car squadron which had inter-ecepted and shot up a German convoy going south from Benghazi. When the action was over there was the usual search for 'loot' in the damaged and abandoned vehicles during which the tankard was found. When he got back to Cairo he made enquiries, and somehow found out that I would be staying in that particular hotel that weekend. That is the saga of the silver tankard, which is still one of my most prized possessions. Taken by Italians: recovered from Germans.

Unfortunately my companions in both these desert interludes did not survive the war. Wg Cdr Bowman was killed on 30 November, 1941 soon after our Stuka adventure, when he was shot down on his approach to a remote desert airfield. Sgt Burney, who by then had been commissioned, was killed in June 1942 on a fighter bomber sortie. It was part of the tragedy of war that men such as these were lost. They were brave, resourceful, determined and so cheerful, even in adversity.

My third and last Desert story is quite different in character. In the offensive which started in November 1941 we had advanced almost to the bottom of the Gulf of Sirte before being pushed back to what became known as the Gazala line. We had a radar unit at Gazala; the fighter force was based on the Gambut airfields; and I, with some of No 211 Fighter Group, was based at El Adem. After some extremely heavy rains our airfields were seas of mud; our aircraft were all bogged down and operations were impossible. The enemy, however, were in a better position for they were still able to operate from the Martuba airfields to the north west of Gazala. On this particular occasion our resident 'Y' Service unit, which monitored enemy radio transmissions, reported signs of activity at Martuba, following this with a report that a raid was building up, that the target was Tobruk, and that the Italian Air Force was involved. Knowing that the enemy also had a radio monitoring organisation I decided to try to hoodwink them by scrambling imaginary fighters and by instructing and directing them to intercept the enemy raid. To add realism to such spoofing I told the controller at the Gazala radar unit to respond to any instructions given to the imaginary fighters with the single word 'Roger' meaning 'received'. Such a short response was unlikely to lead to the Germans finding the source by direction finding.

As soon as we began to receive radar plots of this raid, which we now knew from 'Y' was composed of Italian Stukas escorted by German Me 109s, I scrambled the imaginary fighters, told them what the task was and started vectoring them towards the raid. In turn the 'Y' Service reported that the enemy formation had been warned that allied fighters were airborne and on their way to intercept. I was beginning to think that the ruse had failed because the formation was already nearing Tobruk and had been told that our 'fighters' were close to it, when there was an excited shout from 'Y'. The Stukas had jettisoned their bombs and had turned back whilst the very angry leader of the Me 109s, was saying what what he thought of them. I kept up the pretence by telling our 'fighters' that the raid had turned away and that they were to return to base.

I was surprised but naturally delighted that the ruse had worked. It had not been premeditated and I suppose I thought of it only because the Italian Air Force and particularly their Stuka units had not been showing anything like the aggressive spirit of their German allies.

My time with the Desert Air Force ended soon after we reached Castel Benito (Tripoli) in January 1943. Although delighted to be returning to the UK I was sad to leave some of the finest men that it was ever my privilege to serve with. Their spirit was magnificent.

Above right: Messerschmitt Bf 109 undergoing maintenance under a baking African sun.

Right: Victim. Junkers Ju 52 adapted for mine-sweeping role comes under attack from an RAF fighter.

Behind German Lines in the Western Desert

Marshal of the RAF Lord Cameron GCB, DSO, DFC

Marshal of the Royal Air Force Lord Cameron flew as a pilot in the Battle of Britain and thereafter on several wartime tours on fighter and fighter bomber squadrons, being twice decorated.

After the war he had a wide and varied career, when apart from his official appointments he became known as a wise and profound thinker on defence matters; and also played an active part in Royal Air Force rugby. In 1976 he was appointed Chief of the Air Staff and in 1977 Chief of Defence Staff, where he established a considerable reputation for outspokenness and grasp of the political realities.

Since retirement in 1979 he has retained a close interest in defence matters, speaking and writing extensively in defence journals and the media; and acting as Chairman of the Trustees of the Royal Air Force Museum.

He is currently the Principal of King College, London and was recently awarded a Life Peerage.

The Western Desert is undoubtedly the right place to fight a war — that is if wars have to be fought. Wilfred Thesiger, one of the great desert travellers and writers, has said about the desert — 'No man can live this life and emerge unchanged. He will carry, however faint, the imprint of the desert, the brand which marks the nomad; and he will have within him the yearning to return, weak or insistent according to his nature. For this cruel land can cast a spell which no temperate climate can match.'

There were of course many who hated the Western Desert but they would have hated most places. For many the operations there were their first wartime or perhaps any adventure. The desert can cast its spell. There was comradeship, the operational esprit de corps of a good squadron, the meeting up with many friends, the patrols and air fighting during the day (and sometimes at night). The celebrations after a victory in the air, the uplift with the arrival of the beer ration. The rising before dawn to get up for a patrol. The smell of the dawn desert and of Merlin engines being run up as aircraft came on to readiness. The nervous, queasy stomach, the mud-like tea, the breakfast eagerly eaten after a sortie. The return to readiness as the sun came up and the full heat of the desert came into the body. The hanging about waiting for a scramble or a set operation, the terrible heat of climbing into the cockpit of a metal aircraft at midday, the formation manouevring for take-off on the ground in dust clouds, the delicious feel of cold air flowing into the cockpit as you gained height. The comfortable feeling of seeing your friends and colleagues forming up around you. The voice of the controller giving the first indication of enemy activity over the Alamein positions — the first tally-ho. The few hectic minutes of life and death. The order for home. Wheels down and back safely to the duty operations tent. The

Left: The author. *Popperfoto*

probing questions of the squadron intelligence officer and the Army liaison officer. This was a typical day. Perhaps you operated or flew three or four times. Then came release as the desert dusk spread. A bath of some sort, a drink if there was one, some food and the camp bed.

Yes, the Western Desert is a marvellous place to fight a war. There were few local people to get hurt. The Senussi nomads move freely about the desert and they got the message that it was a good time to be elsewhere. The main sufferers were the combatants who introduced themselves into this strategic area. The surface of the desert is on the whole a mixture of rock and sand but often there are areas which are hard sand and from which it is possible to operate an aircraft. These areas, some treated artifically to an extent, became the landing grounds for the Desert Air Force. They were very adequate, though aircraft systems could get very badly eroded by the constant dust storms that were generated by vehicles, aircraft and certain meteorological conditions.

Maintenance of aircraft was difficult and as usual the Royal Air Force ground crews worked miracles to keep operations going. They were of course handling aircraft that were mostly old and had been out in the area for some time. Many of the reinforcements which had been intended for the desert war had been sunk in various convoys in transit from the United Kingdom. The flow of Spitfires to the theatre had been abysmally slow and the Hurricane Mark IIC force was coping with Messerschmitt Bf 109Fs and Bf 109Gs — both aircraft with a greatly superior performance to the Hurricane except perhaps in the turning circle. Two of the four cannons had been removed from the Hurricane IIC to give it a better performance. But while it is useful to be able to turn inside your enemy in air combat, if the speed differential is so great then it is difficult to take offensive action against your enemy. Such was the case in the desert. This, coupled with the operational direction that the Hurricane force was to operate at about 10,000ft, made the Hurricane very vulnerable to the German and even Italian fighters. The reason was that the commanders felt it was useful for the Army to see they were being protected, particularly against Ju 87 attack. It was quite common for a squadron or wing from its patrol line in and around El Alamein to be able to see the German and Italian fighters taking off from their airfields at El Fuka and El Daba. Within minutes they had climbed above the Hurricane force and could carry out their dive and climb attacks almost at will. The Hurricane tactic was to turn the wing or the squadron into the enemy whilst they were in their attack dive with the hope of someone in the formation getting a deflection shot whilst on the turn or if one of the German fighters got a little careless. This tactic, defensive though it was, got some surprisingly good results. But really one of the main aims of the Hurricane force was to protect the Army from the Stuka attacks which were not infrequent and of which the Royal Air Force got little warning because of the almost total lack of radar cover. There is no doubt that these Hurricane anti-Stuka patrols helped to reduce the weight of attack

Right: 'Bivvy'. Typical Desert Air Force 'accommodation', 1940–43.
Imperial War Museum, CM.3969

Above: Take-off. Douglas Bostons of No 24 Sqn SAAF leaving their desert landing ground for an operation.
Imperial War Museum, CM.3540

Left: Hurricane IIC, AK-W HL883, of 213 Sqn and a Lockheed Hudson of 117 Sqn at LG 125, behind the German lines, November 1942.
Imperial War Museum, CM.4099

against the Army, but in putting themselves in such a vulnerable position in the sky the Hurricane force took heavy losses.

The morale of the Desert Air Force after the retreat to El Alamein was on the low side and no wonder. They had been on the move nearly every night, flying and operating hard during the day, and living very rough. Yes, so were the Army, but the Air Force had to keep some fairly sophisticated equipment working and also to keep operational flying skills going amongst aircrew so that the maximum effectiveness was obtained from them.

Living conditions were tough and aircraft stood out in the desert storms and took their chance of surviving. The tented camp was designed so as to be movable at very short notice. There was an HQ trailer and the squadron doctor also had a trailer used as a consulting room, but otherwise it was tents for all concerned to make their home as best they could. The officer and NCO pilots shared a mess and there were usually six to a tent. The first action on getting the tent erected was to dig some sort of slit trench fairly close by so that refuge could be taken in the middle of the night when the desert airfields came under attack by Ju 88s or Dorniers — which was most nights. The equipment for hygiene was a canvas wash basin and the occasional use of a canvas bath when the supply of water permitted.

Before and during the Alamein battle the fighter squadrons were based back on the Cairo-Alexandria Road in the Amiriya area. This meant that Alexandria was within a two hour drive. The difference of the desert tent to one of the fine suites of the Hotel Cecil in Alexandria was quite out of this world and to drive out of the sand storm of the desert to the clear air of the sea coast as one approached Alexandria was a never-to-be-forgotten experience. The excursions to Alexandria did not, of course, last long but every moment was made to count and if the squadron did not manage three night clubs during the evening they felt they had failed. There was a very popular dancing act of two Lebanese sisters who performed at all three night clubs and they were assured of a following if the squadron was in town. Alexandria, the summer home of Egyptian kings and queens was a much tried city. Certainly life in the Desert Air Force had a mode all of its own. As the El Alamein position consolidated, the two great and historic cities of Cairo and Alexandria became the main goal posts standing behind the 8th Army and its associated Air Force. If the Afrika Korps had driven through to the goal posts of these cities and the Nile Delta, then the war would have taken a very serious turn for the Allies. Few realise how very close the Axis came to achieving this aim. At the time

of the Battle of Alma Halfa for instance in September 1942 they were certainly within a reasonable day's drive of the capital of Egypt. In the meantime life went on in these two cities as if nothing very much was happening. True, some of the braver staff officers in HQ Middle East were beginning to burn their papers and think longingly of the Levant, but the hoteliers and the Club owners in Cairo and Alex were made of sterner stuff. So if it was possible to get back to the 'Delta' for a moment for some reason or another one quickly entered a very different world. The great hotel 'Shepherds' in Cairo (later to be burnt down) was still very much in business — if you could afford it. Certainly there were others less dignified but quite adequate. The Continental Savoy bar was a good meeting place for the Air Force and if someone was in town he would usually appear there sometime during the evening. During the day it was swimming and drinking in the Gezhira Club where there was golf, tennis and adequate food and drink. The Gezhira 'John Collins' was notorious. There was no shortage of restaurants which always seemed to be well stocked — so one lived in some style.

It was always a levelling experience to fly back from, say, Cairo's Heliopolis airfield to your landing ground in the Desert — straight from a bedroom and bath and a good lunch to a dusty tent shared with several others with bullybeef and biscuits for supper, and a patrol over Alamein at dawn. But the change of environment was so great that most who experienced it remember it with the most vivid feelings.

I have often wondered why the Desert Air Force never had its due recognition from historians who have studied the Desert campaign. The Commander Eight Army survived to write his memoirs and indeed to influence military thinking to a significant extent for a considerable period after the war was over. Air Marshal 'Mary' Coningham, a New Zealander, who was Commander Desert Air Force, was killed in the ill-fated airliner 'Star-Tiger' which crashed near the Azores in January 1948. His memoirs were not published nor his analysis of the operations of the Desert war. They would have made interesting reading. After all the Desert campaign saw the start of the close co-operation in the field between the Army and the Royal Air Force which was the pattern to be carried across to the great operations in North West Europe.

To give General Montgomery, as he was then, credit, he was a dedicated advocate of army-air cooperation and the techniques that emerged were largely the result of the liaison that developed between him and Coningham. Relations between them were turbulent at times but no more than you would expect from two characters of powerful personality. The historians have suggested that Montgomery was sometimes over-cautious in his build-up before a battle and certainly he liked to have an element of superiority before launching an attack. He has also been criticised for being a little slow in the follow-up after a successful action such as El Alamein. The Air Force on the other hand manged to achieve a significant degree of air superiority from a fairly early stage when things were going badly on the ground but this was not achieved without a casualty rate equalling that of the Battle of Britain — at times it was worse.

I know the squadron I was in lost six aircraft in one day. During the retreat to the Alamein position and during the battle of Alma Halfa and thereafter, the Desert Air Force kept up a continuous assault against the Afrika Korps positions. Without this assault there would have been no Alamein and no victory and the course of the war would have been considerably different. The air cover produced by the Hurricanes and, at first, the few Spitfires and the constant attacks by Bostons, Baltimores, Tomahawks and latter Kittyhawks, (and Wellingtons by night) established not only air superiority, but helped the Army to fight the land battle; all as it should be.

The purpose of this piece, however, is not to write a history of the Desert Air Force but to describe an interesting operation which took place soon after the Battle of Alamein was over. The Battle started on the night of 23 October 1942 with the first penetration of the enemy minefields and an intensive artillery barrage, and a wide variety of air attacks. The early morning Alamein fighter patrols witnessed an incredible sight of burning tanks and vehicles and clouds of smoke rising to our operating height. The battle was to continue for nine long days until the break-through came on 1 November. The Desert Air Force played its full part and was going to play a key role in the pursuit of Rommel.

By 12 November 1942, the German and Italian Afrika Korps were in retreat and heavy fighting was taking place in the Bardia-Tobruk area. Rommel was fighting a staunch and determined rearguard action. General Montgomery and Air Marshal Coningham, decided that the Afrika Korps in retreat was not being harassed comprehensively enough. It was therefore agreed to deploy two Royal Air Force squadrons well behind the German lines to carry out a series of attacks against Rommel's lines of communication. It was a bold and imaginative plan.

As mentioned before, there are certain areas of the Western Desert which are of hard sand, and it was possible for a wide-undercarriage aircraft like the Hurricane to operate from such a surface. The task force was to consist of Hurricane squadrons No 213 and No 238, armed with two 20mm cannons. Both were well-tried Desert squadrons already with some experience in ground attack operations, which was unusual in fighter squadrons at that time.

The main operational problem could clearly be navigational. Landing Ground 125

Below: Hudsons of 117 Sqn which conveyed personnel and supplies for No 243 Wing to LG 125, November 1942. *Imperial War Museum, CM.4094*

(as it was numbered) was deep in the desert and the area involved had few landscape features of use. Radio silence was to be maintained, as far as possible, for the whole operation. There were no navigational aids. The compass and the watch were to be the main aids. The map was useless.

The plan was for the two squadrons to be led to Landing Ground 125 by a Lockheed Hudson, an American aircraft much used by the wartime Royal Air Force in the Western Desert in an air transport role. The Hudsons would also ferry in essential supplies to keep the squadrons going for the length of time they would be behind enemy lines. The plan was that the operation would go on for three or four days depending on how long it took for the enemy to find out where the attacks were coming from and to retaliate.

The two squadrons were allowed to take only the bare operational necessities to keep them flying. Arrangements were made for the aircraft of a large amount of 20mm ammunition, as it was expected that considerable quantities would be expended in the type of attacks envisaged. Pilots were allowed the basic minimum of personal equipment, only flying clothing and escape kits. Most of us slept in our aircraft, shaving was not required, indeed there was precious little water for even the most basic hygienic purposes. Two cooks came with the party with basic rations for keeping the squadrons going for a few days. Some expert travellers amongst the aircrew managed to find room in the Hurricane for a few cans of beer and those enlightened ones became extraordinarily popular. Supplies did not last long.

The three Hudson aircraft positioned on our departure airfield (if you could call it that) on 12 November and loading operations started immediately and went on all night. The main briefings were completed and all was ready. There was no denying the adventurous nature of the operation, and the more experienced pilots were selected to take part. There was of course the chance of a total debacle if our landing ground was discovered. There was much apprehensive excitement in the aircrew mess the evening before departure.

The Intelligence was clear. Rommel and his forces were retreating and our task was to make life as difficult for them as we possibly could. This type of subversive operation was new to us all. Some of us had been involved in the Battle of Britain and the first offensive sweeps over France, but this was entirely original and exciting. At dawn on the morning of 13 November 1942 we set course for 'Landing Ground 125'. We settled into loose formation with the Hudsons and hoped their navigators were well on the ball. The flight was due to last about two hours. The Hurricanes were fitted with long range tanks. The operations envisaged (as we soon found out) would stretch fuel capacity to the limit.

Before the operation started the Long Range Desert Group had carried out a reconnaissance of the area and the RAF's No 2 Armoured Car Company had been selected to provide ground support. The existence of this

Below: LG 125 scene, November 1942, as Hudsons of 117 Sqn unload supplies.
Imperial War Museum, CM.4092

famous RAF desert unit dated back to the Trenchard concept known as the 'Air-Pin', of using air forces to control local tribes in Iraq without using large numbers of soldiers. The technique had worked well and the RAF Armoured Car Companies were kept in existence, later becoming part of the RAF Regiment. No 2 was commanded by a fabulous character called Squadron Leader Cassano who had been in one desert or another for many years. He knew his Senussi desert well and the Company boasted several other experienced desert warriors.

It is worth pausing here to look for a moment at this man Squadron Leader Cassano. He had joined the Royal Air Force to fly. I don't know what happened to his flying career, but he became one of the great characters of the Western Desert. He was a man of medium height with jet black hair and a black moustache. He could have been taken for an Arab. His uniform when he was in the desert was unconventional to say the least. Some declared that they had seen him in Cairo looking quite smart and he seemed to know where the ladies were to be found. As the Commander of No 2 Armoured Car Company, which he led for two years, he became quite a legend and even the Army were prepared to acknowledge his operational effectiveness. He had operated with the 11th Hussars — the Cherry Pickers — and they knew him well. He had been decorated with the Military Cross for an action when his Company had been attacked by force of German and Italian bombers when operating in the open desert. They suffered many casualties and there was much heroism but the squadron recovered and was soon operational again.

I would like to quote from his operational log when he accompanied us behind the German lines. It ran like this:

'11 Nov — At 1215hrs Sqn Ldr Cassano MC received order to proceed to a secret forward landing ground well into enemy territory. Company moved off at 1230hrs (no waste of time).

12 Nov — Company reached "the wire" (the Egypt/Libyan border) at Fort Maddellena. At 1415hrs a German warrant officer who was proceeding back to his unit was taken prisoner having walked five days due west (presumably he joined the party).

14 Nov — Company arrived at LG 125 at 1200hrs and immediately formed a defensive screen 50 miles out from airfield to observe hostile air or surface enemy forces.

16 Nov — Half section under Flt Lt Palmer proceeded to area 60 miles SE of LG 125 to search for crashed aircraft.

17 Nov — Withdraw from area at the end of the operation. Squadron Leader Cassano was eventually badly wounded in Tunisia and had to hand over command of the Company. (The Royal Air Force has some exciting characters who do not necessarily fly aeroplanes.)'

So the armoured cars had worked their way behind the German lines and thrown a defensive screen around LG 125 ready for the arrival of the aircraft. The screen had a radio warning link with the main control car, situated close to the airfield.

Left: Iron Maiden. RAF armoured cars in the desert, 1942.
Imperial War Museum, CM.203

Our course took us well south of the area of operations and after two hours flying over pretty featureless desert the Hudson leader led the formation down over the strip that we were to use for the next few days. The actual strip was marked out by a line of petrol drums and it was on to this patch of relatively hard sand that the Hurricanes landed. Once on the ground, the first task was to disperse and refuel the aircraft from petrol drums already flown in by Hudson. There was very little cover. The refuelling was achieved by using stirrup pumps originally intended for putting out fires during the Blitz. This method was to prove extremely handy in the days ahead. The second task was to dig slit trenches so that there would be some sort of protection if things started to go wrong.

That afternoon 213 Squadron operating as two flights, one of which I led, took off for an attack on road communications in the Agedabia area. It was to be an eventful sortie. We set out in a loose grouping which was less tiring on a long trip. After about 45 minutes I called my flight into closer formation. When we were about 10 miles from the target I took them down to about 200ft so that the radar at nearby Agedabia airfield would not pick us up. As the formation lost altitude one of my pilots, a Canadian, flew straight into the ground. Whether he was hit by ground fire or it was an error of judgement, we shall never know, but I had lost a fine aggressive operator and the crash resulted in a huge fire and an oil-smoke plume visible for many miles. We had little

time to worry about this as the coast and the road we were to attack was already in view.

As we approached the Agedabia-Benghazi road, with the coast in the distance we turned on our gunsights and placed the firing button on the control column to fire. The formation started to fly a more erratic course to put off enemy gunners. This was the moment when one forgot fear and an exhilarating sense of total commitment took over. The harder you attacked now the less chance there was of being shot down. We approached the road at right angles and only pulling up at the last moment to get a sight on a target. There were targets in profusion because the Afrika Korps tanks and vehicles were nose to tail and some in 'lagger' brewing up. We picked on batches of vehicles and soon we had explosions going and a large number of fires. It is never wise to go back and attack a target a second time unless it is absolutely necessary, so I indicated a turn to the north where further soft-skinned vehicles could be seen in large numbers. Again our attack brought fires and explosions. Unfortunately the Afrika Korps were beginning to wake up and anti-aircraft fire, particularly heavy machine gun fire, was crisscrossing our course with the occasional burst of lazy-looking red tracer. It was about that time that I lost another aircraft but in the heat of the action I did not see exactly what happened. I had exhausted my cannon ammunition and imagined that others in the formation were in much the same situation so I made a right turn back into the desert calling the flight on R/T as all surprise had

Below: Tiffin. Mechanics of a Messerschmitt Bf 109 Staffel take their midday 'meal' alfresco.
Imperial War Museum, MH.5854

now been lost. The important thing was that the enemy did not monitor our radio transmissions thus discovering where we had come from so it was silence again after that first call.

As we left the target, and the excitement of action subsided the problem that was very much in my mind, as leader of the formation, was how I was going to find LG 125. To get there we had to cross 200 miles or so of featureless desert with no sort of navigational aid. We were at fairly low level lest the enemy radar got some idea of the location of our desert base. So it had to be the watch and the compass. On this occasion it was helped by a clear day and patch of a most white sand which was the only real feature close to our landing ground. The whole sortie had taken two hours. The other flight had also lost an aircraft to ground fire so we were already three aircraft down.

The evening was spent digging in and briefing for the following day's operations. I slept in the cockpit of my aircraft, not the most relaxing couch, and I woke several times during the night. By dawn I was stiff and uncomfortable. However, the operation had not been designed for comfort. Next day the plan was to attack Agedabia airfield which was known to be pretty active. Again the operation was to be undertaken in separate flights. After a typical desert breakfast of soya sausages and beans (which several of those troubled by nervous stomachs could not face) we were off again and heading west.

The flight to the target was uneventful. As we approached I ordered my flight down to low level and into a loose formation designed to give maximum manoeuvrability for stafing attacks. Locating the airfield was made simpler by sighting an Italian SM82 transport aircraft which was circling it. I detached two aircraft to deal with it hoping it was full of generals. There were several Italian CR42s parked on the strip. We swept across them with cannon fire and then turned our attention to the airfield installations. It was a successful attack and we claimed the poor SM82 and the CR42s as destroyed. The light anti-aircraft fire from emplacements surrounding the airfield had been quite intense and one of my aircraft had been shot down. It was with some sense of relief that I headed the flight back to the desert. It was to be an eventful journey. As one of my wingmen came abreast of me I could see that his port long range tank was on fire. What should I advise him to do? He was leaving a long trail of smoke across the sky. The danger was that the fire would reach the main fuel system and the aircraft would explode. I was about to tell him to make a speedy forced landing in the desert and hope to be picked up, when the

problem was solved for me. An explosion in the burning tank blew it off the aircraft's wing. I did not know what damage this might have done, but the pilot was a calm Autralian and I felt that he should risk carrying on as he was, as we were, by now, over some pretty inhospitable desert.

Our troubles had only just started. The sky was by now overcast and the desert had taken on a grey colour. Again I tried my best dead-reckoning navigation but this time, when my watch told me that we should be in sight of the landing ground, there was no sign. Certainly the white sand dune was not showing up against the grey of the desert. There was nothing for it but a square search in the hope that one of us would pick up the strip. But it was not to be, and with considerable self-condemnation concerning my navigational technique, and anxious glances at the fuel gauges, I decided that our only chance was to bear north in the hope of running into the British 8th Army which I knew to be advancing fairly rapidly in the direction of Benghazi.

The aircraft that had been on fire seemed to be under control, so we set off north. I hoped to strike the coast at or near Tobruk, but had we enough fuel? We climbed in order to have better visibility and conserve fuel. We pulled back our engine revolutions and put our fuel control into weak, only clearing the engines occasionally to stop rough running. Unhappily our course took us over a substantial element of the retreating Afrika Korps though because of the dust haze we were unaware of this until it was too late. Luckily there were no enemy fighters in the air. Had there been, we would have been sitting targets as no one in my flight had any ammunition left.

The whole sortie to Agedabia airfield should have taken about two hours but we had now been in the air for over four hours. Things were getting pretty desperate. A landing in the desert and possible capture were very much on the cards. Then, through the haze in the distance, I saw the coast appear. The remaining questions were whether we could make it on the fuel we had left and, if we did, whether we could find a landing ground in allied hands. Luckily the answer to both was yes. We struggled to Gambut airfield which had just fallen to the Allies. All pilots landed safely, although the aircraft which had been on fire was a write-off.

At dawn next morning, after some sleep and refuelling, I set off with my remaining aircraft to try and find LG 125. I was a little apprehensive about what sort of reception I would get and felt that my navigation might come in for some criticism because my squadron CO, leading the other six aircraft,

Above: Junkers Ju 87D-1-Trop, ex-S7+LL of 33/St G.3, 'liberated' and repainted in fresh markings by 213 Sqn. *C. Bowyer*

had been due to attack the same target a few minutes after us. Once more we headed behind the German lines, although this time I took care to steer well clear of the Afrika Korps. It was a clear morning and this time my navigation put me right on to the strip. We landed without further incident.

To our surprise we learned that the CO and his flight had also failed to return. As far as the ground crew were concerned the whole of the squadron had been lost and near total catastrophe had struck the operation. Our return brightened the situation somewhat.

I had a pretty good idea that the CO had got into the same sort of trouble that had affected my navigation and that he and his flight were down in the desert somewhere. We refuelled our aircraft and set off to search for the other flight and with a stroke of inspiration took along with us two stirrup pumps.

We spent about an hour searching likely areas for a forced landing when we spotted Verey lights being fired. We found five Hurricanes (one having been shot down over the target) which had apparently landed in the desert with wheels down and were in reasonable order. They wasted no time in marking out a safe landing strip for us. By skilful and energetic use of the stirrup pump we transferred fuel from our long-range tanks

into their empty main tanks. The aircraft batteries were all in good shape and 20 minutes later the whole circus was back at LG 125. What had at first looked like a total catastrophe for the squadron had been to a large extend retrieved.

During our adventures in the desert the other squadron, which had not been on the airfield attack, had been briefed to make further attacks on the Benghazi-Agedabia road. On their way to their target they spotted an Italian armoured column of about 50 vehicles some 60 miles from our strip. The column had obviously been sent to winkle us out of our secret landing-ground. Our security was blown. The squadron abandoned their sortie and got stuck into the column, destroying all the vehicles.

The column was now no longer a threat, but chancing on it had been a great stroke of luck. Given a few hours and the Italians might have made a terrible mess of our whole operation. We had to accept that they had sent out a wireless warning. We spent a restless and vigilant night, on guard against another possible attack, as other columns might have been in the vicinity. Time was clearly running out for us.

On the next day, the fourth behind German lines, the morning's task was to attack the airfield at Galo which was being

Above: Desert Debris.
Remains of an Italian vehicle
park.
Imperial War Museum, CM.4039

Left: Bent Bird. Heinkel He III
at Catania airfield.   *C. Bowyer*

Above: Remains of a Heinkel He III, marked with appropriate desert insigna.
C. Bowyer

used by both the Germans and Italians. It was situated just outside an oasis of the same name. It was a flight of about one hour almost due south into the desert without even a coast line to help us judge our target position. However, on this occasion, the navigation was good and we found and attacked a very surprised airstrip indeed. There were few aircraft on the strip, but a lot of transport and many swiftly scattering troops. It was possibly the HQ of an enemy long range desert group. Ground fire on this occasion was not intense and we had no losses. We had achieved good surprise.

After the previous navigational experience the journey back was made at a higher level, with the aircraft spread well out to give maximum desert coverage. The day was clear and on the hour the welcome white sand dune was in sight. We were soon on the ground.

During our absence two Hudsons had appeared with orders for us to pull out before our strip came under air attack itself or we were attacked from the ground. As soon as refuelling was complete we were off and a two-hour flight brought us back to our slightly more established desert base and the comforts of a shave and a camp bed in a dusty, sand tent. Even now we had to forego a bath, because of the shortage of water.

Our squadron had lost five aircraft with their pilots during the operation. Three of them in fact survived to become prisoners of war. No 2 Armoured Car Company was left to make its own way back to more friendly territory. This they did by disappearing into the desert and flanking the southern elements of the German Army. They had done a great job and their redoubtable commander's reputation as a real desert hawk was further enhanced, but he also had a fine team.

There has been much retrospective discussion amongst military historians about whether Montgomery harassed the Afrika Korps sufficiently during their retreat. Certainly the Desert Air Force played their full part and though our operation was but a small part of the overall air assault it was an important one and a worrying one for the enemy. Our squadron took 14 aircraft on the operation and lost five with one hopelessly damaged. Three pilots prisoners of war. I don't know what Rommel thought about it all but I think he would have been worried about his flank and the knowledge that relatively short range fighters were already operating against his rear areas. It was a good plan of psychological and operational effectiveness. Some fighter formation leaders learnt a thing or two about desert navigation!

Yes, as Wilfred Thesiger wrote of the desert, 'No man can live this life and emerge unchanged'. The squadrons that operated from LG 125 would agree — wholeheartedly.

A Rather Personal War

Terence Kelly

Terence Kelly first saw action on fighter sweeps over France in 1941. In the autumn, his squadron, No 258, was posted to Africa but diverted to the Far East following Pearl Harbor. He remained in Java when the majority of No 258 still surviving were evacuated, and flew with No 605 Squadron. Taken prisoner he spent seven months in the local gaol of Boei Glodok before being transferred to Japan to a camp close to Hiroshima.

His career aside from writing includes his own professional practices in the UK, Jamaica and Trinidad. He has written many plays which have been staged in the West End and provinces and has produced or co-produced many more. He has also written for radio and television. His books include the novels *The Blades of Cordoba*, *Play in a Hot Summer* and *The Genki Boys* set in his own prison camp in Japan: and the non-fiction *Hurricane Over the Jungle*.

In the limited air war against the Japanese which preceded the fall of Singapore and the Dutch East Indies, just one New Zealand and three British fighter squadrons were involved. The New Zealand squadron was No 488 which arrived in Singapore in October 1941 to be joined by No 243 Squadron and a Dutch unit later. Meanwhile two further squadrons, Nos 232 and 258, diverted from the Middle East, were on their way. In the main it will be of No 258 I write because, as one of its pilots who flew until operations in this theatre ended, I am able to give a continuous account while, hopefully, painting a picture of what those exciting weeks were like to all pilots involved in them.

Space prohibits detail of the events leading up to the arrival of the squadron in Singapore. Suffice it to say that we, a very international squadron consisting of five American, one Australian, two Canadian, five New Zealand, one Rhodesian and 10 British pilots, flew off aircraft carrier HMS *Indomitable* on 28 January, 1942 to Kemajoran airport, Batavia, Java and on the following day some of us flew up to Singapore, refuelling en route at Palembang in Sumatra, where 13 of us landed at Seletar. The next day was spent getting as many Hurricanes as possible serviceable and on the 30th those which were, were flown to Tengah airfield. Within an hour there was a scramble. We managed to get eight aircraft into the sky and, encountering a force of bombers and fighters outnumbering us five to one, had two of these shot down and three more badly damaged. One pilot, a New Zealander, Bruce McAlister was killed but the other, a Scot named McCulloch got away with it as was to become something of a habit with him. By afternoon we had just four Hurricanes available to pit against the Japanese — a somewhat lesser number than the 48 it had been intended we should have — and already the squadron was scattered with some pilots on

Left: Terence Kelly, Debden, late 1941, author of this chapter. *via author*

the island, some in Sumatra and some still in Java while our groundstaff were on the high seas. And this situation was soon further confused by Wavell's ill-thought-out decision that one makeshift squadron should be formed to operate from Kallang (the one airfield on Singapore reckoned still to be out of artillery range of the Japanese now just across the Johore Baru Strait) while all other aircraft were to be withdrawn to Sumatra. Our contribution to this makeshift squadron was to be five pilots: 'Denny' Sharp, two of the Americans, Donahue and Kleckner, 'Pip' Healey and myself. However Healey didn't go at once as his aircraft was unserviceable and I didn't go at all as mine had been damaged in the morning's business and was undergoing repairs. It was a solitary feeling being the last pilot on an empty airfield chivvying unenthusiastic ground staff to put an aircraft right, but the gloom lifted when, on the evening of 2 February, the balance of No 258 unexpectedly flew up from Palembang to Tengah on a mission to escort Blenheims and Lockheed Hudsons on a dawn up-country raid on the enemy-occupied airfield of Kluang. Elation, however, was short-lived. Going out to our aircraft next morning it was to find that while their gun panels had been removed there were no groundstaff in sight. The Hudsons, due to bomb at dawn were already on their way, and the Blenheims which we were intended to protect and which were to follow at first light and attack after strafing by their attendant Hurricanes, were already waiting. So the bombers went alone and the Japanese were waiting for them. It was disaster. The Hurricanes returned in shame to Palembang and I went with them.

There were two airfields near Palembang, the civilian airport and a huge, cleared area some 40 miles to the south west, a secret field the Japanese were never to discover. To distinguish them from each other we dubbed them respectively 'P1' and 'P2'. We landed at P1 which lay about ten miles to the north of the town and possessed a 1,300-metre runway and a shorter one making a boss-eyed cross. The road from the town passed by the west side of the field which was otherwise hemmed in by light jungle. There was a decent terminal building but no hangars nor much in the way of buildings from which to operate the forces which were, for all practical purposes, to comprise the defensive effort for a country large enough to include the whole of Italy. There was little transport, no cooking facilities, no dispersal huts, no heavy anti-aircraft guns and few slit trenches, while the defence consisted of a few Dutch Bofors guns and a handful of Dutch troops. There were no Hurricane tool kits, aircraft spares were all but non-existent, and ammunition, glycol and oxygen supplies were low. Aircraft had to be serviced by crews who had never worked on Hurricanes before. For warning of approach of enemy aircraft there was a small operations room in Palembang with a single and bad telephone line to P1. There was no means of plotting enemy or friendly aircraft, aircraft recognition hardly existed, and such warning as was received was telephoned by watchers at posts ranged in a circle about 50 kilometres from the airfield giving us at best five minutes to be airborne. There was no radio direction finding and no direction finding for homing aircraft, while radio communication between ground and air, and air to air, was always unsatisfactory and often non-existent.

This last was the most serious want of all. One flew deaf and dumb over hundreds of miles of unbroken jungle where each mile

Above left: Pilots who ferried Hurricanes at Port Sudan. L-R: Glynn, Lambert, unknown, Sheerin, Keedwell, Scott — all Sergeants. *via author*

Above: Arthur Gerald — 'Art' — Donahue DFC, an American, who was later killed in action on 11 September 1942. *R. F. Donahue*

looked identical to the rest and where, once lost, the only hope was to fly until one found a river and, hoping it was the Moesi on which Palembang lay, fly along it until one saw the town. One could watch with horror a friend about to be attacked and be powerless to warn him; one could not inform that one had insufficient petrol to reach base or a faulty engine in the hope one might be sufficiently pinpointed to make the chance of being found at least a possibility and, as will be seen, this grave shortcoming was to have the most extraordinary and disastrous consequences.

But at least, or so we encouraged ourselves, extricated from the hopeless confusion of Singapore and with the enemy fully engaged in investing it, here in Sumatra we would have a breathing space in which to build up to reasonable strength and sort things out. It was not to be. That very afternoon we were attacked.

The usual afternoon's torrential downpour having abated, we were sitting in chairs on the verandah of the terminal building, chatting and smoking. Our readiness state, that is to say the list of pilots due to fly that afternoon, was chalked on the glass walls behind us and with the shortage of aircraft covered about every other pilot. Expecting more Hurricanes up from Java, we were not surprised to hear aircraft approaching and I remember being impressed that with the sky still covered almost entirely by thick clouds they had found P.1 at all and musing on the good fortune of there being just the one break in it straight ahead of us without which they could never have landed and might have been very pushed to make it back to Java. And it was then we saw the first Hurricane. It came through the small blue gap to the north and was followed, one by one, by others, still little

more than specks, pouring through the gap, diving on us in the traditional beat-up. We watched delightedly... until suddenly we realised these aircraft had radial engines! That they *weren't* Hurricanes!

Realisation coincided with attack! The air was filled with the whine of bullets and cannon shells and the roar of engines! The first Navy O* pulled out of its dive and climbed away not 20ft above our heads, the blood red circles on its wings mocking us. Behind was the sound of shattering glass and only yards away a man was screaming and clutching at his stomach. The second Navy O, seeming to be aiming directly at us, was not a hundred yards away machine guns and cannon blazing. I dropped, and, as it pulled up, ran. P.1 was filled with running men: pilots on readiness running to their machines, ground staff racing out to help them in and get them started up, others with no purpose in remaining running for the cover of the jungle... But as *I* ran, I had to stop. For I saw something almost beyond belief. One of No 258's pilots, one of the Americans, 'Red' Campbell, was standing calmly, revolver in hand, aiming at the next Navy O. Useless, of course — but not a gesture. One reads of men who have no fear. They are very rare — but Campbell was one of them.

There is a difference between being the recipient of general bombing and being the *specific* target and there was certainly drama in that first blooding of this particular type of warfare. One's friends taxying past at dangerous speed and tearing down the runway to do battle. The strafing of Navy Os. The shriek of aircraft, the shattering of

*To British pilots at this time the plane now known as the 'Zero', was called Navy O (Oh) or Navy Nought, never Zero.

**Above: Kallang Airport,
Singapore, in late 1930s.**
C. Bowyer

**Right: Air and ground crews,
258 Sqn at Kallang dispersal
hut, early 1942.** *R. F. Donahue*

glass, the spatter of machine guns, the pop of cannon and the slow cudumph, cudumph, cudumph of Bofors guns. The added heartening chatter of the Brownings. Air battles to witness against a background of heavy cloud, a Navy O hurtling earthwards in a screaming dive into the jungle. A Hurricane eluding a Japanese which had been sitting on its tail apparently pumping bullets into it. Another hit, showing the thin white thread of Glycol thicken, yet managing to land. And Campbell, nerveless, reloading his revolver.

Curiously that attack proved an almost total failure. Of the aircraft which managed to get airborne all landed safely, mostly at P.2. No aircraft were damaged on the ground; but a few ground staff personnel were killed or wounded. However the following day was another matter. This time there

were bombers and the Japanese did not repeat the error of having all their fighters strafe; again there was no warning and this time there were Navy O's waiting to pick off Hurricanes taking off to do battle with them. We flew several times and by the end of the day nine of No 258's Hurricanes were missing or shot down and others damaged; in fact out of the entire force the only pilots who managed to bring back undamaged aircraft to P.1 were Bertie Lambert and myself. Three No 258 pilots were dead, one was dying, two were missing and three Hurricanes had been badly shot about and their pilots either baled out or crash landed in swamp or on the field. The latter were (Sergeants) Scott, Nichols and Nash; the missing were White and McCulloch; the dying was a Canadian, Keedwell; and the dead were (Pilot Officers)

Left: Hurricane in its brickwalled dispersal pen, Singapore, 1941.
R. F. Donahue

Scott, Glynn (our youngest pilot) and Kleckner who, with others of No 258, had just returned to Palembang from Kallang.

As it had begun so it was to go on with the days between 4 and 14 February hectic and the 14th the most hectic of them all. One was either flying and involved or not flying and watching the involvement of others. Much of the action was within sight of the airfield and there was continual incident what with strafing and bombing raids, searches in the jungle for pilots shot down near enough to P.1 for this to be worthwhile and so on. After such lapse of time it is difficult to disentangle one day from another but flashes of incidents remain: hoping against all hope that a Blenheim quietly passing at some distance, (its crew clearly unaware P.1 was under attack), would get by unnoticed and the sickening feeling of seeing it all of a sudden surrounded by Japanese Navy Os like a shoal of piranhas scenting an open wound; a bombed up aircraft on the field exploding in a huge ball of yellow flame and some poor devil standing near enough to touch having most of his stomach gouged away by a lump of flying shrapnel; and something else, something remarkable, and of value later.

Eight of us had been ferried in a Lodestar down to Kemajoran to ferry up replacement Hurricanes. Led by Wing Commander Maguire (now Air Marshal Sir Harold Maguire) we broke formation to land and, flying two to Maguire, I was second down. As we were taxying in we were attacked, the sky suddenly being seemingly filled with Navy Os presumably tipped off by some fifth columnist. But their timing was just less than

perfect for seven of the eight were safely down and the only one caught was Scott, well into his final approach. Just below him, I saw with horror the Navy O on his tail, slim, jungle-green, with its disproportionate radial engine and cannon shells thudding from its gun. I saw smoke begin to pour from Scotty's engine, even saw his head as he hauled back on his stick to get enough height for baling out. And he succeeded, jumping at eight or nine hundred feet and landing by parachute close by. But what was even more remarkable was what happened to the Navy O. Its speed would not have been great, hardly 300mph, and its recovery from its dive with plenty of air space not particularly severe. Yet it was more than the airframe could take — both wings simply folded upwards like those of

Below: Hurricane BF163 of 258 Sqn, Singapore 1941, investigating a concrete monsoon ditch. *R. F. Donahue*

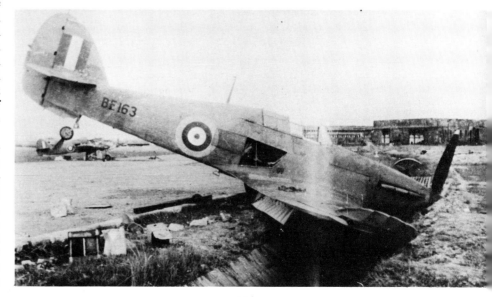

carrier borne aircraft, which fold for stacking purposes, and it crashed beside us in the jungle.

Above all I remember the incident of Dicky Parr, one of the 232 Squadron pilots, also flying from P.1. Shot up, with throttle jammed open, he made an efficient job of land wheels up and fast, by switching off his engine at just the right moment to end, on his nose, tidily positioned at the very end of the runway thus not interfering with others taking off and landing. Lambert (I believe) and I tore across in a truck to find Parr, already out of his upended Hurricane, awaiting us. 'I guess', he said, 'I won't be needing this any more.' And fishing into his pocket he drew out from it the little finger of his left hand which had been taken off by the bullet which jammed his throttle open.

But the day not to be forgotten was 14 February 1942. It started with promise. A Japanese invasion force had been sighted in the Banka Straits on the east coast of Sumatra. Blenheims were detailed to attack escorted by as many Hurricanes as could be mustered. We managed 14 — so far as I know the largest number of Hurricanes which ever flew a mission together in the entire campaign. When the Blenheims, presumably from P.2, failed to rendezvous overhead, we took off. It was a splendid morning with some cumulus and a thin skein of cloud through which as we climbed we saw, obscured but recognisable, the heartening sight of a large formation of Lockheed Hudsons evidently heading for P.1. Promised reinforcements were at last arriving! Stimulated we pressed on to Banka. But we didn't find the convoy — why I do not know; it certainly was there. Anyway, Thomson, our CO, ordered a return to base, an instruc-

tion I personally didn't hear as my R/T wasn't functioning. Nearing P.1, I spotted Navy Os above us at the very moment when, for some unaccountable reason, the entire formation turned abruptly southwards. Unable to communicate, I flew to its head and started waggling my wings and gesticulating like mad but earning no more than a glower from Thomson as he bellowed into his mouthpiece presumably for me to get back into place. Something had to be done. Ruefully I observed the formation flying blithely southwards as I headed up, joined by one other Hurricane, to take on the enemy.

The next hour or so was rather a busy one and apart from being involved with several Navy Os in the vicinity of P.1 one of which I shot down and another possibly, I was also chased halfway round Sumatra by one which managed to get on my tail and which I only shook off by flying at zero feet and turning violently between trees than than a wingspan apart, a nefarious practice I had improperly learnt in training and which I doubted the more disciplined Japanese pilots would have contemplated trying. Fortunately unscathed after an hour and forty minutes flying (which is a long time in a Hurricane), my gauges showing my tanks all but empty, I returned to P.1 landed and taxied to my Hurricane's usual place facing the east-west cross runway. Astonishingly no ground crew came running out to help me down, refuel the tanks, re-cover the gunports, reload the guns and check oil and glycol. I was very put out — after all I had quite a line to shoot. But there was no one. Mystified I undid my straps, unclasped the parachute harness, hastily turned a forgotten gun button away from 'Fire' and put my helmet over it, stripped off my gauntlets, hauled myself out

Below: Pilots of No 453 Sqn RAAF at Sembawang, Singapore, December 1941, 'scrambling'.
Imperial War Museum, CF.764

Left: Japanese 'Navy-O' (later termed 'Zero').

of the cockpit, felt for and found the step in the fuselage and jumped down to the ground.

Only then did it really hit me. The airfield was empty, abandoned. There was not a soul; there was not a sound. I stood aghast, bewildered. All but two hours before I had taken off from a bustling airport; now it was deserted. Dead. All, except for human beings, was exactly as I had left it; the unserviceable Hurricanes, petrol bowsers, Parr's machine. All the paraphernalia of an active fighter base was there. Everything. Everything except the men. The terminal building glinted in the sun, silent, abandoned; the chairs we had sat in were empty. It was something from *Beau Geste*. The deserted fort with tables laid but only stillness. In all my life I never felt more alone. Then, thankfully, I head a sound, a comforting sound in that hot and steamy empty place, the sound of another Hurricane returning. Joyfully, I watched it all the way, landing, taxying, drawing up beside my own, the pilot doing all the things which I had done getting out and down to join me. Bertie Lambert.

We talked in whispers — two pilots beside their Hurricanes on an abandoned airfield in Sumatra.

'What d'you make of it?'
'Haven't a clue. Hear anything on your R/T?'
'U/S . . .'

We broke off as a man came racing from the jungle, a 258 Squadron pilot — 'Micky' Nash, shouting: 'What the hell are you doing here? Didn't you get the gen on your R/T?'
'Duff.' I wondered if there were unexploded bombs.
'So was mine,' said Bertie. 'What's up?'
'Paratroops. Hundreds of the buggers! You can't walk out! You can't drive out! They're all around the place!'

With horror I remembered those Lockheed Hudsons. 'But . . . but they were Lockheeds. Those trailing flaps . . . You must have seen them, Bertie. They *were* Lockheeds.'
'Definitely!' The awfulness had struck him too. 'Buggers must have bought them from the Yanks. Jesus Christ on a bicycle. We passed right over them. What a beano we could have had!'
'You've got one now', said Micky grimly. 'Listen!'

We listened and heard rifle fire. I forgot the Lockheeds.
'You're lucky,' Micky said. 'You've got kites.'
'If they start,' said Bertie.

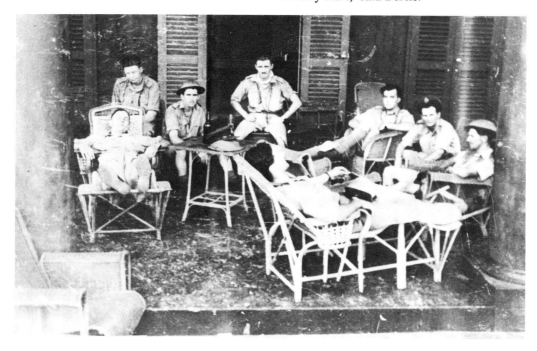

Left: Verandah of Officers' Mess, Tengah, Singapore. L-R: Thomson; Campbell; Dobbyn; Macnamara; Tremlett; Klechner; Brown; de la Perelle. *R. F. Donahue*

Above: AVM S. F. Vincent
CB, DFC, AFC, DL.

Above right: Sqn Ldr 'Ricky'
Wright DFM; 'Cam' White;
'Joe' Hutton; 'Art' Brown.
R. F. Donahue

Right: Hurricanes on P.1
airstrip. *R. F. Donahue*

'And if there's any juice left. Mine's showing sweet FA'

'Well you'd . . .' Micky broke off at a thumping sound.

'Mortars!' said Bertie, solemnly.

'Hand grenades.'

I wasn't disposed to argue it. 'What are you going to do, Micky?', I asked.

'Get the hell out of sight. Before they start shooting us.'

I didn't like the look of the green perimeter but there was a certain form to things. 'Micky . . .'

'If you aren't quick, you damn well won't start.'

'Okay,' I said, 'Best of luck, Micky.'

'Ta, ta!', said Bertie, 'I'm off!

We got into our aircraft all fingers and thumbs grabbing at parachute straps and shoving the ends in the quick release, scrabbling for webbing harness and shoving home the pin. I didn't bother with gloves and simply jammed my helmet on my head with everything dangling. I saw Bertie's propeller turn, pressed my own starter button and watched my own prop slowly, jerkily start to turn as well and then there was a cough and, thankfully, the engine roared to life. I turned for a final wave to Micky — but he had vanished. Opening the throttle, I turned left along the secondary runway to where it met the main one. Normally I'd have taxied to the

end of that: now I didn't bother. Even so, I did my drill; I was, by nature, a careful pilot.

PRAFT. P — Petrol . . . That's a laugh! R — Retractable undercarriage . . . Lights red. Okay. A — Airscrew . . . Fine pitch. Okay. F — Flaps . . . Lever up. Okay. T — Trim . . . Neutral. Okay.

Taking the most cursory of looks around the sky for waiting Navy Os, I slammed the throttle open. The Hurricane began to gather speed, the tail came up, the nose went down and I could see the runway ahead, the mess of Parr's machine, the jungle. Halfway along I unstuck and banked immediately and looking down could see odd parachutes, like handkerchiefs, upon the trees. That was all. Odd parachutes and the green jungle of Sumatra which hid the Japanese and 19 year-old Micky and God only knew who else besides. But I didn't dwell on it, not with a petrol gauge flickering on empty and 40 odd miles to go. I never flew a Hurricane so slowly, wobbling through the sky, a sitting target for a Navy O. Fortunately there were none. And I made P.2. As did Bertie. When they checked my tanks I had two gallons left. The next day, 15 February, there were at P.2 eight serviceable Hurricanes remaining. These were ordered to strafe the substantial force of Japanese who were advancing on Palembang in self-propelled barges up the Moesi River. It was arranged that Nos 258

Above: Servicing a Hurricane at Palembang. *C. Bowyer*

and 232 Squadrons should take turn and turn about with 258 making the first attack. We took off through an apparent haze which, once pierced, proved to be a thin level layer of cloud stretching as far as the eye could see, a serious thing for without RDF there was no way of refinding the airfield. Fortunately one of our Americans, 'Art' Donahue, was alert to the danger and the moment he had passed through the haze at once went back down through it, landed (P.2 fortunately being huge) and, grabbing a Verey pistol, started firing upwards through the mist. There shot through what was to the seven of us and the single Blenheim, presumably intended to guide us to the barges, a green ball bursting like a Roman candle around which we began to gyrate using it as a centre. Thenceforth it was a strange, nervewracking business. One pilot, like an unenthusiastic swimmer on a winter's day, lowered wheels and flaps and circumspectly dipped the nose of his machine and disappeared — only almost immediately to rear up again in a fierce, clumsy, evasive climb having obviously barely avoided collision with the trees. Back he went into the circle. Another tried only to rear up again. So it went on. Another tried and failed to reappear leaving the rest of us only able to surmise whether he had crashed or made it. The Blenheim vanished, perhaps to Java for which he would have had the range. For the

rest of us it was now P. 2 or crash landing in swamp or jungle. I took my turn and gingerly descended. For a moment all was white and then as quickly I was in clear air and hurtling at the green of jungle, slamming the throttle open, rearing like a startled animal through and above the mist again. So it went on, a circle of Hurricanes of diminishing numbers looking unreal as they crept round with lowered flaps and slowly spinning wheels. Someone tried again and failed to reappear. One felt the onset of loneliness. I tried again, found the field but was crossing it diagonally. I tried half a dozen times and was always too much to one side, overshooting or not quite straight. I steeled myself to work it out, made an intentional feint to give me the direction of approach, climbed through the murk and turned by guesswork sufficiently to put me along the line of correct descent. All that was needed was an accurate circuit. I counted to 30, performed an essentially accurate rate one turn, counted again, turned, counted, turned and came into land. When I broke through at perhaps a hundred feet it was not too bad for I was within the field and correctly on line. But much too far along. But one thing was sure — I wasn't going through that muck again!

P.2 was huge, studded with clumps of trees and broadening at its northern end like an old type key. I steered towards the starboard

jungle boundary and when as close as I dared be, opened the throttle full bore and at fifty feet did a split arse turn to take me round a hundred and eighty degrees plus within the field's perimeter. It was memory and guesswork now for, turning, the trees could not be seen. But it worked. I got round and took off the bank — only to find myself heading straight for one of the tree clumps. So it was another split arse turn and recovery and then it was clear ahead and room enough. Thankfully I put her down. As I taxied in, I saw two Hurricanes on their noses. We were down to six.

When the mist cleared we took off and strafed the barges. It was carnage. A 12-gun Hurricane had battalion power, 12,000 rounds a minute. Moreover armed for aerial combat the ammunition included armour piercing, tracer and incendiary bullets. The barges were filled with Japanese packed like matches stood vertically in a box and their only defence was a machine gunner in the stern.

I flew with Donahue. When we came on the barges we had become detached from the others so I don't know how they fared. Donny went in first. There were about six barges each with about 200 Japanese. Moving slowly against the stream of turgid, chocolate-coloured water you would have thought them stationary but for the thin creaming line of engine wakes. They were unfortunate to have been found on a long straight stretch for even tucked as they were tight to the jungle margin they had no cover.

I watched Donahue's bullets turn the water ahead of the nearest barge into a pincushion which then moved along both sides of the first barge with only the flashes of striking bullets and tracer lines showing in the body of the barge before the fusillade had passed beyond it and the pincushion was in between the first and second barges. And so along the line. Then it my turn and I lost sight of Donahue; when I completed my turn to bring me in line for my second strafe, he was not ahead of me. In fact he had been hit on his initial run, a minor foot wound which sent him back to England where he was later killed leading his own Spitfire squadron.

Afterwards, when I was a prisoner of war, the Japanese talked of the horror wrought amongst those barges and we destroyed our brevets lest they revenge themselves. It was the only aspect of war I heard the Japanese speak of with awe. Yet we didn't make a second attack. Why, I do not know. We had the means and the enemy, however shaken, was still a cohesive force crawling up a fast flowing river. Sufficiently pressed strafing would have so devastated that force has to render it inoperative and Sumatran bases were vital to the Japanese to mount their onslaught yet to come on Java. But there it is. Someone, somewhere ordered P.2, which the enemy did not even know existed, to be evacuated. So we left it. Some by boat up the Moesi ahead of the advancing Japanese, some by road southwards to the port of Oosthaven. Some by train. And a few of us by Hurricane.

Operations 'Wildhorn III'

Air Marshal Sir Edward Chilton KBE, CB, FRIN

The Royal Air Force career of Air Marshal Sir Edward Chilton focused largely on Coastal and Maritime operations; but he also saw much service in the Far East and the Mediterranean. He retired as Commander in Chief of Coastal Command.

His Service interests have coloured much of his career in retirement, particularly his specialist qualifications in the field of navigation. He has also over recent years established a notable reputation as writer, historian, lecturer and raconteur, travelling widely and being in much demand by public and private bodies in these capabilities. He has also maintained close contact with the RAF through his many sporting interests of rowing, sailing and swimming.

His main business interests since retirement have centred on consultancy on Defence Systems and Data Processing.

If you should be in the company of Polish people and get drawn into a discussion about World War 2, you will quickly discover that they regard three episodes as being especially significant. These events are: their role at Narvik (Norway), the taking of Monte Cassino (Italy) and the theft of a German V2 rocket in Poland. The Royal Air Force was privileged to share in the last event and I shall try to lead the reader through this rather complex story, which brings out to good advantage all of the elements of a job well done. The accurate preparation for the flight, the precise navigation, the excellent airmanship, the courage and the resourcefulness of the crew shine in every respect.

Before I can introduce the reader to the details of 'Operation Wildhorn', it is necessary to sketch in some of the details for the gathering of information about Hitler's so-called 'Secret Weapons'. Before the war there had been agents' reports about these weapons but little solid fact. Oddly, it was Hitler himself who let the cat out of the bag by saying, at a massive rally in Danzig on 19 September 1939, that Germany possessed a weapon 'which is not yet known and with which we ourselves cannot be attacked!' This phrase was to set the alarm bells ringing, but towards the end of 1939 we had a most unexpected windfall which could only be described as a vast 'Pandora's box'; an anonymous letter from a well-wisher from Germany. The sender is now known but the name is still kept secret. This letter was secretly delivered to the British Naval Attache in Oslo and sent on to London. It covered a very sound outline of all the latest German technical developments, which included, amongst many items, a long-range rocket which was being tested at Pennemunde in the Baltic. Sadly, this report did not get the attention it deserved as the Admiralty regarded it as a plant although Dr R. V. Jones, who was searching for clues

Left: The author. *Popperfoto*

about Hitler's secret weapons, gave the report much study. Perhaps one can understand the apparent lack of interest because, with France and the Low Countries still intact, the risk for the UK from such a weapon appeared to be minimal. Dr Jones felt that the report was too detailed to be a hoax and when he was personally charged with finding out about the rocket he gave urgent attention to the details. However, events suddenly moved very swiftly and, with the unexpected fall of the Low Countries and France in 1940, a rocket with a possible range of 250 miles became a real menace.

Furthermore, we also became aware of the close proximity of the German Air Force at their new airfields, and it was Dr Jones who solved our immediate danger from their accurate radio beams which led the GAF Bombers over our cities. We were lucky in that the necessary counter measures were brought into play at an early date. Dr Jones was now under greater pressure to find out the truth about the rocket but information was hard to come by, especially as most of Europe was virtually closed to our agents. All was not lost, however, as since 1941 the well-organised Polish underground had maintained a constant watch on strange events going on in certain parts of their country, especially in the Blizna area. Although there were great difficulties in finding ways and means of getting the information to London, by 1943 there was a constant stream of intelligence, but often confusing, especially when there were two weapons under development, which became known as the V1 and the V2. The fact that there were two weapons was not known to us until later, and it is easy to imagine the confusion as there were so many apparent contradictions. Some underground reports referred to 'cigar-shaped' missiles while others talked of a small pilot-less aircraft. I shall not prolong this aspect of the story except to say that, even after the UK had by 2 December 1943 established that there were two weapons, there were still several missing pieces of information, such as the size of the war-head, the range of the rocket missile, its fuel, its reliability and, above all, was it possible to introduce any form of counter-measures? Perhaps the most curious detail to be forwarded was the 'Air Burst Phenomenon' of the V2 which, unknown to Dr Jones and his staff, was proving a major headache to the Germans. In May 1944 the first break occurred, since a virtually-complete V2 rocket thrust chamber was located by the Poles in a soft river bank. It was photographed at once before the German recovery team arrived on the site. To outdo the Germans (who usually arrived on the impact site very quickly) the thrust chamber was pushed into the river Bug with the hope of finding it later on after the Germans had left. The German recovery team failed to find the thrust chamber and left empty-handed. Unfortunately, notwithstanding a great effort, the Poles also failed to find it. However, their courage and tenacity was rewarded a few days later since an entire V2 crashed into a riverside marsh with remarkably little damage as it did not have an explosive head, being a test vehicle. The Poles promptly pushed the whole missile into the river while a local farmer contrived to drive his cows in and around the area, stirring up the mud and the river. Thus, when the German recovery team arrived there was nothing for them to see except the cows watering in the river. The Germans gave up the search after a few days and left the area. The reader will immediately appreciate the fact that, if this missile could somehow be transported to the UK, many of Dr Jones' problems would be resolved. Apart from the distance involved, the Poles had to evolve a complex organisation to recover the weapon, the first major headache. Once the weapon was relocated it would be necessary to dismantle it without design, drawings, without the proper tools, and then to convey the vital parts to some area in Poland where an RAF aircraft could land to collect them. The security aspects alone were extremely difficult, while the simple act of locating a tractor to haul the missile out of the river, and a steel cable strong enough for the task, appeared well nigh impossible.

Let it suffice for me to say that all this was devised by various cunning ways; the vital parts were moved to a safe area for detailed technical inspection and a very comprehensive report prepared. Once this vital information had been evaluated in London by early June 1944, plans for Operation Wildhorn 3 were put in hand, but action to implement them had hardly started when news came in that a Peenemunde-launched V2 had impacted in southern Sweden. This was only a week after the start of the Normandy landings. Unfortunately, the Swedish rocket tended to lower the priority for the recovery of the Polish V2, with consequences which could not have been foreseen at the time. The recovery of the Swedish parts was comparatively simple; they were examined on the impact site and then flown to England. These parts solved many of Dr Jones's missing links, especially the nature of the propellant and the size of the war-head. However, with the benefit of hindsight it would have been wiser to have pressed on with the recovery of the Polish V2 because the Swedish V2 parts contained components of 'Wasserfall,' a surface-to-air missile with a radio guidance system, a very different

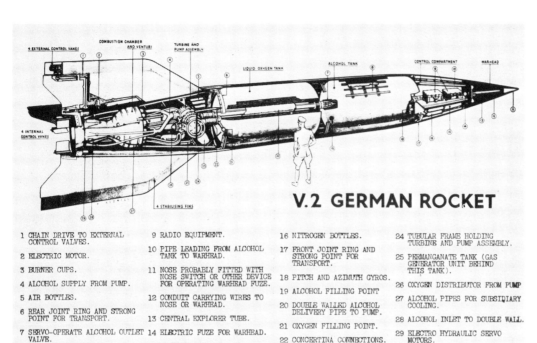

Left: German A.4 (V.2) rocket.
Imperial War Museum, C.4832

V.2 GERMAN ROCKET

1 CHAIN DRIVE TO EXTERNAL CONTROL VALVES.

2 ELECTRIC MOTOR.

3 BURNER CUPS.

4 ALCOHOL SUPPLY FROM PUMP.

5 AIR BOTTLES.

6 REAR JOINT RING AND STRONG POINT FOR TRANSPORT.

7 SERVO-OPERATE ALCOHOL OUTLET VALVE.

8 ROCKET SHELL CONSTRUCTION.

9 RADIO EQUIPMENT.

10 PIPE LEADING FROM ALCOHOL TANK TO WARHEAD.

11 NOSE PROBABLY FITTED WITH NOSE SWITCH OR OTHER DEVICE FOR OPERATING WARHEAD FUZE.

12 CONDUIT CARRYING WIRES TO NOSE OR WARHEAD.

13 CENTRAL EXPLORER TUBE.

14 ELECTRIC FUZE FOR WARHEAD.

15 PLYWOOD FRAME.

16 NITROGEN BOTTLES.

17 FRONT JOINT RING AND STRONG POINT FOR TRANSPORT.

18 PITCH AND AZIMUTH GYROS.

19 ALCOHOL FILLING POINT.

20 DOUBLE WALLED ALCOHOL DELIVERY PIPE TO PUMP.

21 OXYGEN FILLING POINT.

22 CONCERTINA CONNECTIONS.

23 HYDROGEN PEROXIDE TANK.

24 TUBULAR FRAME HOLDING TURBINE AND PUMP ASSEMBLY.

25 PERMANGANATE TANK (GAS GENERATOR UNIT BEHIND THIS TANK).

26 OXYGEN DISTRIBUTOR FROM PUMP.

27 ALCOHOL PIPES FOR SUBSIDIARY COOLING.

28 ALCOHOL INLET TO DOUBLE WALL.

29 ELECTRO HYDRAULIC SERVO MOTORS.

system from that employed in the normal V2. The electronic experts at RAE Farnborough had located an elaborate anti-jamming device amongst the Swedish rocket remains with some five million combinations, which rather dampened any ideas we might have had for interfering with the V2's guidance system! Had the Polish parts arrived before the Swedish parts, the result would have been profound, especially as the former would have arrived with a detailed technical report. By luck, the SOEHQ's in London had already asked the RAF to continue with the planning for Operation Wildhorn 3. It was decided to make the flight from Brindisi in Italy in a long-range Dakota of No 267 Squadron. This squadron had been operating in the Middle East and the Balkans for a long time and the crews were very experienced in SOE operations and had already successfully carried out Operation Wildhorn 1 and 2, also into Poland. This RAF squadron had gathered together a somewhat cosmopolitan band of brothers; there were a great number of Dominion and Colonial members, especially amongst the aircrew, as well as Poles, French, Dutch and even a Russian. Perhaps more extraordinary, for an RAF Squadron, one of the medical officers really belonged to the United States Air Force.

It was decided that the landing site would be at Zaborow near Tarnow; ideally this site should not have been used again as it was thought to have been compromised, but it was virtually impossible to find another. Furthermore, it would have been too difficult to reorganise the Polish reception team, the system of lights and patrols, the hide-outs as well as an adequate security guard to protect the landing area from German intervention. It would be appropriate to spell out the requirements for one of these landing sites for night 'SOE' operations — many pilots of today would regard them barely adequate in daylight and in the fine weather. The aim was to have five-eighths of a mile — if possible — square in shape — no obstructions on the approaches — flat — smooth and firm land — no hidden ditches or tree stumps etc.

The crew selected were Flight Lieutenant Stanley George Culliford, the captain and

Left: Flt Lt George Culliford DSO in a Dakota cockpit.
E. Chilton

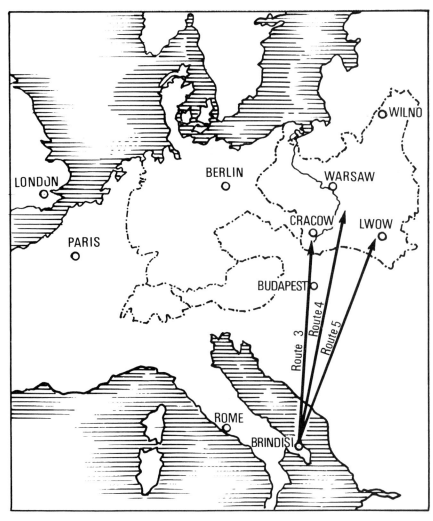

Route 3
Route 4
Route 5

pilot, Flying Officer John P. Williams, the navigator, Flight-Sergeant Appleby, the wireless-operator, and as a second pilot (borrowed from a Polish Liberator Squadron to act as an interpreter and as a standby pilot in the case of accidents) Flight Lieutenant Kazimier Szrajer. This team had already established a reputation for flying when the weather conditions were very poor; they were often in the air when all other aircraft were grounded, German or British, and this was especially important on their supply mission to Tito's partisans in the valleys of Yugoslavia. Often during these flights the clouds would suddenly merge with the mountains and the pilot would urgently demand, from the navigator, an immediate new course and height to fly for safety or, with equal urgency when enemy fighters appeared, to seek the security of the clouds. This form of flying demands the highest skills and a special navigational technique.

The Squadron Commander selected a new long-range Dakota Mark 3 for the task, KG477, for the aircraft had to carry sufficient fuel for the return journey from Zaborow. Unfortunately, endless delays now occurred due to a prolonged period of wet weather especially at the selected landing site, the

code name of 'Saucepan', which was already known to be less firm than was desired. The delay did have some advantages, in that much more detailed preparation could be made, especially as the site had been used once before and a rough target map of the landing site had been made. All non-essential equipment was removed from the aircraft and the crew would not have the luxury of self-sealing fuel tanks, no armour plate and no guns! Every piece of equipment which was to be used was checked on the ground and in the air. The accuracy of the compass, upon which so much depended, was verified several times in the air, as was the drift sight, which was of a rather primitive type.

On the morning of 25 July 1944, the 'All Clear' was given for the flight to be made, as weather conditions at the landing site were said to be acceptable, a fact which was not entirely true as subsequent events were to show. The 'All Clear' was given through a secret radio message and then reconfirmed by the BBC later than morning in 'Code Tunes'. All this may sound complicated to the reader but, once started, this operation brought into play hundreds of individuals, all of whom were risking their lives. In fact, while the last minute preparations were in hand at Bari (the airfield near Brindisi being used), at the other end of the operation, on the proposed landing site, some German troops with an AA battery had most unexpectedly turned up. For good measure, two German Storch light reconnaissance aircraft had also alighted on the landing strip. All this confusion was inherent in a changing situation as the German forces were retreating through that area from the advancing Russians. Worse still, it suddenly started to rain again, making the already soft ground softer still, so much so that the reception committee wanted to call off the operation by sending off the agreed secret signal. The committee were prevented from so doing because there were several very important Polish would-be passengers who hoped to return in the Dakota. In the event, all the Germans on the site moved off as suddenly as they had come, so the secret confirmation signal was sent off. Strangely, the German AA battery did not move very far, only a few miles away, where it took up a position on a commanding site, another headache for the partisans.

Back at Bari, Dakota KG477 was loaded with 19 suitcases of 'special equipment' and four passengers. As the names of these brave men have been hidden away for so long, I propose to list them. They were: Captain Kazimierz Bilski; Second Lieutenant Leszek Starzynski; Major Bogusslaw Wolniak; and Lieutenant Jan Nowak.

The Dakota took off at 2000 hrs on a perfectly calm evening and headed for the

Dalmation coast of the Adriatic Sea. To start with they were escorted by a well-armed Liberator but this could not climb as well as the Dakota and it was slower, so it was soon left behind. The Dakota crossed the Yugoslav coast at Dubrovnik just as the daylight faded and the navigator managed to get a fix near Sarajevo. The pilot elected to fly in the vicinity of the high ground south of Belgrade by which time it was very dark (no moon — unusual for an SOE flight), so that astro-navigation was the order of things for the navigator as it was a clear night and all the stars were visible. They continued up the Rumanian border, then across the eastern part of Hungary. A sudden change of wind direction took them rather closer to Budapest than they wished but this provided an unexpected but valuable navigational check as that city was entirely lit up — the navigator's first war-time experience of finding such an easy check. They then went on across Czechoslovakia and the Carpathian mountains and so on to the landing site, exactly on their planned time of arrival, a fine effort after a flight of some 680 miles. What was much better, they arrived right overhead and could make the recognition signal at once. The signal to land was given but the pilot tended to overshoot as he was uncertain of the approach, so he went round again and this was unfortunate as it woke up the entire area. Furthermore, the aircraft's landing light had also lit up the local farmhouses as well as the houses where Germans were billeted. Fortunately the Germans remained silent, discretion overcoming their valour, knowing that they were surrounded by well-armed partisans. The Germans were also well aware that the ever-advancing Russian front line was not too far away, and German morale was already starting to slip.

As soon as the aircraft landed, the Polish passengers with their heavy 'special baggage' vanished swiftly into the darkness while the west-bound passengers immediately boarded the aircraft in strict order of priority *after* the V2 parts had been carefully stowed. Ten minutes was to be allowed for the entire turn-round for the homeward flight. Alas, the best of plans or intentions often fail just when a little luck is most needed, and this was to prove one such case. When all was ready and the pilot opened the throttle, the Dakota refused to move and it was quickly appreciated that the wheels had sunk too deeply into the soft ground. The five passengers and their luggage were disembarked. After several attempts the pilot came to the conclusion that the hand-brake had locked on, as he had already had some trouble with it, so he decided to cut through the connections supplying the hydraulic fluid to see if this would solve the difficulty, but all to no effect.

After more attempts to free the wheels with no success, it was decided to burn the aircraft and for the crew to go off with the partisans. Petrol was splashed around the aircraft but at the very last moment the site dispatch officer, Captain Wlodek, suggested yet another go at digging out the wheels, this time digging slopes away from the wheels and with the help of straw and wood planks. This time the wheels pulled free and the passengers reboarded the aircraft. The pilot had had to use full boost on the engines to achieve this success and the noise was very considerable, certainly waking up the entire neighbourhood with a real risk that the Germans would move out to attack. All this had delayed the aircraft for one hour and ten minutes instead of the planned ten minutes and this would add difficulties to their return because of the shortage of darkness, and this in turn would call for very different tactics. On the flight there, the pilot's plan had been to fly around the likely areas of night-fighter patrols. They had dog-legged around PECs to avoid the area of Lake Balaton where German night-fighters had been shooting down the Halifaxes and Liberators on SOE operations. There was also a heavy concentration of anti-aircraft batteries there. The plan was to fly below 8,000ft wherever possible so as to use the ground return from the night-fighters' radar and to keep as near to the high ground as possible, with the valleys nearby to duck into in case of emergency. As the pilot said afterwards — 'We regarded timidity as a virtue.' Clearly these tactics would now need a quick readjustment as the return would have to be made by cutting corners and taking great risks. The outward flight had taken 4hrs 55min, and already 1hr 10min was lost. Before we leave the ground I should record for posterity the names of the passengers: Jerzy Chmielewski, the V2 technical expert; Jozef Retinger who had earlier parachuted into Poland (his first and only jump . . . probably the oldest parachutist of World War 2, age 56); Tomasz Arciszweski; 2nd Lieutenant Tadeusz Cheiuk, and finally Czeslaw Mieinski . . . all men who gave so much for their country.

Returning now to the pilot — in great haste of take off — he was beset with new difficulties, the first of which was to taxi the aircraft in an uncertain area without brakes or proper guiding lights. The partisans with some hand-held electric torches for the flare path had either gone home (thinking that the operation had failed) or were out along the site's perimeter standing guard against the possible arrival of German troops. However, the take-off was accomplished in a somewhat hair-raising manner as the pilot lacked outside reference points and the ability to control a straight take-off. He also had the added nightmare in that he would have to recross the area in which he had so recently been bogged down. With great skill and a certain degree of good luck, the aircraft was safely airborne so that the crew could apply to themselves the problems that lay ahead. The most immediate of these was to retract the undercarriage which was not now operable by the normal means as the hydraulic system had been severed on the ground. This was eventually achieved by pouring water and coffee from the emergency rations into the hydraulic reservoir and pumping up the undercarriage by hand, a time-consuming process. The navigator then had to re-adjust the flight plan for the return so that the aircraft would be relatively clear of enemy fighters by first light. The pilot's task was to climb as quickly as possible so as to clear the Carpathian mountains, their first hurdle, but this was easier than expected as the aircraft was getting much lighter as the fuel was consumed. As soon as the mountains were safely cleared, the pilot put the aircraft's nose down and kept the engine settings as for the maximum continuous climb to give the maximum speed. As the pilot expressed it in his report, he planned 'to skither across Hungary as close to the ground as safety permitted'. For the other members of the crew, the urgent need was for everyone to keep a sharp lookout for enemy fighters; several Ju 88's were seen but if they saw the Dakota they did not attack it. They were also lucky in that their flight path was either too low for the enemy AA batteries or that their selected route by-passed them.

At first light, the Yugoslav coast was crossed and the way was clear for a successful return to the Brindisi airfield — well, almost so. After a flight of 4hr 15min, some 40 minutes quicker than on the outward journey, the airfield controller at Brindisi warned them that there was a very strong wind blowing across their single runway. This was very bad news for the pilot since his brakes were inoperable and several SOE aircraft had already crashed there when landing in bad weather with strong cross winds but the Dakota was not especially difficult to land under these circumstances. Fortunately, the pilot was at least able to lower the undercarriage notwithstanding the lack of hydraulic power, as it was an excellent design feature of the Dakota in that the undercarriage would fall down and lock, and with water in the hydraulic system it was still possible to pump down the wing flaps, both so essential for landing. All was not lost, however, as a new runway was under construction which by good luck was facing into the strong wind, and sufficient of it had been completed to enable the pilot to land as soon as various obstructions had been removed.

The flight was concluded at 0550hrs on 26 July 1944. The Dakota was left there for the repair to the hydraulic system, and the crew and passengers plus the vital V2 parts were transferred to Dakota KG496 to continue the flight to Bari, their home base. By the next afternoon Dakota KG477, now repaired, was flown to Bari by a reserve crew and then the two crews, together with the V2 parts and the passengers, left on the long flight to London. The safe route was via Rabat Sale and Gibraltar, and they arrived at RAF Station Hendon on 28 July, the end of a truly remarkable flight.

As so often happens in war, the rewards for great risk and skill are not always recognised at the time because it is somewhat ironic that much of the valuable information that this flight brought to London had been somewhat devalued by the information obtained from the rocket which fell in Sweden. Perhaps more extraordinary was the fact that the same fate overtook the report of an Allied Mission which had been sent to examine the Blizna rocket-testing area. This area was in Russian hands by early August and in spite of strong Russian objections to the team's visit it eventually arrived and found much interesting information and an assortment of rocket parts which confirmed the Swedish and Polish information. However, by the time that the Mission's report arrived from Russia, V2 rockets had started to arrive in London, on 18 September 1944. Thus, with unwelcome parts now arriving in the UK, once again events in Poland had been overtaken. In passing, it would not be out of place to record that the Russians — our so-called Allies — showed their true colours by sending on the Mission's carefully-collected V2 samples... not the real samples, of course, but carefully-collected old engine parts marked as V2 parts!

The rewards for this epic flight were soon to follow. Flight Lieutenant Culliford RNZAF was awarded the DSO and the Polish 'Virtuti Militair', Flying Officer Williams the DFC and the Polish 'Cross of Valour', while Flight Sergeant Appleby was awarded the DFM and the Polish 'Cross of Valour'.

In concluding, I have written about a particular SOE event because it covers an operation about which so little is known, even within the Royal Air Force. To me, this story typifies the courage, tenacity and skill of the RAF's aircrews in World War 2. By the same token, we must remember the ground crews who so carefully serviced the aircraft and also the aircraft, engine and weapon designers who produced the tools for the air war which could be stressed to the limit when the need arose. This was just one such case when the need did arise.

The author would like to acknowledge the assistance given to him in the preparation of this story by: The Public Record Office, London; The Air Historical Branch, MOD; S. G. Culliford, DSO, VM (Pilot of Wildhorn 3); J. P. Williams, DFC, KW (Navigator of Wildhorn 3); J. A. Wells (Navigator of Wildhorn 2); Professor R. V. Jones CBE (*Most Secret War*); F. I. Ordway and M. R. Sharpe (*The Rocket Team*); Josef Garlinski (Poland, *SOE and the Allies*); David Irving (*The Mare's Nest*); RAF Personnel Management Centre, Innsworth, Glos.

Below: German rocket base at Wizernes after RAF bombing; seen here on 4 November 1944.
Imperial War Museum, C.5637

Aegean Interlude

Air Chief Marshal Sir Christopher Foxley-Norris
GCB, DSO, OBE, MA, CBIM, FRSA

Air Chief Marshal Sir Christopher Foxley-Norris was commissioned in the Reserve of Air Force Officers in 1936 through the Oxford University Air Squadron. His wartime service included the somewhat unusual record of having been on flying duties throughout the six years of hostilities.

Much of his postwar career was spent in Fighter Command and in the Far East Air Force, including considerable experience of anti-guerilla operations. His last two Service appointments were as Commander of NATO's Second Tactical Air Force and as Chief of Defence Personnel and Logistics.

In his eight years since retirement his chief activity has been as Chairman of the Leonard Cheshire Foundation; he is also Chairman of the Battle of Britain Fighter Association, General Portfolio Life Insurance and the Freedom Organisation for the Right to Enjoy Smoking Tobacco. He is an Honorary Fellow of Trinity College, Oxford. He writes and speaks extensively in the media and has published a book of memoirs *A Lighter Shade of Blue* (Ian Allan).

The following account covers some events following on the disastrous and ill-conceived attempt to invade the Aegean Islands of Cos and Leros in the early autumn of 1943. I was myself posted as a flight commander to No 252 Beaufighter Squadron at this time; and later I took command of No 603 Squadron, similarly equipped.

Turkey had remained neutral throughout the war, a fact for which I suppose we should be grateful, for she must have been sorely tempted on several occasions, eg after the German invasion of Greece and Crete or Rommel's apparently unstoppable drive through the Desert, to throw in her lot once more with her World War 1 ally. Now the tide of war had turned. The Germans had been driven out of Africa and Sicily and were being steadily pushed back in Italy. More importantly, their failure to score a quick victory in Russia indicated an inevitable eventual defeat there. It was felt by Churchill that a dramatic military stroke under the direct gaze of the Turks might persuade them to declare war against an apparently helpless Germany, thereby much improving the prospects of one of his pet hobbyhorses, a Balkan thrust against the allegedly soft underbelly of Europe. The targets selected were the two large German-occupied Greek islands of Cos and Leros. They were to be taken by an amphibious *coup de main*, including paratroops, and held as a base for further attacks on the vulnerable German garrisons and communications in the Aegean.

Politically it may have been sound thinking, but militarily it was a nonsense. We, of all people, should by now have learnt the lesson that without local air superiority such an operation could not possibly succeed; and it did not need much military genius to appreciate that air superiority must lie with the enemy. He could operate high performance fighters continuously over the target islands and their approaches from Rhodes

Below: Wg Cdr C. Foxley-Norris OC 603 Sqn (rt) and his sqn adjutant, Flt Lt R. Oddy, circa September 1944.
ACM Sir C. Foxley-Norris

and Crete, which straddled the invasion route, and from the Greek mainland. Since Air Marshal Tedder firmly refused to divert any fighter aircraft from the Western Mediterranean for the purpose, all that we could pit against them were Beaufighters, operating from Cyprus at maximum range against defenders superior both in performance and numbers. The result was a foregone conclusion. We got a bloody nose and our unfortunate troops, whom we could not cover and the Navy could not resupply, were forced to surrender. It seemed unlikely that the watching Turks had been very impressed: certainly they did not rush to join us. The air side of the operation had been conducted by the Middle East Air Force. Air Vice-Marshal Saul was apparently made the scapegoat for a failure which was inevitable from the start; and was no more seen. One could not help wondering whether the consciences of his superiors were entirely clear over the casualties sustained and the share of the blame.

No 252 Squadron, like Achilles, retired to its tents. These particular tents were located by the banks of the Suez Canal and here we were re-trained in attacks with rockets, only then being introduced into the area. When we were not flying ourselves, we could sit on the mess verandah and watch with fascination the mine-sweeping of the Canal by special Wellington aircraft. The Germans had taken to dropping magnetic mines into the Canal by night. The Wellingtons were fitted with huge cartwheel devices under their fuselages. These emitted a magnetic discharge which detonated the mines. This sounds very simple but the selection of the right height at which to fly called for very nice calculation and precise flying. If the aircraft flew too high, the magnetic discharge was not strong enough to do the job; if too low the mine exploded and destroyed the aircraft. The pilots were phlegmatic men of reflective mein, who drank a great deal of beer. We admired them very much.

The operational role now given to 252 Squadron was to participate in the interruption of supplies to the German garrisons on the Aegean islands, in particular those on Crete and Rhodes. These garrisons had been

Above left: Beaufighter 'K', 252 Sqn, setting out from Malta.
Imperial War Museum, CM.5108

Left: 252 Sqn Beaufighter strike on a Crete radar station. *V. Cashmore*

established in 1941 after the enemy's successful invasion of the area. They constituted the means of suppression of our unfortunate Greek allies, and they also offered a serious air and sea threat on the northern flank of our own Mediterranean communications. For reinforcement and military supplies they depended on shipping or on the old three-engined Ju52 transport aircraft, the supply routes running from the mainland, usually Athens itself but also from Salonika and other smaller ports (the shorter the sea crossing the better, but even in harbour they had no guarantee of safety).

Our job was to try to starve the smaller garrisons into surrender, and to render the large ones operationally ineffective or at least eliminate their offensive capability. The difficulty arose of course that in starving the Germans we were likely also to starve the native Greeks. In attacking shipping it is usually impracticable to distinguish between those loaded with military stores and those carrying the ordinary necessities of life — with some exceptions of course such as fuel tankers. Sometimes we had intelligence information on cargoes and knew which were ammunition or troop carriers — but usually they were just ships and had to take their chances. Luckily some of the bigger islands were more or less self-supporting for food; and the rest were maintained by small sailing or powered caiques, which we left alone unless they shot at us. On one memorable occasion we encountered about dawn a 16-oared boat, which might have come straight out of Homer, its crew rowing like mad to make harbour before the light came; we wished them well but naturally they could not hear our ribald cries of 'Well rowed, Leander', or 'Give her ten, Argonauts'.

Our own counterforce, as well as 252, included No 603 Beaufighter Squadron, two South African light bomber/reconnaissance squadrons, and a squadron of torpedo-dropping Wellingtons for night work. Additionally of course the Royal Navy threatened the sea routes with the occasional submarine and with a varied force of small attack boats, dashingly commanded in the family tradition by George Jellicoe. The leading British representative with the Greek resistance forces on the mainland was Monty Woodhouse. We had all been contemporaries at Winchester, which made things matey.

Unlike some of the better publicised resistance movements in other occupied European countries, the Greeks never gave up their bitter and unrelenting campaign against their occupiers. Their coasts, islands and mountains formed admirable terrain for guerilla activities and only in the larger towns and more developed areas was there any considerable degree of collaboration. The fact that a great proportion of the resistance forces were Communist-infiltrated and finally Communist-dominated only reflected the higher standard of foresight and unscrupulous manipulation that existed in the Russian organisation and policy staffs than in our own. At least they fought and tied down numbers of German forces — which was all that mattered at the time. A German soldier guarding a railway in Thrace was not available to serve at Stalingrad or Caen.

The enemy's defences against our squadrons consisted of anti-aircraft guns on the ships and shore installations, special flakship escorts and the ubiquitous Messerschmitts on the larger islands; they also, unusually, included some Arado 196 seaplane fighters but these were too slow to worry us — indeed the boot was on the other foot and the they tried to keep out of our way on most occasions. The Messerschmitts could outperform us, but could not pick us up on radar at our low operating height, and interceptions were mercifully rare.

We were ourselves stationed at various landing fields in the Western Desert, of which Mersa Matruh with its lagoon for sailing and swimming (it is now a holiday resort) was much the most attractive; Gambut, further to the west, was perhaps the least. Why we were moved so often when the land fighting was now so remote and the enemy air threat negligible, was difficult to understand; and it irritated the NCOs and airmen who were great hands at making purses out of sows' ears and could convert the dreariest bit of sandy scrub into a home-from-home, given time to put some roots down.

There is a lesson here for all who ever have to command troops, and particularly British troops. When you are compelled to mess them about if humanly possible explain to them why. 'Their's not to reason why' is a military principle which has long lost its validity — if it ever had any.

On paper the lumbering Ju52s should have been easy meat and indeed one of my pilots shot down two on his first operational sortie. However, they were normally used at night and made skilful use of their very low speed. If they suspected we were after them, they flew at about 60kts at below 100ft above sea level, which presented great difficulties to the Beaufighter. Our efforts proved discouragingly unsuccessful, partly due to the fact that being basically anti-shipping aircraft rather than specialist night fighters we were not equipped with Airborne Interception (AI) radar. Our discouragement generated a classic instance of leadership by example.

We were being briefed one evening for a night of attempted aircraft interception around Crete. A light aircraft descended on

our desert land ground and out of it stepped Group Captain Max Aitken, by then the Senior Air Staff Officer of No 201 Group, our parent formation. He listened to the briefing (he was of course already a night fighter pilot of established repute); and then asked me if I could let him have an aircraft and observer so that he could join the programme. I naturally complied, and shortly after midnight he took off.

Four or five hours later he returned. He reported, as was confirmed by his observer, that having had no luck on the approach lanes to Crete, he had joined the actual circuit of the main German airfield at Heraklion, the most heavily defended point on the island. He had caught the enemy napping and had destroyed three enemy aircraft and damaged two. He completed his sortie report and departed. He had not lectured to us or rebuked us; he had merely shown that it could be done. He recommended his observer for a DFC. We had learned a valuable and well-proven lesson — actions speak louder than words.

Our anti-shipping operations were predictably more effective. The Germans tried to complete their passages by night which gave some cover. Our Beaufighters were equipped with ASV (Air to Surface Vessel) radar but it was not really accurate enough for completely blind attacks, and we needed a helpful moonpath to give us a good chance of success. It was about this time that I was given another insight into the phenomenon of fear.

Formation attacks by night were obviously impractical; to try to concentrate the weight of attack, we adopted a so-called 'Daisy Chain' tactic, a series of single aircraft conducting a west to east patrol across the Aegean to intersect all the enemy's north-south shipping routes. The aircraft were

Top left: The 1,500-ton *Tanais* under rocket attack by 26 Beaufighters of 252 Sqn, 1 June 1944. *V. Cashmore*

Centre left: The 2,300-ton *Sabina* being RP-strafed by 252 Sqn on 1 June 1944. *V. Cashmore*

Bottom left: 252 Sqn Beaus' attack in the Symi area, 14 May 1944. *V. Cashmore*

Above: Dornier Do 24 downed north of Crete during Beaufighter attack on an enemy shipping convoy. *Imperial War Museum, C.4036*

told us that the enemy had been driven to the comparatively desperate measure of sailing large daylight convoys; desperate, because he did not have adequate aircraft or warship resources to defend them effectively against concentrated attack. When we got at them, their losses were consequently high: but so were ours. On one major attack, our CO, Wing Commander Willie Meharg, who was leading the wing, was badly hit on his run in. His starboard engine became a flaming torch, he flicked over and went straight into the sea at high speed. Unhappily there was plenty of both eyewitness and photographic evidence of exactly what had happened. So, when I had the painful duty of breaking the news to his wife, who was a Wren officer in Alexandria, I could not offer her any hope of his survival. She took it very bravely.

I was considerably embarrassed, although of course personally delighted, to hear a few weeks later that both Willie and his observer were prisoners of war, the only injury they had between them being some burns to the observer's exposed right arm. To this day, neither remembers anything until they found themselves safely floating in their Mae Wests amid the wreckage of the enemy convoy.

The severity of our losses was due to the inflexibility of the tactics imposed on us by our weapons, the rocket and the cannon. Both had to be fired in a shallow dive with the aircraft pointed at the target, ie directly down its gun-barrels; the maximum accurate range for the rockets was 800 yards and for the cannon considerably less. Furthermore, since the enemy's flak defences were naturally strongest at the beginning of our attack, it was the leading sections of our squadrons that suffered the most. Casualties were thus heavy both in quality and

spaced at 10-minute intervals. If a pilot found a target, the others following behind or flying ahead could be directed on to it. This worked fairly well on several occasions; but one night one of the leading pilots sighted an enemy warship and called up the remainder, informing them of its location, course and speed, and that he was climbing to attack with rockets. As he did so, still transmitting, he must have been hit and set on fire. He screamed piercingly all the way down to the sea for perhaps 10 or 15 seconds. It was the most appalling sound any of us had ever heard. That night none of the other crews reported sighting or attacking that or any other ship.

Our daylight anti-shipping activities occasionally flared into major operations when reconnaissance or intelligence reports

quantity; we could perhaps afford the former even less that the latter as time went by. Discussion was endless on how we could improve matters — particularly among those of us who were normally to be found in the front row.

I remember two solutions being attempted, neither with success. One was by a squadron commander who decided to lead from the back, ie leading the last instead of the first section of aircraft. There was no comparison with the Duke of Plaza Toro. He was a provenly brave man and nobody on his squadron doubted it. He merely reasoned that his survival was operationally important, and that from the more rearward position he could also apply more tactical flexibility to the attack, ie if the first sections had clearly lethally damaged the main target ship, he could switch the remainder to other targets. It worked very well for a time; but higher authority discovered what he was up to and disapproved. I thought they were wrong, and I still do.

Another imaginative and perhaps more acceptable solution to our difficulty was along these lines, 'If we have so many losses because both our aircraft and our weapons have to be pointed directly at heavily defended ships, why not modify the flight path of the weapons so that only they have to be so pointed?'. The idea was that the aircraft would fly at a safer distance parallel to the convoy and fire salvos of rockets which would themselves turn through 90° in mid-air and head for the target. This was to be accomplished by fitting the rocket with a sort of aerodynamic spoiler. As the weapon accelerated under the thrust of its cordite charge to a given speed, the spoiler was to be forced open by the wind speed, interrupt the

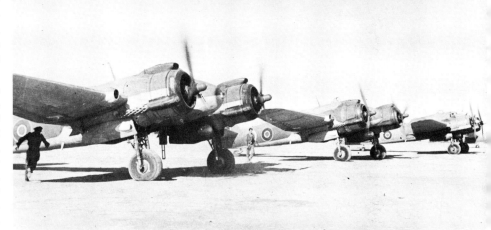

airflow and divert the rocket at right angles before snapping off under pressure.

It seemed worth a try, although it sounded somewhat haphazard; and so it proved. A demonstration was arranged and a distinguished audience of interested spectators gathered for the trials. A battery of rocket launchers was mounted to the flank of their observation stand and the first salvo was fired. Unfortunately owing to some miscalculation or misfortune (surely not with intent?) the rockets duly diverted; but through 180° and not 90° as planned. They screamed back over the heads of the terrified spectators (for some of whom it was the first time they had really earned the Africa Stars they proudly displayed) and crashed into the sand behind them. There were no casualties, but the experiment was abandoned.

We continued assiduously with our established tactics and were kept pretty busy. Even at base life was not without incident. While at Mersa Matruh we had the pleasure of the company of a squadron of Royal

Top: Wg Cdr C. Foxley-Norris OC 603 Sqn (L) with Flt Lt Tuhill (nav) and ground crew of Beaufighter NV248.
ACM Sir C. Foxley-Norris

Above: Beaus about to bite, 1944.
Imperial War Museum, CM.5575

91

Above: Arado 196 under attack from a 603 Sqn Beau, 6 September 1944.
ACM Sir C. Foxley-Norris

Hellenic Air Force Spitfires (the enemy was by now trying very little in the way of counter-attack but sensible precautions had to be taken). In the spring of 1944, we had the privilege of a visit from one of the best known and bizarre figures to emerge from the Desert Campaign. His name was Jasper Maskelyne, well known before the war as a partner in the great team of theatrical magicians and illusionists, Maskelyne and Devant. His natural talents for deception had been put to excellent use and his neatest trick was the production of dummy aircraft in large numbers. Made of wood and fabric, they were startlingly lifelike from the air, defying both visual and photographic reconnaissance. Dressed up as a Colonel in the Camouflage Corps, or some such, he would arrive on an airfield with a few truckloads of materials and a band of enthusiastic specialists and, hey presto! In a matter of hours squadrons of bombers or fighters materialised where God and the Air Ministry had created none.

As a man he was vastly entertaining and a great raconteur and personally always a welcome arrival on a desert airfield. Professionally his visits tended to be less acceptable, since in the nature of things as soon as the enemy detected these instant reinforcements a rain of bombs tended to follow.

At this time the Allies were going to great lengths to try to confuse and deceive the enemy as to where our invasion of Europe, by now clearly pending, would be directed. The 'soft under-belly' could by no means by ruled out of German calculations (and indeed as

noted was at one time Winston Churchill's favoured solution). Naturally everything possible was being done to foster this illusion, and Colonel Maskelyne's 'Circus' was kept hard at it, generating squadrons of cardboard bombers up and down the coast of North Africa for the enemy to detect and draw false conclusions from. At Mersa Matruh we were honoured with the appearance of two squadrons of lifelike Liberator heavy bombers.

Now enemy activity against us at this stage was confined as a rule to a weekly visitation from a special reconnaissance Ju86P which came over at very high level indeed and photographed our airfields; the old Spitfires dutifully chased it but its height and speed were usually beyond them. With Teutonic thoroughness it visited us regularly on Thursdays (or Fridays if the weather prevented the Thursday trip). Our massive Liberators sat there waiting to be photographed and strict instructions were given to the defences to make sure that the photography was not prevented. Thursday came, and Friday; but no reconnaissance. We were a little disturbed but rationalised that the weather was probably bad at the Greek bases; all would be well next week. But next week came and went still without sight or sound of our regular customer; and now there was growing cause for concern, for sand, sun and wind soon undid Jasper's work, which was not designed to last and only retained its realistic appearance from the air for quite a short period.

It was with some relief that a day or two later we received a report from the Air Defence Centre of an incoming track, fast, very high and headed straight for us. All would soon be well and the deceptive photographs duly taken. Alas! for the best laid plans etc. In a moment of mental aberration, carried away by the lust for battle, or merely through lack of linguistic communication, one of our gallant Greek allies managed to haul his ageing Spitfire well above its normal ceiling and to shoot down the intruder. Amid yells of Hellenic enthusiasm and bellows of British fury the Junkers crashed into the sea in flames a mile or so from the airfield. By what must have been a unique statistic, this one sortie achieved for the pilot at the same time a Greek DFC and a British court martial.

These incidents illustrate and typify what I have entitled 'Aegean Interlude'. It was a serious and often hazardous campaign, with a major objective which was eventually attained. But it had a highly individualistic flavour, was never dull, routine or monotonous. If all campaigns were the same, war might become dangerously and deplorably attractive and entertaining.

**Above: 603 Sqn, late 1944.
Seated, L–R: Flt Lt Rogers;
Flt Lt Oddy (Adj); Sqn Ldr
Pain; Wg Cdr C. Foxley-Norris
(OC); Sqn Ldr Deck; Flt Lt
Simpson.**
ACM Sir C. Foxley-Norris

**Left: Beau V8502 of 46 Sqn at
Mersa Matruh, 1943.**
via C. F. Shores

**Below left: Beau 'R' of 46 Sqn
after landing at Edcu, March
1943 with its starboard wheel
not locked down.**
K. G. Thomas

PRU to Prison

Lord Barber

Lord Barber's military career started in the Army. After escaping from Dunkirk he was seconded to the RAF and flew as an operational pilot until he was shot down and became a prisoner of war in 1942. His experiences of such are recorded below; but in spite of his adventures he found time as a POW to take a first class honours degree in law to add to the economics degree he had previously attained at Oxford.

However after the war he turned from the law to politics. Specialising largely on the economic side he finally held office as Chancellor of the Exchequer, and was also Chairman of the Conservative Party Organisation.

In the mid-1970s he forsook politics for commerce and at the present time holds the post of Chairman of the Standard Chartered Bank.

Below: The author and his Spitfire at Gibraltar, 25 January 1942, prior to his ultimate flight. *Lord Barber*

It was in the late afternoon that I was taken from my cell and, after the final interrogation, out into the yard to be shot. That was in March 1944 at the Gestapo Headquarters in Schneidemuhl. But more of that later.

It all started during the winter of 1939-40 when I was serving with the Territorial Army at a small town in Northern France called Seclin. I sometimes wonder whether it was just coincidence that it was there, at Seclin, that the first Photographic Reconnaissance Unit Spitfires in France were based. Little did I know at the time that, after Dunkirk, I was to be seconded to the RAF and that, in due course, I was to join the Unit. And then came the day, in January 1942, when I had to bale out and was captured by the Germans.

In the history of PRU I played an insignificant part, but my involvement was sufficient to produce a lasting admiration for the men who conceived and developed what must surely rank as one of the most remarkable outfits of the wartime RAF.

One of those men was Sidney Cotton, whose determination and unorthodox approach created what became known as 'Cotton's Circus', the precursor of PRU. To gauge the character of the man, it is necessary to retail only one story taken from Andrew Brookes' book, *'Photo Reconnaissance'*. He tells how, in September 1939, the First Sea Lord was pressing Air Marshal Sir Richard Peck, the Director General of Operations, for photographs of the Dutch coast between Flushing and Ymuiden where a German force was reported to be concentrating.

Cotton, who at that time was still a civilian, was asked for his advice as to how to overcome an apparently unsurmountable technical problem. Eventually the frustrated Cotton told the meeting that if the RAF would lend him a Blenheim, he would get the pictures straight away. Not surprisingly, the

possibility of a civilian being shot down in an RAF aircraft was unacceptable. Cotton left Whitehall a disappointed man. He said later: 'I went back to my office high above St James's Square and stared dejectedly out of the window, over the hills to the twin towers of the old Crystal Palace and beyond... Then I looked again at the blue sky and the clouds. It was one of those days when anyone who loves flying longs to get airborne. Why not? Why not take the Lockheed and go and get the pictures now?'

Before long Cotton was crossing the Kent coast in his civil aircraft bound for the mouth of the Scheldt. The cameras turned over both Flushing and Ymuiden, and then it was back across the North Sea to Farnborough. The School of Photography worked all night developing and printing so that Cotton could be in Peck's office at 1000hrs the next morning with an album of enlargements in his brief case.

Peck opened the meeting and the talk proceeded much as it had done the day before. After half an hour Cotton produced the album.

'Is this the sort of thing you want?' he asked.

Peck examined each print critically and was full of praise for the photography. The places were clearly marked with the respective place-names, but it was taken for granted that they were of pre-war origin.

'These are first class', said Peck, handing the album round, 'but we wouldn't expect this sort of quality in wartime'. Cotton said nothing. Then someone asked when the prints were taken, and Cotton pulled the pin.

'At three-fifteen yesterday!'

News of the audacious incident soon spread and the next day the Chief of the Air Staff asked Cotton to take charge of photographic reconnaissance in the RAF.

By the time I joined them, the principal aircraft being used was the Spitfire — but a Spitfire with a difference. It had no guns and no radio. The purpose was to save both weight and space in order to carry as much fuel, oil and oxygen as possible to keep the aircraft airborne for as long as possible. So, whereas the basic fighter Spitfire had 85 gallons of fuel, the PRU Spitfire carried 220 gallons, and many flights were made of more than five hours. An additional reason for removing the radio was, we were told, that the lack of a radio mast gave the aircraft another 10mph which was a distinct advantage for a completely unarmed aircraft being chased by Messerschmitts deep in enemy territory! The optimum height for the longer sorties was 30,000ft, and at that height the cold was intense. Not only was there no cockpit heating until later but, of course, in those days there was no pressurisation.

The navigation was primitive in the extreme. With no radio, no navigator, and unreliable weather forecasts, you simply plotted your track and set your course, climbed to 30,000ft, hung on to your map of Europe and prayed that when there was a break in the cloud you might recognise some configuration of railway lines or a bend in a river which would enable you to check your position. If you were over ten-tenths cloud, there was simply nothing you could do but press on and hope for the best. You could not go down below the clouds, first because your fuel consumption increased the lower you descended and second, because, being unarmed, you would stand no chance against enemy fighters attacking from above.

The lack of a radio or of any kind of navigation facilities other than a simple map made long flights over cloud particularly hazardous. Occasionally you would be over

Below: Spitfire PR VII, X4786 in May 1943. *C. Bowyer*

95

cloud for the whole of the outward and return journeys. And, with cross winds of up to 100mph you frequently had little idea where you were when you finally broke through the cloud — hopefully somewhere over Britain where the land was reasonably flat and low. If you were not able to determine your position you landed where you could. On one occasion, as dusk was descending and with no airfield in sight, I chose what seemed in the half light to be a suitable large field only to find out the hard way, almost immediately on touch down, that it was dotted with large poles to prevent the enemy from landing! The aircraft was a write-off, but the photographs were safe.

On my last flight I was returning from Gibraltar. Very soon after reaching 30,000ft I was over ten-tenths cloud and it stayed that way without a single break until I had used up more than half the fuel. Eventually came the first welcome break in the cloud but, to my dismay, there was nothing but water as far as the eye could see. I knew that I must be somewhere over the Bay of Biscay, but by this time I should have been hitting the Brest peninsula. What I did not know what that I had been flying into a strong and wholly unexpected head wind which now made it impossible for me to reach England before the fuel ran out. I plodded on and got as far as the Channel coast.

Because it was thought (erroneously as we later found out) that the Germans did not know that our aircraft were unarmed, there was a standing instruction that, in the event of trouble over enemy territory, the aircraft should always be abandoned to destruction. This was doubly important in my case because I was carrying some particularly sensitive photographs of ports in neutral Spain, which were suspected of harbouring German submarines. The obvious answer

was to bale out, and I can still see so vividly that beautiful Spitfire spiralling to destruction while I floated slowly down to be greeted by the enemy waiting for me on the coast near Mont-St-Michael. Fortunately, a second set of the photographs was being sent home by more conventional means.

There was one other consequence of having no radio. If that single Rolls-Royce Merlin engine failed, for instance over the North Sea, you had no means of alerting anyone or giving your position, and you knew that, even if you ditched safely in the sea, there would be no action by the air-sea rescue services. Later on the Unit was equipped with Mosquitos with twin engines, radio and navigator. But I am pleased that I served in those early days.

Our CO was Wing Commander Geoffrey Tuttle who was later to become Deputy Chief of the Air Staff. Our confidence in him was absolute, not least because we knew that he had chosen us himself. He was one squadron commander in the RAF who could select any pilot he wanted and to get him.

To return to that fateful afternoon in Schneidemuhl. Since being taken prisoner, I had tried one means of escaping after another. There was the attempt to saw through the floor of a cattle truck on the long journey to Silesia. There was the attempt to get out of Stalag Luft III in a laundry bag, which nearly succeeded. There were others. But there are two which I think are worth recounting in some detail. They both involved tunnelling, but of a very different kind.

One of the major problems of tunnelling was the dispersal of the earth. Remember that, day and night, the camp was patrolled by specially trained security guards, known as 'Ferrets'. So the first difficulty to be overcome was to avoid being seen carrying the earth away from the tunnel, and the second was to put it somewhere where hopefully the 'Ferrets' would not find it. Nobody had yet found any way of avoiding these problems. Indeed, they were assumed to be inevitable, for how could you possibly dig a tunnel without carrying the earth away and dumping it somewhere else? But it was not inevitable.

I do not know who first thought of the idea but, one day, talking and plotting with Tommy Calnan (also a PRU pilot who after the war became Chief Test Pilot at Farnborough) he mentioned the concept of the 'mole'. Suppose, instead of digging the traditional type of tunnel of 100ft or more, we were to dig a tunnel only long enough for three men to lie horizontally, one in front of the other, with a reasonable amount of spare tunnel behind. Suppose then that the earth was to be passed to the back of the tunnel but, instead of being taken out of the tunnel and secretly dispersed, it was simply used to fill up the spare space in the tunnel behind us. The theory of the 'mole' as it came to be called was strikingly simple and clearly had great advantages. First, of course, all conventional tunnels had a trap at the entrance and, the trap being inside the camp, this was the part of the tunnel most likely to be discovered by the Germans, however cleverly camouflaged and hidden. In the case of the 'mole' there would be no entrance to be discovered for it would be filled in and no longer exist. The second advantage was that moling would avoid most of the delay involved in the secret dispersal of the earth, which was extremely time consuming and frequently had to stop with the approach of one of the 'Ferrets'.

The problems were obvious. In the traditional type of tunnel with a trap at the entrance, it was not too difficult to provide fresh air for the man at the face. But moving along mole-like in a completely enclosed underground 'capsule' there would be no fresh air. We had to find an answer to this. Furthermore, we doubted whether we could stand the strain of lying prostrate working in such a confined space for more than 24 hours. This meant that the tunnel had to be reasonably short. And, of course, unlike the traditional tunnel which was shored up with bed boards, there could be no such support in the 'mole' and we had to face the very real danger that the earth would give way and collapse upon us.

As luck would have it, sometime later the ideal situation presented itself to us. The security arrangements round the perimeter of the compound consisted of two high barbed wire fences, about six feet apart filled to the top with coiled barbed wire. Between this impregnable barrier and the camp proper there was a strip of ground some 20ft wide, at the inner border of which was a single strand of trip wire. The whole of this 20ft strip was visible to the guards in the high observation towers which were placed round the perimeter barrier. The guards were armed with machine guns and it was well understood that, if you stepped over the trip wire into the 'no man's land', you would be shot without warning.

The opportunity to put our theory into practice came when the Germans started to dig a trench in this 'no man's land', the purpose of which was to intercept any shallow tunnels. The trench was sufficiently deep to enable a person to lie in it and — crucial to our plan — to be out of the angle of fire of the guards in their observation towers. We were assured beyond doubt that this blind spot existed. It had been carefully worked out by one of our colleagues, a navigator, who in private life was a chartered surveyor. The problem was how to get over the trip wire and into the trench when the guards in the two nearest observation towers had an unobstructed view of the whole area apart, of course, from the bottom of the trench.

The answer was two completely successful diversions which were set up to attract the attention of the guards. In the first case a group of prisoners rushed to the trip wire to ask the guard in one of the observation towers to telephone for help because of a fire in one of the huts. He obligingly turned his back and went to the telephone. In the other case, two prisoners started a mock fight surrounded by a small crowd near the second observation tower. I was told afterwards that the scene would have done credit to any Western.

The diversions worked perfectly, and before long all three of us had leapt into the trench unseen. We got to work immediately. We tunnelled only a few feet under the surface, where the earth above was firm with the roots of pine trees which had been cut down. Every so often we pushed up a rod to provide an air hole. As time went on we were faced with two problems, one manageable and one fatal. The first problem was that our third colleague, who shall remain nameless, became claustrophobic. An otherwise tough airman, he began to panic. We had packed a considerable amount of earth behind us and were moving along quite well. He wanted to go into reverse and to dig our way back to the entrance. There we were in the middle of the night, three sweating individuals lying prostrate in the narrowest of tunnels, blocked at both ends, arguing as to which way we should go. The truth is that Tommy and I were also pretty whacked. And we were worried because, although the scheme was working, we were not inching forward quite as fast as we had hoped. We knew that we had to get out before dawn, because we were going to surface in a ditch which was only just beyond the far side of the outer wire. We hit the compound side of the wire before first light, but we had still six feet to go to get to the other side of the outer wire, and we knew that there was no chance of making it. Our third man had calmed down and, to his credit, he agreed that we should lie in the tunnel throughout the day ready to break out when darkness fell. Whether the three of us could have stuck it for another 12 hours, we shall never know.

We were resting as best we could, when we heard excited German voices. The alsatians which accompanied the regular perimeter patrol had sniffed at the air-holes and started to bark. Our fear was that the earth might collapse on top of us, so we broke the roof ourselves to see the muzzle of a rifle and looks of absolute astonishment on the faces of the guards. It seemed only seconds before the whole camp had assembled to witness the end. They gave us an almighty cheer as we were marched off for yet another period of solitary in the cooler.

It was shortly afterwards that some of us were sent to Schubin in Poland. The idea of moving as much further east was to make escaping more difficult. In the event, it proved to be easier and 30 of us escaped through what I believe to be the cleverest tunnel of them all.

One of the problems which faced aircrew attempting to escape was that the Germans had decided that, for security reasons, we should never be taken outside the camp to work. On the other hand, we had among us almost every kind of expert and tradesman you could think of, and we received very considerable help, by devious means, from the authorities in London. So it was that, soon after arriving in Schubin, we set about organising a series of tunnels most of which were discovered by the Germans at an early stage, but one of which was to prove to be completely successful.

The Germans knew that the normal trap at the entrance to a tunnel was horizontal. You lifted it up, went down a short shaft and then entered the tunnel itself. One reason why almost all tunnels were eventually discovered before they made much progress was that, however well the traps were disguised, there was only a limited number of places where they could be located. The huts were pretty spartan, and it was therefore very difficult to hide or disguise a trap. The Germans knew all about false floors. On one occasion, after much preparatory work, we moved the whole of an inside wall of a hut some two feet, and sunk a shaft in the resulting gap. For a time that looked like being a real winner, but

eventually it was discovered, and thereafter the Germans regularly went round meticulously measuring the internal dimensions of each hut in the camp!

It seemed that every conceivable type of trap had been tried, and that the Germans were now familiar with all the old tricks. And yet there was, in theory at least, one concept which had never been pursued because it seemed to be a contradiction in terms. This was the concept of a vertical trap which would be below ground level and out of sight. No one had ever found anywhere where such a trap could be located. But there was such a place at Schubin — in the latrine. It was a remarkable communal 50-seater and, provided the relevant seats were occupied, no inquisitive German would suspect the work was going on in the enormous pit below. The plan was to make a trap in the side of the pit, below the seats. This would enable us to work in the tunnel undisturbed and, furthermore, we could disperse the earth in the pit itself. The working conditions could hardly be described as ideal, but the whole concept became a brilliant reality.

There was no great difficulty in making part of the seating detachable, but making the trap in the side of the brick wall of the pit without falling into the pit itself proved to be quite a task, but it was accomplished. Behind the trap and under the concrete floor we dug out a large chamber six feet high, some 12ft long and 10ft wide. Nothing on this scale had ever been accomplished before. The great advantage was that the earth from the tunnel could be temporarily stored in the chamber, so enabling digging to continue without the need for immediate dispersal. Some 30 men were involved in the whole operation.

From time to time Polish workmen were brought into the camp under armed guard to pump out the great pit. They soon realised what was happening but typically, despite the risk to themselves, they kept their silence and made our escape possible. We had noted that the pit was never wholly emptied. The level was simply kept down. This meant that the earth from the tunnel would always be covered. We had some 300ft of tunnel to dig to reach a potato clamp which was well outside the perimeter wire, and we aimed to be 20ft below ground at the lowest point under the wire. Fresh air at the tunnel face was essential. Our air-conditioning system was both simply and effective — a kit bag with circles of wire stitched round it so that it acted as a bellows leading into a pipe made of tins laid along the tunnel floor to the man at the face. The operator pumped the kit bag like an upright concertina. The only disadvantage was that the 'fresh air' intake had to be located in the latrine. There was no such thing as a torch, so our light was provided by small tins each filled with fat into which was stuck a piece of pyjama cord. Work at the face was hard, and hauling back the earth through more than 200ft of a tunnel which was only about two feet high and two feet wide was a considerable task.

While we were making steady progress with the tunnel, all the back-up services were hard at work to prepare for the actual escape. 'Tailors' were transforming uniforms into civilian clothes. The forgery department were turning out identity documents. Others were preparing chunks of concentrated high-energy food consisting mainly of chocolate, oatmeal and glucose which had been saved from Red Cross parcels over the previous months.

Once the tunnel had reached beyond the wire, the excitement was intense. The Germans had not the slightest suspicion. Then came the day when we estimated we had reached the point just before the potato clamp and a hollow in the ground next to it. This was to give maximum cover when we broke ground. I shall never forget the moment when I gingerly peeped above the exit hole and waited for the roving search-light to pass by before wriggling out and along the potato clamp and then away into the woods.

Although I was then out of the camp, I should recount now what I was later told happened within the camp.

The following morning everyone was assembled as normal for the first count of the day. The report to the commandant was that 30 prisoners were missing. Twice more the count took place. On each occasion with the same result. The commandant's reaction was precisely as we had hoped and expected. He simply refused to believe that the missing 30 were not hidden somewhere in the camp. Hour after hour the search proceeded and still the commandant refused to sound the alarm and report to his superiors that 30 of his prisoners were missing. Meanwhile, those of us who were on the run were given a head start.

My plan was to travel by train from the Polish city of Bromberg back into Germany and up to the Baltic port of Kolberg, where I knew I could get to the Danish island of Bornholm. My mother was Danish and relatives on Bornholm would certainly be able to arrange for a herring fishing boat to take me to neutral Sweden. I spoke some German and any deficiency in my accent was accounted for by my posing as a Danish 'Freiwilliger' — a Danish volunteer workman. I had a forged foreign worker's identity card and I was dressed in trousers dyed brown, wearing a RAF raincoat, which to the Germans bore no resemblance to a military coat, and a cap which a helpful Pole

had conveniently left behind on one of the visits to clear out the latrine. I had a small attache case in which I had some concentrated food, shaving kit, a cloth to keep my shoes clean and so on. Most of my fellow escapees would be walking by night and hiding by day. For them appearance was secondary. For me, travelling by train, it was essential not to appear deshevelled.

I had 16 miles to walk to the railway station at Bromberg and I had to be there to catch the morning train. My plan was to leave the train at Schneidemuhl and then to travel north to Kolberg. I had plenty of German money, cleverly smuggled into the camp from London, and I was therefore able to ask for a return ticket, as a means of avoiding suspicion. It was with some trepidation that I went up to the ticket office and said 'Schneidemuhl, hin und zuruck, bitte.' No problem. So I checked the platform and when I got there who should I see walking up and down but Tommy Calnan and Robert Kee who were travelling together. Prudently we should have ignored each other, but we could not resist a subdued 'Heil Hitler!'.

There were three classes of travel on the train. Although I had plenty of money and was reasonably well dressed, I was not quite smart enough to appear as an obvious first class passenger. Because the Germans would naturally assume that any escaped prisoner travelling by train would be short of cash, they would expect him to travel third class. So I travelled second class. I entered the compartment and took my seat as casually as I could and I raised my eyes to glance around. For a moment I froze. There sitting opposite me and looking out of the window was a German NCO whom I immediately recognised as one of the camp guards. I dared not move for fear of exciting suspicion, so I stayed put. The man never recognised me and, in fact, although I did not know it at the time, no alarm had yet been given by the camp commandant.

When I got to Schneidemuhl I found that there was no train going north until the following morning, so I walked out of the town and into the woods where I eventually settled down for the night. I had nothing to keep me warm and by midnight it had started to drizzle and I was shivering in the damp cold of a East European March night. With the temperature falling, it was impossible to spend the night in the open and, in any event, I had to keep up a reasonably clean appearance. I could see no buildings in the countryside. To wander round in the middle of the night looking for shelter in some out-house on the outskirts of the town would inevitably have appeared furtive to anyone who might have spotted me.

So often on such occasions the least risky

course is the brazen one. I walked back into the empty town and, with all the false confidence I could muster, I entered the railway station and made for the waiting room. It was packed with German soldiers drinking beer from the buffet. There were virtually no civilians. I went up to the counter. '*Ein bier, bitte*. This, together with a bowl of potato soup, made me one of the crowd and, with a limited amount of conversation, a few more beers and the occasional doze, the night passed uneventfully.

It was on the next leg of my journey that some plain clothes police came through the train checking the papers of each passenger. I sensed that this was no routine check, and my suspicion was confirmed when I overheard a reference to escaped prisoners of war. But all went well. My identity papers were accepted without demur, as was my story that I was travelling to see my brother, also a Dane, who was ill.

My confidence was growing, I was getting used to being in the company of Germans, the sense of being hunted was receding and more than ever before I really began to believe that I was going to make it. I had now reached a small town in northern Pomerania, and had only one more comparatively short train journey to complete before reaching the port of Kolberg where I knew I had every chance of boarding a Danish boat to the island of Bornholm. There were a couple of hours to wait for the train, it was a glorious crisp sunny Sunday morning, and I set off to walk round the town, not strolling, but always with a purposeful air. There were plenty of people about, I was

Right: The author (2nd from rt) and fellow prisoners of war. *Lord Barber*

many miles from the camp and there was nothing to excite suspicion.

I saw the two elderly SA men, 'Brown-shirts', walking slowly along the footpath towards me. Quite casually, it seemed almost on the spur of the moment, they stopped as we were passing each other and they asked for my papers. They were not in the least aggressive, but they exuded the dogged perseverance of the minor oficial. They returned my identity papers and they accepted my story but they pointed out that, as a foreign voluntary worker I should have a letter from my German employer giving me permission to be away from my place of work. I knew before the escape that this was the one piece of paper I was lacking, but the camp's forgery department had simply not had time to prepare it.

'You say you are here to visit your sick brother. Where is he living?' one of them asked. I had noticed we were in a street called Friedrichstrasse. '*Friedrichstrasse siebzehn*', I replied, hoping they would leave me to go on my way. Not so. They may not have looked particularly bright, but they were stubborn. They said they would come with me. We arrived at the door of number seventeen and I rang the bell. A lady answered the door.

I explained that I had come to visit my brother who was ill. She replied that the only people who lived in the house were her own family. I knew in my heart that the end was not far away, but I thought that there might be just a chance that, although the SA men were armed, an opportunity would arise to make a dash for it. So it seemed worthwhile to play them along for a little longer. We walked together to the police station where they said they would telephone my employer. Once we had entered the building, all chance of escape had gone, and the game was up. '*Ich bin ein offizier in der Britische Luftwaffe.*'

Depressed as I was, I shall never forget the astonishment on their faces. Instead of checking out some poor little Danish workman who was taking a couple of days off without permission, they had made a great catch. Within the hour I was bundled into a car and taken to the Gestapo Headquarters back in Schneidemuhl.

For a week I was kept there, interrogated for long periods during the night and made to stand up in my altogether for several hours during the day. I was never physically ill-treated, but on several occasions I heard the cries of others who were. I was repeatedly reminded during the interrogations that none of my colleagues knew where I was or what had happened to me and that I was entirely at the mercy of the Gestapo. They could do with me whatever they wished and nobody would ever know. Who had given me the money? Where had I got the cap from? What were the plans of the others who had got out of the tunnel?

How I longed to be back in the camp with my friends.

My mind went back to a discussion some of us had had soon after being taken prisoner. We had concluded that once you told your inquisitors anything, even if false, they would know that you were on the slide. And in those circumstances the Gestapo would not hesitate to use physical force and, if you were left a wreck, to dispose of you.

One day, during the afternoon, I was collected from my cell, and taken upstairs to what turned out to be my final interrogation. My reaction to the questions was the same as on all the previous occasions. This time there were two interrogators and one of them pointed out yet again that, as far as my comrades were concerned, I had simply disappeared, that I was entirely in the hands of the Gestapo and that, unless I co-operated, I would be taken out and shot there and then. I referred lamely to the Geneva Convention, and they smiled. There was a short silence, and I was taken roughly by the arms, out of the room, down the stairs and into a yard. I was then told I had one last chance to co-operate. I cannot now recall what I felt, except that I accepted that the end had come and I longed for just one friend. I said nothing.

To me it was desperately real. I did not know that to the man who had interrogated me for a week it was a ruse — one last attempt to get me to talk. 'Take him back to his cell.'

Within what I seem to remember was an hour or so I was taken to the same railway station which I had last seen a week previously. I was then escorted under armed guard back to the camp in Poland. Just before I left my cell I had torn off the bottom of the prison instructions which were hanging on the wall. On that bit of paper was a large and very clear rubber stamp with the swastika in the middle and around the edge the dreaded words '*Geheime Staatspolizei*' — Secret State Police, or Gestapo. I hid the bit of paper in my shoe and I knew that our forgery boys back in the camp would be thrilled. They were!

Eventually, after a period of solitary, I learned that all 30 of us had been caught and brought back to the camp, except for two who had been shot while making a run for it. Our only satisfaction, apart from the excitement and a short spell of freedom, was that we had caused untold havoc to the German authorities. There was nothing else to do except to settle down to plan the next escape. But that is another story.

The Year of the Tempest

Roland Beamont CBE, DSO, DFC

Wing Commander 'Bee' Beamont established a unique reputation in World War 2 for participation in and leadership of tactical fighter operations, for which he was decorated four times.

After the war he retired from the Royal Air Force but continued an extremely active flying career as test and experimental pilot, first for English Electric and then for British Aerospace. Among his achievements were the development of our first jet bomber, the Canberra; he was the first to fly the supersonic Lightning fighter; then was first Briton to fly at twice the speed of sound. He was also mainly involved in the initiation and progression of the Tornado programme. For all these activities he received a number of major awards and medals in aeronautics.

He is a prolific writer on aviation matters. His books include *Phoenix into Ashes*, *Typhoon and Tempest At War* and many others. He is a senior official and active member of the Guild of Air Pilots.

Above right: Tempest with 'short' cannon on test at Langley, flown by Sqn Ldr Cotes-Preedy.
British Aerospace

Below right: Early production Tempest V with 'long' cannon, at Hawkers' Langley factory, January 1944.
British Aerospace

Right: Wg Cdr Roland Beamont DSO, OBE, DFC.
Imperial War Museum, CH.13623

In early 1944 the Maintenance Unit at Aston Down was beginning to receive the first aircraft from the new Hawker production line at Langley, the Tempest V series 1.

This was the first new Hawker fighter of the war years, its predecessor the Typhoon having made its first flight just before the outbreak of World War 2, both flown by Philip Lucas. The Tempest, though developed from the Typhoon, was virtually a different aeroplane having not only all the improvements and modifications of four years of Typhoon development and operational experience but also an entirely new wing, thinner and of elliptical plan form, with spring-tab ailerons, increased fin area and a Napier Sabre 11A engine giving 2,200hp.

The thin wing was aimed to provide a high dive-speed capability and improved low-altitude performance; and the spring-tab ailerons, designed by Freddy Page (currently Chairman and Chief Executive of the Aircraft Group of British Aerospace), were to provide greatly improved lateral controllability to speeds of over 500mph. They were the first application of the spring-tab principle in this country, possibly in the world, and the intention was to provide sustained fast rolling power for this new fighter at speeds well in excess of all other contemporary fighters. The Me 109 was severely limited in this respect from about 350mph, but the Fw 190 might not be so easy to improve upon.

The first Tempest wing began forming in March 1944 with No 486 (NZ) Squadron and 150 Wing Headquarters at Castle Camps, and No 3 Squadron at Bradwell Bay; and after about two weeks' formation practice, day and night, these two squadrons completed an intensive and successful armament practice camp at Ayr later in March during which the exceptional gun-platform stability of the Tempest began to show in their gunnery scores on the 15ft square ground

Above: The first Tempest delivered. JN751 at 486 Sqn, Castle Camps, March 1944, bearing Wing Leader's markings (Beamont). *Imperial War Museum, CH.13959*

Right: Tempest JN766, SA-N, 486 Sqn, Castle Camps, 1944. *Imperial War Museum, CH.13955*

targets at the Irish sea coast range south of Ayr. For these exercises the two inner 20mm cannon only were loaded with 100 rounds ball ammunition each, and pilots were soon recording more than 50% hits per sortie, with 75% and more not infrequently.

The wing then headed south, arriving at the forward base selected for it, Newchurch on Dungeness, on 28 April 1944. No 56 Squadron joined the wing there still with its Typhoons as sufficient Tempests had not yet been received from the makers to re-equip them at that stage. With the ingenuity and adaptability traditional to the RAF, the wing servicing echelon under 'Digger' Aitken soon organised themselves in their new tented and agricultural surroundings and the Tempests were quickly on to final work-up prior to being declared 'operational'. Of course no formal information was available but all ranks knew that the great day — the invasion of France and Germany — could not be far away, and it was with a sense of pride and no little excitement that the pilots of 150 Wing considered their new circumstances. The new Tempest fighter was a joy to fly and clearly had better performance at low altitude than the fastest Spitfires and Mustangs which were themselves faster than most of the enemy; and now they were positioned to

put this new fighter into operation just in time to gain fighting experience with it before the biggest battle of all since the Battle of Britain. It was a good feeling.

Guns were fired in anger for the first time on 7 May during a moonlight 'Intruder' sortie to Lens/Mons, and a train was stopped with much steam at Guines. In a second sortie that night a flak-defended train was successfully attacked near Evreux. On both sorties the aircraft serial No JN 751, code 'RB', was flown by the wing leader. The first daylight Tempest operation was on 11 May when the same aircraft led No 3 Squadron on a low-level 'Ranger' sweep to Evreux and Amiens, meeting heavy defensive fire from Amiens marshalling yards. The Tempests shot up gun posts, and the leader's wingman Van Lierde sustained superficial flak damage to wing and fuselage.

Following a defensive patrol at dusk in the Thames estuary area on the 12th, No 3 Squadron flew a deeper penetration 'Ranger' to Rheims and Laon on 15 May with JN 751 leading, but again with no sightings of EA; and further sorties on the 17th and 20th to Boulogne and the Lille-Cambrai area produced good experience of the flak defences but no other targets.

Then on 21 May No 3 Squadron with

JN 751 in the lead flew a 'Ranger' to Brussels-Courtrai and attacked a mini-submarine on a heavy multi-wheel trailer passing through a village, and set it on fire. This was subsequently confirmed as destroyed and was the first significant operational success of the Tempest. Four motor barges were attacked on the way home (barges and freight trains being legitimate targets at that period).

This had been an excellent final training for the Tempest pilots, and actions followed swiftly. On 22 May JN 751 with No 3 Squadron successfully attacked five trains in the Lille-Mons area, two of them heavily defended with light flak. The last near Bethune was carrying inflamables and burnt strongly. Wehrmacht vehicles were attacked with 486 Squadron near Rheims on 26 May and JN 751 was hit in the engine bay by 88mm flak over Boulogne on the way back. Then on 27 May a planned attack on Cormeille-en-Vexin airfield (now Pontoise) north of Paris brought the Tempests' first major success. Twin-engined bombers had been sighted there by a Spitfire wing and were expected by Intelligence to be part of a reinforcement for a raid on UK (target Bristol that night), and attacking fast out of the late evening sun JN 751 with five aircraft of No 3 Squadron destroyed or damaged four Ju 188s in dispersal blast-pens on the south side of the field. Despite much light flak no Tempests were hit. Further 'Rangers' were flown during the next few days and on 30 May JN 751 flew to Tangmere for the briefing of all the fighter wing leaders by the Commander-in-Chief on 'Operation Overlord', the invasion of the continent of Europe. This was a memorable occasion and later that day when flying back to Newchurch at the Tempest's low-level cruise of 330mph IAS and with D-day at the most only a few days away, the writer felt more than privileged to have the best-equipped and (in his view at any rate) the best-trained wing for the job ahead!

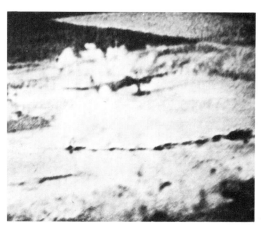

Above: Roland Beamont's Tempest, JN751 in D-Day striping, Newchurch, 5 June 1944. *Imperial War Museum*

Left: Tempest JN751 attacking a Ju 188 on Pontoise airfield, 28 May 1944. *Imperial War Museum*

On D-day, 6 June 1944, the Tempests patrolled the shipping lanes at squadron strength without excitement until, at almost the end of the long day, Nos 3 and 486 Squadrons were scrambled at 2220hrs to patrol the Beachhead at wing strength against much radar-plotted enemy activity. This was where the earlier night training came in useful as the wing climbed out through heavy cloud in the already gathering dusk, and by the time the gun flashes, tracer and searchlights of the fighting area were in sight the sky was already dark and the wing was keeping station with navigation lights. At about 20 miles out navigation lights were extinguished and shortly afterwards 'Blackgang' radar reported numerous EA at low level. Almost at once a mass of lights appeared ahead and curved by to port as another wing headed home. It was clearly by now a night-fighter's job, and after a last look at the fires of the battle flaring ominously in the darkness below and a thought for the brave souls enduring down there, it was time to concentrate on how best to get these two squadrons of the fastest day-fighters back to a safe landing in full darkness and through a warm-frontal weather system which by now must have caused thick cloud and heavy rain over our Newchurch base. Radio consultation confirmed this and instructions were received to divert the wing to Ford which was reported 'clearing behind the front'. Setting the new course and ordering 'nav lights on — close up', it was impressive to look round and see what appeared to be the complete wing still in steady formation under the stars with only cloud sheet below and the faint pale light of the northern horizon ahead at approaching midnight.

At 20 miles from the south coast the order 'squadrons line astern, sections line astern' was given, the also advice that in the event of anyone getting lost Tangmere and Dunsfold were suitable for emergencies. Presently lights appeared through wisps of cloud ahead and they proved to be the navigation lights of two Spitfire wings which Control now reported were recovering to Ford ahead of us. Giving the order 'aircraft line astern — keep loose station and follow your next ahead in to land', the Tempests joined the long procession of lights going left-handed round what could now be seen as a 'Dremlighting' circuit approach and flarepath, and after a seemingly long time with frequent glances at the fuel gauges which were down in the last quarter but in reality after only two wide circuits, the Tempests joined the long stream of lights descending in the darkness towards the flarepath. All the Tempests landed safely at Ford except one who subsequently got down at Dunsfold.

It was one of the lesser-known statistics of

that strange and remarkable time that over 200 day-fighters were landed in darkness at Ford that night without accident.

By the time refuelling arrangements had been completed and cockpits 0700hrs ordered, it was 0130hrs and time for the welcome bacon and eggs provided with seemingly endless goodwill by the WAAFS of the station staff which had planned so well and efficiently in every way for this eventuality. It was fascinating to see so many familiar faces from other wings and squadrons, all grimy and tired after a 20 hour or more working day but full of cheer and enormous morale. The writer remembers briefly exchanging merriment with Johnnie Johnson, whose high level wing sweep on 27 May had reported the Pontoise Ju 188s but had not, we pointed out facetiously, attacked them — why, we wondered — were Spitfires too fragile for the real war low down! Johnson seemed inclined to start a new war right there at this point — so we retired to bed for a few hours in tiered-bunk huts, before getting up again almost at once it seemed to check the wing's departure arrangements.

At 0745hrs the Tempests taxied out and soon roared back low in tight formation over Newchurch. At 0830hrs the wing was declared operational again for 7 June, D+1, but 11 Group in the event kindly did not call us up from standby after the exertions of the 6th; so that by the morning of 8 June there was general relief that we were not to be left out of things any longer when a Form D arrived for an air superiority sweep inland from the British Beachhead, starting from Rouen and coming out over the 'Mulberry Harbour' and shipping supplying the beaches.

The writer, flying JH 751, led 3 Squadron (CO Squadron Leader Wigglesworth), with 486 (CO Squadron Leader Johnny Iremonger) stepped up downsun and the wing climbed to 15,000ft over the Channel in clear sunshine dappled here and there with fair-weather cumulus. It was a perfect flying day and who knew what lay head.

Making landfall on track just west of Dieppe caused the writer a brief memory of the No 2 Base Hospital there in 1940 just prior to being booted out of France, and of the flight home at the end of May to face what we were by then sure would be the battle for Britain, when we were determined that one day we would be back — and now four years later it was happening.

It came almost as a surprise after recent operations in the area without sign of Luftwaffe reaction to hear 'Blackgang' radar give confident voice to 'unidentifieds 30 miles ahead coming your way, probably below you'. The Tempest pilots concentrated on the small cumulus clouds ahead and below in the direction of Rouen and the winding Seine now becoming visible.

'Blackgang' again: 'Probably 6-10 aircraft at 10,000ft, 10 miles slightly to port ahead'.

The wing increased speed in a shallow descent for tactical advantage to about 400mph IAS as 'Blackgang' gave 'Aircraft probably Bandits crossing you left to right head below, five miles — you should see them'.

This sounded like a perfect bounce, and indeed it was as suddenly an untidy string of fighters in dark silhouette against the broken cloud was weaving and crossing our path about two miles ahead and about 5,000ft below us.

'Kelvin leader attacking to port — Harlequin squadron cover us', and the Tempests of 3 Squadron followed JN 751 down at 450mph IAS towards the enemy formation. Seen briefly in plan form the fighters ahead looked like Mustangs but then at about 1,000yd black crosses could be seen and the shapes of Me 109G6s.

'Tally-ho — they are 109s — come on in!'

With the comforting presence of 486 above the decision was made to give away speed advantage and stay in a turning match with the 109s and, with the last in the formation filling and overlapping JN 751's windscreen, two bursts set it on fire and it rolled away to port to crash north of Rouen. At this point JN 751 was hit in the starboard wing by an

Far left: Tempest JN751 attacking transport targets on 22 May 1944. *Imperial War Museum*

Left: Sqn Ldr John Iremonger, OC 486 Sqn, Castle Camps, 1944. *Imperial War Museum*

FLYING BOMB ON
LAUNCHING PLATFORM

HE round and pulled up into a small cumulus cloud to take stock of the situation and to instruct Johnny Iremonger to reform the wing and complete the mission, while JN 751 headed hopefully for home which was eventually reached safely.

In this action Bob Moore also claimed two 109s destroyed and Lefty Witman one, while other 3 Squadron pilots claimed 'probables and damaged', so that this had been a conclusive victory for the Tempests' first air combat. One Tempest lost its engine power with propeller failure, but force-landed on the first forward airstrip available in the beachhead, and the Navy returned the pilot within 24 hours.

In its first month of operations the Tempest wing had demonstrated emphatically that this was a formidable and capable new fighter in a wide range of actions, and all seemed set for a great summer in support of our land forces' drive to Germany. But at 0530hrs on 16 June two Tempests under Ground Control (the writer and Bob Cole) intercepted a pilotless aircraft (V1) travelling at 370mph at 2,000ft in broken cloud and rain off Folkestone and shot it down at Ashford; and this began an intensive six-week campaign in which the Newchurch wing was diverted from all other operations to mount and maintain patrols day and night against the quickly-escalating and sustained V1 attack on London. Sections of two aircraft patrolled continuously under GCI off the coast at Hastings, Dungeness and Folkestone, and it was soon found that high initial cruise speed and height advantage were necessary in order that 400mph IAS or

Top: V1 (flying bomb) on its launch platform, France, mid-1944.
Imperial War Museum

Above: Tempests leaving Newchurch on a 'Diver' patrol, June 1944.
Imperial War Museum, CH.14097

Right: Re-arming and refuelling a 3 Sqn Tempest, JF-G, at Newchurch, June 1944. In background is No 56 Sqn dispersed.
Imperial War Museum

more could be available immediately on sighting, or else the target would most probably get away.

Nearly all attacks developed in the astern cone because of this and initially there were many instances of full shoots without vital hits owing to the small size of the target. After two weeks and in total absence of official support, the Tempest 20mm guns were reharmonised on 'local authorisation' by the wing armourers from 'standard Fighter Command spread' to point-harmonisation at 300yd, and immediately the score rate increased as did instances of V1s exploding with spectacular and damaging but seldom fatal effect, but the Tempests did suffer additional losses in this period unfortunately due to 'friendly' AA fire, and on some occasions to flying into debris from the target and also in the hail of spent 20mm cartridge cases falling from the section leader's aircraft. But it was a time of mixed feelings. It was a far cry from the vigorous air combat over the continent of Europe which we had anticipated but every V1 going through the Newchurch sector was a potential killer in greater London, and the wing tackled this task with resolution and dedication together with the special night flying Tempest unit based at Manston, led by Squadron Leader Joe Berry, whose score of 60 V1s destroyed was the highest attained.

Successes came swiftly. The wings' 200th V1 was destroyed on 29 June; the 500th on 26 July, and with 56 Squadron finally equipping with Tempests at the end of July, 150 wing ultimately scored 638 by the time in mid-August that AA Command became

Far left: Tempest of No 150 Wing chasing a V1 over Kent, 1944. *Imperial War Museum*

Left: V1's destruction, viewed through a Tempest's gunsight. *Imperial War Museum*

generally equipped with the new American radar gun control and proximity-fused shells. These together produced a dramatic change in their accuracy and enabled the Tempests to be withdrawn from the defence of London by the end of August and to rejoin the great battle for Europe.

So, on 26 August the Newchurch wing resumed the offensive having become the highest scoring wing by far against V1s and in the process having obtained unique gunnery experience for all its pilots against small fast targets; experience which was to have a significant effect during the coming months. Until mid-September the Tempests operated daily at squadron and wing strength against a variety of targets such as armoured fighting vehicles and transport; a set-piece attack on a radar 'Freya' at Cassel; suspected V2 rocket sites in Holland in which the CO of 3 Squadron was lost; and long range daylight bomber escorts to Emden and the Ruhr. During these JN751 was hit by flak in the starboard wing, and WO Owen of 3 Squadron ditched off the Hague and was captured.

Then came the good news. With the capture of Brussels by the British forces imminent, the Tempest wing was to rejoin 2nd TAF after intermediate moves to Manston and Matlaske. As a test of overall efficiency a maximum effort was ordered for 20 September, and a formation of 60 Tempests in squadrons-line-astern was practised during the movement to Manston. This was judged moderately successful, and finally on 28 September the writer led out 54 Tempests from Matlaske arriving over Brussels/Grimberghen B60 airfield, in what was described by onlookers as 'perfect and impressive formation'.

No 150 Wing of 85 Group in UK had now replaced the very successful Mustangs of No 122 Wing of 83 Group in 2nd TAF, and no time was lost in getting back into action. On the same day 56 Squadron swept the Arnhem battle area and next day, 29 September, the squadrons on air superiority sweeps along the Rhine and Reichwald Forest claimed four Fw 190s destroyed, one 'probable' and one damaged. Flying Officer Clapperton was lost to flak but survived as a PoW. On 30 September, 486 destroyed an Me 109 and saw Me 262 jets near Nimnegen, and on 1 October the wing moved again by squadrons to the largest forward base in the British sector just captured from the Germans, B80 airfield at Volkel, commanded by Group Captain Pat Jameson, where they were joined by 80 and 274 squadrons newly equipped with Tempests. This airfield was still under fire from nearby forward enemy positions and WO Reid was killed on the way in. The wing leader's new series 2 aircraft (RPB) with 'short' cannon and increased fuel was also hit in the starboard tailplane by flak near Eindhoven when homing to Volkel.

Next day, while 'RPB' was in for repair the writer, flying US-1 serial EJ 578, with 56 Squadron over Nijmegen at 15,000ft, met about 15 Fw 190s which made a high-speed diving firing pass without hitting anyone and tried to dive away. EJ 578 caught one at over 500mph and shot it down near Cleve, clearly demonstrating the superiority of the Tempest in the dive.

Volkel was a very active station except when bad weather intervened as it now began to, but on 12 October 3 Squadron went on an 'armed reconnaissance' low-level penetration to Munster with the primary object of interception of Me 262s near their

Above: Air Cmdre C. A. 'Daddy' Bouchier CBE, DFC, Senior Air Staff Officer (SASO), No 11 Group area fighter defences against V1 bombs. *Imperial War Museum, CH.14618*

Below: Tempests of 122 Wing taking off from Volkel, October 1944. Note long-range fuel tanks fitted. *Imperial War Museum*

Achmer base, but found and attacked a heavily defended military train on the way, losing the wing leader who forcelanded in a wood and was captured. This sortie had been delayed by a low-flying attack by a Me 262 which dropped anti-personnel bombs on the ATC tented complex near the runway causing casualties, and these activities by the very capable Messerschmitt jets, misused as bombers by personal direction of Hitler, were to become a feature of the sector in the weeks to come. The Tempests became quite successful against them, Bob Cole of 3 Squadron getting their first 262 a week later. The method was to penetrate to the known or suspected areas of their bases and patrol in the hope of intercepting the jets on their return, and in one these actions the commander of the Me 262 unit at Achmer near Asnabruck, the high scoring Major Walthur Nowotny, was shot down and killed.

Under the aggressive leadership of both Wing Commander Peter Brooker and, after Brooker was killed in April 1945, of Wing Commander Mackie, the 122 wing Tempests maintained their successful momentum as one of the most effective types for the low-altitude air war with its mix of ground attack against airfields and transport and air superiority combat, and by the end of hostilities in May 1945 had in addition to an exceptionally high score against ground targets, become the second highest scoring wing against enemy aircraft in 2nd TAF.

No 33 and 22 squadrons added their very effective contribution with their new Tempests from 135 Wing at Gilze Rigen from early in 1945, and in the last three months of the war the Tempests remained in the thick of the heaviest fighting. An operational research report of the period stated: 'No other Wing in 2nd TAF could show such an all-round record of air and ground combat success. The aircraft-destroyed total was beaten only by 126 Wing (by half an aircraft!). Nearly 60% of all 2nd TAF loco attacks were made by pilots of 122 (Mustang and Tempest) Wing. At the wing the standard of shooting is much above the average.'

The success of the Tempest in the last and vital year of the war was due not only to the inspired work of Sydney Camm and the great Hawker team, but also in large part to the dedication, skill, courage and high morale of all the personnel of the units involved, never forgetting those who did not come back.

Below: Roland Beamont, with Sqn Ldr Cotes-Preedy, September 1944, shortly after arriving at Brussels/ Grimbergen with Tempests joining No 122 Wing, 2nd Tactical Air Force.
Imperial War Museum, CL.1387

Bottom: Tempest pilots of No 122 Wing at Volkel, B80 airfield, October 1944.
Imperial War Museum

Pick-up By Hudson

Group Captain Hugh Verity DSO, DFC

Born in Jamaica in 1918, Hugh Verity went to Cheltenham College and learned to fly in the Oxford University Air Squadron just before World War 2. In 1941-42, after escaping from internment in Ireland, he was flying night Beaufighters in No 29 Squadron. In 1943 he was Flight Commander of the pick-up Lysanders in No 161 (SD) Squadron. His book *We Landed by Moonlight* was published by Ian Allan in 1979.

After the war, he commanded a photographic and a night fighter squadron as well as teaching at Quetta and Latimer Staff Colleges. In the early 1960s he was Secretary of the Joint Planning Staff in London and CO of RAF Akrotiri in Cyprus. In 1965 he retired early to make a second career and, from 1968 to 1980, he was the Director of the Printing and Publishing Industry Training Board. Now semi-retired, he is the Administrator of Sion College, an ancient library for the Church of England.

No 161 (Special Duties) Squadron, RAF, was one of the two 'cloak and dagger' squadrons based at RAF Tempsford from 1942 until the end of World War 2. Initially, while 'B' Flight's converted bombers parachuted people, weapons and supplies into occupied Europe, 'A' Flight, equipped with Lysanders, did most of the clandestine landings by moonlight in occupied France.

The first squadron commander, Wing Commander E. H. Fielden MVO, AFC, known affectionately as 'Mouse', had been Captain of the King's Flight and had brought with him the royal Hudson. This and a few other Hudsons proved useful for larger scale pick-ups. Thus eventually there was a third flight of Hudsons. Lysanders could use strips only 500 yards long, but could not normally carry more than three passengers. Hudsons, which needed 1,000 yards, could carry 10 passengers and their luggage.

The Hudson was a low-wing monoplane with two Wright Cyclone radial engines. It had originally been a small airliner, built in the USA by Lockheed-Vega who then called it the 'A-24'. It had been developed into a military 'reconnaissance bomber' by the addition of a bomb-aimer's position with perspex windows in the nose and an air gunner's turret projecting from the top of the rear fuselage. Some 161 Squadron Hudsons had had their dome-shaped gun turrets removed to improve control at low speeds for landings and take-offs. The centre of gravity was then adjusted by the addition of some 300lb of lead ballast. The long tail-plane had twin pear-shaped fins and rudders near its rounded ends. Hudsons were mainly used for escorting convoys crossing the Atlantic. One of our 161 Squadron Hudsons had large and elegant lettering on its side *Spirit of Lockheed-Vega Employees*.

There was a door into the fuselage on the port side behind the wing. The interior was crude structural metal with no attempt at

Right: Hugh Verity as a Wing Commander, DSO (Bar), DFC, December 1943.
H. Coster, FRSA

sound-proofing or comfortable seating for passengers. They had to sit on their luggage or on the floor, with their backs to the side walls of the fuselage. Every possible pound of weight had been saved. There was provision for small scale parachute operations with a chute through the floor. Moving forward through this egg-shaped compartment the pilot and navigator could reach their seats in the front through a little door. The navigator could sit beside the pilot on a folding canvas seat on a metal frame or he could sit at his table, or lie down, in the nose position. The wireless operator/air gunner had two work stations: one for each of his functions.

The customers were secret intelligence, resistance or evasion organisations, SIS, SOE, M19 and their French and Belgian partners. All pick-up operations were cleared by the Air Ministry who first had the landing fields photographed by the Photographic

Reconnaissance Unit at RAF Benson. The Lysander pilots trained selected agents to organise pick-ups on the ground, to find and describe firm strips with clear approaches and to lay out 'flarepaths'. For Hudsons these were 450 yards long with four pocket torches at 150 yard intervals with a fifth light 50 yards to the right of the last torch. Before they were switched on, pre-arranged morse letters were exchanged with the aircraft and a hand-held sixth torch near the first lamp. This was an extension of the 150-yard long Lysander 'flarepath' which had been used since 1940. Agents in charge of ground parties were told that their aircraft were coming by coded 'personal messages' after the BBC news in French.

Wing Commander P. C. Pickard ('Pick') completed the first successful Hudson pick-ups. He had taken over command of No 161 (SD) Squadron from Mouse Fielden in

Above: Lockheed Hudson III, T9465, which served with 269 Sqn, Coastal Command before its use by 161 Sqn.
Crown copyright, CH.2653

October 1942. He was already famous as a bomber pilot, partly through his leading role in the film *Target for Tonight*. Tall and fair, he was in his late 20s but looked older. On 13 February 1943, Pick set off for St Yan, west of Charolles, with a Canadian navigator, Pilot Officer Dicky Taylor, and Flying Officer Henry Figg as wireless operator/Air Gunner. They had five Gaullist Resistance agents on board. They followed our most popular flak-free route towards the centre or South-East of France. This was via Cabourg, NE of Caen, the islands in the Loire east of Blois and Nevers. (Coastlines and big rivers gave splendid visual fixes by monlight.)

The field was a large well-drained grass airfield which had not yet been taken over by the Luftwaffe, as it was to be later that year. As the passengers got out, Fernand Gane's hat blew off in the wind from the port propeller and could not be found — until a German patrol came across it next day. They also noticed the Hudson's wheel marks and had the field so ploughed that we could not use it again.

One of the agents landed was Jean Fleury who was to be in charge of General de Gaulle's radio operators in France. In 1981 he wrote to me:

'The reception committee was small and not well armed. In landing, the aeroplane had made a lot of noise and had swept the field with its powerful landing lamp. The passengers were many and bewildered. It was necessary to get away as quickly as possible. I suggested that, without separating, we should go straight to Roanne and get into whatever train arrived first.

'As we arrived, a train for Lyons came into the station. It was stuffed full of German soldiers. They very obligingly made room in the luggage rack for our suitcases which were full of Colts and radio transmitters. As for us, we slept until Lyons, lulled by the snores of our travelling companions.'

On 20/21 February 'Pick' and his crew were successful again, near Arles, but their third landing, on 24/25 February 1943 was to become one of the pick-up legends.

After flying over a lot of thick fog above the Loire, they found the field near Tournus and Cuisery (north of Lyon) at 0130. They were flashed the signal to wait. On the ground the reception committee were frantically throwing bricks about to flatten the heaps that had been piled up 3' high to obstruct the field. It was an hour or two before the flare-path could be lit. During that wait, Pick did 20 circuits with a complete approach and overshoot on each, lowering wheels and flaps each time. His right wrist and thumb were in plaster because of an accident in an officers' mess party which he had given to celebrate the birth of his son. (He had fallen from a beam after hanging upside down by his knees.) Henry Figg remembers working the throttles for him as well as controlling the wheels and flaps.

By pure chance, Peter Churchill was in a ditch watching all this. He was an SOE agent in the South of France and had bicycled there to see how much traffic there was on the main road at night as he was planning a Lysander pick-up. When, eventually, Pick's wheels touched, Peter saw a tremendous splash. The man holding the second torch vanished in a wave of mud.

At the end of the landing run the Hudson dug in on a patch of soft ground. After half-an-hour of digging and heaving by aircrew, flare-path party and passengers, Pick could taxi away and, on firmer ground, slalom between piles of bricks, rolling back a quarter of a mile to the end of the strip where he had touched down. Here he became even more deeply bogged. Full engine power would not move the Hudson. Those involved in the operation were now joined by dozens of people living nearby who had been woken up by the noise of the engines. Peter Churchill saw Pick come to the door of the aircraft and heard his question: '*Qui est le Chef de cette bande de Sauvages?*'

Then two horses were harnessed to the Hudson and, with motors at full throttle and about 30 men pushing, it eventually moved on to firmer ground. Henry Figg described this to me:

'Pick was at the controls and at every

opportunity he opened the throttles to pull out, blowing everyone who was digging and pushing violently away from the aircraft. The problem was the tail wheel locking device. Either Pick was not locking it or the lock had broken. Every time Pick opened up the tail wheel castored and the opposite main wheel went deeper in the mud. Eventually, I obtained a long branch and used it as a steering arm. With the help of horses the aircraft was moved. (On subsequent trips we made sure of a tail arm being carried.) The most annoying and frightening part of the operation was the willing helpers running around the aircraft and I grabbed at least three, preventing them from going into the moving propellers. I must add that I think I suggested burning the aircraft at one stage when cars appeared before the horses arrived. Pick did not agree, thank God.'

Meanwhile, to give a longer take-off run, many more heaps of bricks were cleared. It was 0530 before Pick could taxi to the corner of the field and take off in the direction which he had been advised would give the longest run. Soon after take-off, one wing tip hit a tree, but the damage was not serious. Next morning Peter Churchill found 30 inches of wing tip on the ground. He also found that the wheels had dug in to a depth of 18inches.

The crew were astonished that there had been no intervention on the ground by the enemy after all that noise for four hours. They crossed the coast north of Le Havre at 0703 as dawn was breaking and the Luftwaffe day fighters were taking off on their first patrols.

In April Pick successfully completed two more Hudson pick-ups, with a different crew. His navigator was Flying Officer Broadley and his wireless operator Flying Officer Cocker. Then he was posted to RAF Lissett as a Group Captain. Squadron Leader L. McD. Hodges, who had been awarded a bar to his DFC the day before, was promoted to Wing Commander to take over No 161 Squadron. He had been 'B' Flight Commander, parachuting agents and supplies from Halifaxes. He too would soon train himself to do pick-ups by Lysanders and Hudsons.

At that time I was commanding the Lysander Flight of No 161 Squadron. Pick had begun my initiation to Hudson pick-ups in January by demonstrating how one could land with a run of only 350 yards by coming over the hedge at 60 knots instead of the 75 recommended in Pilots' Notes.

It was not until 19 May that I could do my first operational Hudson pickup. I was lent a crew from 'B' Flight and I was delighted to find that my navigator would be none other than Flight Lieutenant Philippe Livry of the French Air Force. At that time he already had several French decorations. He was a big man ('1.m 86 et 95 kilos', he records in his book *Missions dans la RAF*). His short but wavy black hair and black army-style moustache, his strong nose and chin, his voice like thunder; all these gave him a formidable and unique presence. He was 20 years older than me but he became one of my best friends.

Sergeant Shine was our wireless operator/ air gunner. He was a cheerful young Yorkshireman with wavy brown hair and pink cheeks. He was quiet, absolutely dependable at his work, with no sign of nerves. His long-term ambition was to run a pub. We three normally made up the crew for all the Hudson pick-ups I took part in.

Comparing a Hudson trip with a Lysander trip, I came to the conclusion that the landing itself on the sketchy flarepath of small torches really was very much more difficult; the navigation was, obviously, very much easier. Not only was there a full-time navigator to concentrate on it, with both hands free; there was also a radio loop for getting bearings and a medium range electronic navigation aid called 'Gee'.

Below: Westland Lysander IIIA, V9367, MA-B of 161 Sqn. *PRO, Air/27/1068*

The landing called for a much larger circuit pattern. The Hudson weighed about three times as much as a Lysander and had to approach about 10 knots faster. It was not nearly so manoeuvrable at slow speeds. In these circumstances lining it up for the final approach was by no means easy, however accurately the race-track circuit pattern was flown. It was not unusual for these clandestine Hudson landings to be achieved after a missed approach. This meant opening up the motors to full throttle to go round again. What the party on the field must have thought of the noise, I shudder to imagine. They must have thought it a signal for any security forces within earshot to converge on the field as quickly as possible. This is perhaps one of the reasons why the *équipe de terrain* always included armed sentries on every approach road and track. They had weapons — mainly Sten guns — which had been dropped by parachute.

That same night of 19/20 May, Group Captain 'Mouse' Fielden successfully completed 'Tulip' at his second attempt. Fog in the target area had defeated him four nights earlier. We all knew this was an operation for the Secret Intelligence Service because all their pick-ups had flower code-names and all their air transport forms were typed with purple ribbons while those for SOE were typed in black. It had actually been laid on by Winston Churchill through SIS. The Prime Minister specially wanted to talk to General Georges, a five-star French general. He hoped that he might persuade him to lean on General de Gaulle who was so much his junior. Major Morton arranged this operation through SIS to pick up General Georges from Michel Thoraval's field on the Causse Méjean, west of Florac on the Plaine de Chanet.

With three passengers, Group Captain Fielden did not take off from Tangmere until 2305. After landing at 0215, he had to spend half an hour on the ground in France, partly waiting for his passengers to roll up in a car convoy, without lights. By the time he was airborne, there was no hope of returning directly to England without risking his VIP passenger to German day fighters. He decided to fly south to Maison Blanche, near Algiers. Squadron Leader Wagland remembers: 'That operation was my first landing in France since before the war. After landing we stopped the engines and must have waited 10 minutes or so for General Georges' car convoy to turn up.

'The cars arrived with no lights. Passengers on board, Fielden started the engines. He drove, I held fully open the throttles and kept the mixture controls on 'Rich'. The wireless operator, Flying Officer Cocker, held the pitch control to 'Fine'. Evidently we were taking no chances. Fielden never braked the wheels before retracting the undercarriage. The smell of burning rubber as the rubber door seals scraped against the revolving wheels was alarming as well as unpleasant.

'As we flew South we were "pooped at" by anti-aircraft guns on the Balearic Islands — a gesture of neutrality as they were far away. Frankly, I did not realise the importance of our VIP until we got to Maison Blanche, when the crew tumbled out first. As the VIP left the aircraft, Fielden sprang smartly to attention and gave a magnificent salute — a courtesy I have only seen him extend otherwise to their Majesties the King and Queen on visiting Tempsford. I was quite shaken by the display'.

After landing, instead of coming back to London to meet Churchill, General Georges went straight to General Giraud in Algiers. This caused no little dismay in high places as Philip Schneidau told me, 'That was the end of the story'.

On 15/16 June I landed a Hudson near Feillens, a few miles up and across the river Sâone from Mâcon. We picked up eight passengers including Paul Rivière, who was the most successful reception chief for pick-ups, Admiral Robert, General Arnoult and Henri Frenay, the leader of *'Combat'*.

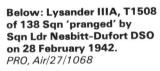

Below: Lysander IIIA, T1508 of 138 Sqn 'pranged' by Sqn Ldr Nesbitt-Dufort DSO on 28 February 1942.
PRO, Air/27/1068

When I was given the thumbs up signal, we took off and climbed up. 'Philippe', I said, 'We must go to Algiers; it is far too late now to go north. The day fighters would get us; dawn will be breaking long before we get to the Channel'. 'OK' said Philippe, 'But I have no maps or charts for the Mediterranean with me. All I have are the frequencies for the Allied radios near Algiers'. He checked through the contents of his canvas navigator's bag. He was right. We had neither of us thought to make sure that we would have the right map-sheets on board in case they should be wanted. Still, I had flown a Beaufighter from Gibraltar to Malta and back two years before and I did not think we needed a map to find Algiers.

We did our best to remember the general shape of the Western Mediterranean and the relationship of Algiers to the French Riviera. We decided to go slightly west of South. Over Provence the cloud had cleared. Just before dawn we could see the Balearic Islands on the starboard side. As we approached the coast of North Africa we called and called on the various Allied frequencies by R/T and Eddie Shine did the same by W/T, but we got no answer. Then there was the problem of which way to turn when we could see the Algerian coast. We planned to strike it to the east of Algiers and turn west. Our guesswork on geography worked well and we landed at Maison Blanche airfield, near Algiers, at 0650 on 16 June.

We had been flying all night and we were all tired but I thought it best to go straight on to Gibraltar, as soon as we had refuelled, had breakfast, signalled home and scrounged some maps. Otherwise it would be impossible to keep my eight passengers together and deliver them, in good order, to their authorities in England.

One of the eight, a grey-haired military looking Frenchman, courteously thanked me for the trip and said he was leaving now to go to Algiers. I, equally courteously, explained to him that my orders were to deliver our passengers to the right organisation in England and that no member of the party could leave it. He then said that General de Gaulle was a personal friend of his and that he wanted to report to him in Algiers as soon as possible to put himself under his orders. As that did not persuade me, he then told me that his ancient mother was in poor health and living in Algiers. If he did not see her now he might never see her again. Finally, in desperation, he asked if there wasn't anybody in authority that he could speak to. (I suppose I did not look specially authoritative, wearing a civilian blue skirt with short sleeves and an open neck.) Although I was captain of the aircraft, I called on Philippe to

back me up. (He was after all, 20 years older than I was.) In his voice like thunder he put an end of the argument and we could go off to get some coffee.

In the unusual glare of the south Mediterranean sun, we took off from Maison Blanche at 0910. We all managed to keep awake until we landed at Gibraltar at 1200. The Rock Hotel found rooms for us when invited to do so by the local military intelligence — who were, no doubt, experienced in dealing with a great variety of unexpected arrivals by various forms of transport.

We stayed the night and took off at 2210 on 17 June for a night flight back to England. By this time we had rested well and had spent some hours shopping. The profusion of fruit, wine, silk stockings and all those things which were unavailable or rationed in England was amazing to see. We loaded a 15cwt Army truck with crates of bottles of sherry and sacks of fruit, such as lemons and bananas, which my family at home had not seen for years. (My five-year old brother-in-law was totally baffled by one of these bananas and had no idea how to zip it open.) The runway at Gibraltar was by now quite long and I judged that we would get airborne in spite of the extra weight. I can now admit that we cut a few corners on that flight home, flying over parts of Portugal and Spain without permission. It was most striking to see the towns lit up after years of flying over blacked-out towns and villages at home and in France.

When we arrived over the south coast of England, Philippe was having some difficulty with the navigation. I cannot now remember what was out of order, possibly the Gee or the R/T. But I do remember that there was a blanket of low could over the coast and that we did not know exactly where we were. Then we saw a flock of tethered barrage balloons floating just above the cloud tops as if grazing on them. We thought it must be Portsmouth that their cables were protecting for low-level air attack. We were right and soon found our way back to Tangmere and breakfast. We landed at 0555 on 18 June — after quite a memorable trip.

I was later told that my tactical decision to stage through Algiers had caused a flap in Whitehall involving four cabinet ministers and a special lunch between the PM nd the Foreign Secretary, but all was well when I brought all my passengers back to England.

The official historical archives show that Hudson sorties for pick-ups totalled 44; of these 36 were successful. These delivered about 140 people to France and collected at least 220. The amazing fact is that not one Hudson was lost on these apparently hazardous operations.

Development and Operation of the Escort Fighter

Lieutenant-General Aviateur Baron M. Donnet DFC

Lt General Aviateur Mike Donnet was trained as an officer and pilot in the Belgian Air Force before World War 2. He first came to public notice by his daring escape from Belgium after its occupation in 1940. He and a fellow-countryman secretly rebuilt an ancient biplane hidden in a farm, and finally succeeded in taking off under the noses of the Germans, escaping their defences and landing safely in England.

Thereafter he had a distinguished career as a fighter pilot and leader for the duration of the war.

After the war he held various appointments in the Belgian Air Force and rose to high office in NATO. Always a good friend of Britain and the British, he also served as Defence Attache to the Belgian Embassy in London, where as doyen of the Attache's Corps he made and renewed many friendships.

The earliest military use of aircraft, in the first stages of World War 1, was for reconnaissance and the aircraft so employed were unescorted. But when the role of bombing was undertaken it aroused sufficient fighter opposition to necessitate the provision of escorting fighters and many heavy air battles occurred in consequence.

The lessons of war are too often forgotten in peace and it is difficult for planners to forecast military developments with accuracy. Between the world wars, bombers were designed which were sometimes faster than contemporary fighters, particularly by the Germans in the 1930s; it was considered that they had the range, speed, armament and general performance to reach their targets unescorted. Fighters were basically interceptors and their range was consequently short. Only the United States Army Air Corps and the Luftwaffe envisaged long-range fighters (Lockheed P-38 Lightning and Messerschmitt 110) but both were twin-engined and lacked the manoeuvrability to deal with defending interceptors.

When World War 2 was launched in Poland, the Luftwaffe rapidly gained air supremacy and their bombers were able to operate more or less regardless of opposition. The German fighters provided area cover and doubled as ground attackers when appropriate. When the fighting transferred to the Western front, fighter opposition from the French and British proved stiffer but their numbers were inadequate; most bombers continued to operate unescorted although they, particularly the Allies, sometimes suffered heavy casualties in consequence. Once again the Luftwaffe attained sufficient air superiority for it to operate freely without much heed of the enemy or need for fighter escorts as such.

All this changed when after the fall of France the Luftwaffe was launched against Great Britain. Unescorted bombers proved

Below: The author as a Pilot Officer at Hornchurch, 1942.
M. Donnet

Above: Lockheed P-38 Lightning, this particular aircraft being a PR variant.

Left: Messerschmitt Bf 110s of ZG 79 Haifischgruppe 'Shark Group'), 1940.

Below left: Douglas Bostons of 107 Sqn.

Right: Hurricane IIC, BD962 of No 3 Sqn. *C. Bowyer*

Below: Hurricane IIB, BP173, armed with eight 3-inch rocket projectiles' rails.

Bottom: Spitfire Vbs of No 243 Sqn, based at Custon in 1942.

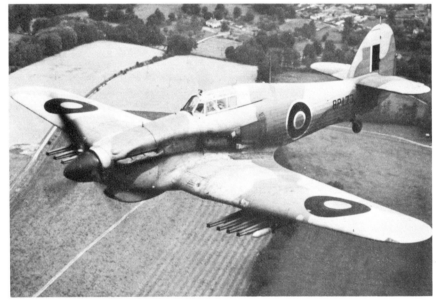

highly vulnerable to well-organised fighter defences and the need for escort fighters of equal performance was clearly demonstrated, the inadequacy of the Me 110 being soon apparent. When, because of bad planning, weather or navigation, the bombers arrived unescorted, their losses were heavy and unacceptable. As the battle developed, fighter escorts were flown more and more closely to the bombers and reach a proportion of one to one. Flying at the limit of its range the Me 109 which was not designed for this work encountered serious problems, but little was done to resolve them by improved design or modification.

As soon as the Battle of Britain was won, Fighter Command started planning its own offensive. Before the end of 1940 fighter sweeps were covering France and the Low Countries. Initially the Luftwaffe re-acted strongly and contact between fighters was constant and heavy. To force the enemy into the air, bombers were introduced to attack targets of importance, first the twin-engined Blenheim and then the four-engined Stirling and even the occasional RAF Flying Fortress. To get the bombers to their target and back was a major operation, involving many squadrons of fighters operating under wing organisation. Besides close escort and escort cover, these wings operated on target support, on rear cover and on diversions. Thus up to 300 fighters might support a formation of six or twelve Blenheims, or three, or even a single Stirling. Practically every flying day brought scenes of fierce fighting. Losses on both sides were high including some of the most experienced pilots, such as the famous legless Douglas Bader.

The first six months of 1942 were largely a repetition of 1941. The RAF introduced the new and faster Boston bomber and also operated Hurricanes as bombers (Hurribombers) but they also required escort. This at the time was provided largely by the Spitfire Mk V which was matched by the Fw 190 and the Me 109 F&G. Escort operations demanded very careful planning. The rendezvous of fighters and bombers was usually over England, at very low level to defeat radar cover and in radio silence, the fighters taking up their allotted roles and stations as the bombers climbed to bombing altitude. By such tactics the targets, which were dictated by the limited range of the escorting Spitfires, were usually reached but heavy fighting nearly always developed as our aircraft headed for home.

The Hurribombers usually operated low-level cannon and bombing ground attacks; but they too required help in both flak-suppression and in defence against German fighters. In one example in 18 April 1942 the Hurribombers were briefed to attack Göring's own train in the station at Neufchatel and were given three squadrons of Spitfires as escorts. Unfortunately, owing to navigation error, this particular attack was abortive but others were more successful. On 18 May for instance Hurribombers were briefed to attack a merchant ship, accompanied by two flak ships, lying off Dunkirk. The attacking Hurricanes approached at minimum level, with another squadron (No 64) suppressing the flak, and a third (122) giving fighter cover. All did their job well and by the time the force left all three ships were sinking and two hours later were at the bottom of the North Sea.

The summer of 1942 saw a major change in the pattern of our offensive. The Americans introduced the B-17 Flying Fortress and B-24 Liberator on high level daylight operations. The first of these operations were again against short-range targets such as Rouen, allowing three squadrons of the newly introduced Spitfire IX to provide

Left: Six stages in the destruction of a Focke Wulf Fw 190 by an RAF Typhoon.
Imperial War Museum, C.3847A

escort (Nos 64, 403, and 611). The height at which the tight formation of bombers attacked, 25,000ft, surprised the Germans and the defending Fw 190s could only attack from behind and at the same level. They did not reach the bombers and were beaten off by the Spitfires, which were of at least equal performance at that altitude, two Fws being shot down. Two days later the Fortresses accurately attacked Abbeville airfield with the same escort, acting as a valuable diversion to the Dieppe operation. Similar attacks were continued for two weeks but the Luftwaffe soon worked out effective methods of re-action, particularly in how to deal with the bombers' own defensive armament.

At this time the USAAF had the twin-engined Lightning available for escort but although fast and long-ranged it was unmanoeuvrable. Also the pilots were inexperienced. On their first operation they flew beautiful formation but failed to notice the Fw 190s creeping up behind the bombers which had to be chased away by the top-cover Spitfires. The size of the bomber formations increased steadily, flying in boxes of six for self-protection, giving added cover problems to the fighter escort. Until American fighters became available, the RAF provided that escort but its lack of range imposed unwelcome restrictions on the bombers' radius of action, the Rhine constituting the absolute maximum distance.

Top left: Boeing B-17 Fortresses of the 390th BG, USAAF over Paris on 15 September 1943 prior to bombing the Renault factory. *P. Vance*

Centre left: 'Little Friend'. Republic P-47D-11-RE, Serial 42-75587, 'B8-V' of the 379th FG, 362nd FG, 9th AF, USAAF based at Wormingford, Essex in early 1944.

Bottom left: Sound and Fury. The mighty 'Jug' — nickname for the P-47 Thunderbolt.

Right: Spitfire Vbs at Kenley, July 1942. *M. Donnet*

Below: No 64 Squadron at Turnhouse, September 1941. The author is 5th from left, centre row. *D. R. Stuart*

When the bombers attempted further penetration without fighter escort their losses proved prohibitive, as their self-protection was outweighed and outranged by the armaments developed by the Germans, including air-to-air rockets. Somehow the true long-range fighter had to be provided to escort effectively.

In due course the solution to the escort of the American daylight bombing raids far into Germany was provided by the arrival of the P-47 Thunderbolt fighter, and later and more decisively of the B-51 Mustang. An earlier version of this aircraft, equipped with an Allison engine, had been tried by the RAF but its performance, particularly at high altitude, proved disappointing and it was relegated to army co-operation duties. The inspiration of fitting it with a Packard-built Rolls-Royce engine converted it into what was arguably the best fighter of World War 2. Its all-round performance coupled with remarkably long-range gave it the ability to match and eventually dominate the Luftwaffe over German skies; and once again the provision of a really affective fighter escort was demonstrated to be the key to efficient offensive air action.

To return to the RAF's own offensive. In 1943 the twin-engined Ventura light bombers of the RAF appeared on operations and

joined the Boston light bombers for the attacks against targets in the occupied Low countries and the north of France. The escort had to be flown in the well tried manner and if all the defenders were not intercepted, there was always the threat of the enemy fighters which when it materialised brought casualties to both bombers and fighters alike. The B-26 Marauder twin-engined bomber of the USAAF began its operation in the middle of 1943. These fast bombers would fly in formation of 36 aircraft made up of 12 times three aircraft all well grouped. The formation of 36 aircraft would follow each other closely. Escorts would be placed on both sides well above. The Marauders flew at heights of 12,000 to 15,000ft, which was a dangerous altitude in relation to the 88mm AA guns.

Many of their targets seemed to be odd to the escorting fighters. They were concrete buildings in the middle of the open country. It is only later that one learned that they were the future launching sites for the V1 flying bomb. When attacking these targets which were so close to each other that often the bomber formations followed each other like the trains on an inner circle. The fighters then provided an area cover. The Marauders were joined in the second half of 1943 by Mitchels both of the USAAF and of the RAF.

At sea the enemy was trying to bring in supplies by merchant ships. The sea lines of

Top left: Hornchurch Wing, Spring 1942. Author is seated extreme right. *M. Donnet*

Centre left: Flg Off Patterson and his Spitfire IXA, 64 Sqn, October 1942. *M. Donnet*

Bottom left: Mustangs of No 19 Squadron. *MoD, CH.12725*

Above: No 64 Sqn at Fairlop, March 1943. Author is 2nd from left, standing on Spitfire's wing; while seated astride the propeller spinner is the New Zealand 'ace' W. V. 'Bill' Crawford-Compton DSO, DFC. *M. Donnet*

communication were constantly under observation and any enemy ship would immediately have to expect a destructive air attack. This would be carried out by twin-engined Beaufighters of the RAF, by far the best anti-shipping offensive weapon system. Armed with four 20mm cannons, this aircraft could carry rockets or bombs. Over the sea it would represent a target difficult to spot. The Beaufighters carried their own anti-flak capabilities. On the other hand they had to be protected against enemy fighters especially during their bombing or strafing attacks. The fighters would be grouped on both sides of the twin-engined strike aircraft and fly for long periods at nought feet over the sea.

For a while after D-day all allied fighters were pre-occupied with protecting the invasion forces and their beach-heads and on interception duties but, on 7 and 30 July 1944, large escorts were provided for hundreds of Halifaxes and Lancasters used in daylight attacks against the enemy defences around Caen. Additionally the Mitchells and

Right: Flying Officer 'Mike' Donnet, 64 Sqn, July 1942. *M. Donnet*

Below: Lockheed Venturas of No 21 Squadron.

Bottom: North American Mitchell of No 320 Sqn attacking a steel works at Caen, late 1944.

Far right: North American P-51 Mustang with long-range fuel pods under wings. *C. Bowyer*

Below right: Martin B-26 Marauder of the 9th AF, USAAF bombing Ijmuiden E-boat pens on 26 March 1944. *E. Rowe*

Bostons, attacking communications, troop concentrations and eventually the main retreating German forces, had to be protected against fighter interception.

Operating from airfields north-east of Brussels, after its capture, large forces of vulnerable Dakotas were used to supply 21 Army Group and later in all forms of support for the Arnhem Operation. The Luftwaffe was never far away and continual fighter protection was essential. When it could not be provided losses were heavy. For example the escort planned for the Stirlings and Dakotas on resupply for the paratroops at Arnhem could not on one occasion meet the task because of very bad weather over England and the Low Countries, and many were shot down in consequence.

Many of our fighter squadrons were now located well forward and as a result the Spitfires could provide escorts for large forces of Lancasters and Halifaxes operating against many German targets. These escorts were usually successful, although shadowing enemy fighters were always on the look out for stragglers. Special airfields were earmarked for re-arming and refuelling the Spitfires to enable them to fly to the limit of their range. A notable raid was carried out on 5 January 1945 by 200 heavy bombers against Ludwigshaven. The escort included No 450 (Australian) Squadron, newly arrived from Italy, to whom the act of flying in a cold and uncomfortable Spitfire for two hours at above 25,000ft proved a most unpleasant and unwelcome experience. After landing back at Hastings three almost frozen pilots had to be carried out of their cockpits.

A more pleasant interlude occurred when

Above: Sqn Ldr M. Donnet and Flt Sgt Gebreugh, Hawkinge, October 1944, 350 Sqn. *M. Donnet*

Above right: Flg Off Wusterfeld of No 350 Sqn and Spitfire XIVs at Lympne, October 1944. *M. Donnet*

Right: Gestapo Headquarters in the Shell Building, Copenhagen, March 1945, before the RAF attacked. *M. Donnet*

Below right: Shell House, Copenhagen after the attack by Mosquitos on 21 March 1945. *M. Donnet*

Far top right: Messerschmitt Me 262A-1a, 'Schwalbe'.

Far centre right: Messerschmitt Me 163B-1a 'Komet'.

Far bottom right: A and B Wings, Bentwaters, March 1945. L-R: Sqn Ldr Drew; Sqn Ldr Gale; Sqn Ldr Thompson; Wg Cdr J. Plagis; Wg Cdr M. Donnet; Sqn Ldr J. Storrar; Sqn Ldr Green; Major Austeen. *M. Donnet*

two Spitfire squadrons escorted to Paris two Dakotas, the leading one carrying Winston Churchill on a visit to General de Gaulle. The pilots found it a welcome change to be able to look down on Paris without being greeted by a hail of AA fire.

At the end of 1944 the RAF followed the USAAF example and introduced some Mustangs for escort duties for our own heavy bombers in raids over Germany. They welcomed all the advantages and capabilities that the Americans had already experienced in this aircraft. Targets for such raids included the Lancaster attack with the 22,000lb 'Grand Slam' bomb against the viaduct at Bielefeld. The watching fighter pilots could follow the fall of the bombs from 20,000ft and observed the destruction of the target. Over 1,000 bombers were used in escorted attacks in March on Essen and Dortmund and the vast size of the bomber stream set special problems for the escorting fighters which however succeeded in beating off all Luftwaffe attacks.

RAF Mustang escort was not confined to four-engined heavy bombers. They also carried out very long range sorties to Norway with the anti-shipping wings of Coastal Command and to various targets with the Mosquitos of 2 Group. Notable among these was the raid on the Gestapo Headquarters at Copenhagen which was brilliantly taken out

Above: Lancaster PO-N, 467 Sqn RAAF bombing by day on 10 September 1944.
H. Lees

Below right: View of Hitler's private retreat, the 'Eagle's Nest' at Berchtesgaden, at 09.53hrs on 25 April 1945, from Lancaster 'A' of 153 Sqn (Flt Lt Kilner) at 18,000ft.

tactics, the performance of the Me 262 was so high that, had Hitler allowed large numbers of them to be used in their designed role of interception, the problems for our bombers and their escorts would have been far greater.

Some operations made special demands on the skills of both bombers and escorts. For example on 16 April 1945, 35 Lancasters attacked a German battleship at Schweinemunde. The escort wing of three squadrons of Mustangs had to take off from England, climb through 20,000ft of cloud, and make a rendezvous with the bombers over the middle of Germany; this, and the return journey in the same conditions, were accomplished with complete succeess.

Perhaps the last escort operation of the war was flown on 4 May when Beaufighters flew from Holland to join operations designed to prevent the escape of German shipping to Norway. They were escorted from base by Nos 64 and 126 Mustang squadrons and succeeded in sinking a considerable number of ships. A heavy anti-aircraft ship was also attacked off Kiel by No 126 Squadron, unhappily losing their Norwegian CO, Major Austeen, who thus gave his life for his country and for liberty in the very last hours of the war.

The Mustangs landed back at Luneborg after five hours and 20mins. It was their last wartime sortie, as they learned that evening of the German surrender. They had contributed much to the story of the RAF fighters which had conducted so many successful escort missions. Once again it had been proved that against heavily defended targets such escort is the key to effective daylight offensive operations.

by pin-point bombing although anti-aircraft fire from German warships destroyed three Mosquitos and two Mustangs. When the latter landed back at Fiesfield they had been airborne for over five hours in the bumpy air of low-level flight.

Another major and successful escort task was to accompany the vast mass of aircraft and gliders supporting the Rhine crossings. But when some days later 400 Lancasters attacked Hamburg, the Me 262 jet fighter was brought into the defence with considerable initial success. Although the Mustang pilots evolved successful defence

Operation 'Taxable'

Group Captain Leonard Cheshire VC, OM, DSO, DFC

Leonard Cheshire has attained unique distinction in two quite separate careers, in war and in peace.

Joining the RAF through the Oxford University Air Squadron he was posted to bombers in 1940 and remained with Bomber Command throughout the war. His record of courage, skill and cool determination was unparalleled even in that remarkable force, including the leadership of the elite 617 Squadron and the pioneering of highly successful low-level target-marker systems. He was awarded the DFC, the DSO three times, and finally the Victoria Cross after the completion of 100 operational missions against heavily defended targets. He was also the British observer at the dropping of the atomic bomb over Nagasaki.

Since 1948 his life has been dedicated to the relief of suffering and the care of the handicapped. There are now over 220 Leonard Cheshire homes for that care in 48 countries across the world. His faith and dedication have been an inspiration to many thousands of handicapped people and those who work with and for them. He has been recently awarded a papal knighthood of the Order of St Gregory and made a member of the Order of Merit by Her Majesty the Queen.

The morning of 3 May 1944 was sunny and bright and there was a feeling of expectancy in our hearts as we made our usual way up to flights. The night before 617 Squadron had returned from a week's special leave granted by 'Bomber Harris' himself, the Commander-in-Chief, because of what he considered the unparalleled success of the attack on Munich which we had led eight days previously. The sole reason for our continued existence as a Special Duties Squadron, after the spectacular breaching of the Mohne and Eder Dams under Guy Gibson's leadership nearly a year previously, was that we should discover a means of dropping a very large bomb with an accuracy of the order of 30ft from a height of 16,000ft or more. They way to do it, we had discovered, was to drop a small cluster of brightly coloured magnesium markers at point blank range, verify their accuracy and then call in the heavies up above at 16,000ft to drop their bombs on a very long and careful run-in. But the weakness of the system was that we were obliged to use four-engined Lancasters for the low-level marking and, if we were to survive against heavily defended targets, we would need the vastly superior and more versatile Mosquitos. Bomber Harris had said: 'Hit the Gestapo Headquarters at Munich with your markers and wipe out the surrounding area with the heavies of 5 Group which I will give you for the occasion and you can keep your Mosquitos'. It had been one of those nights when everything had run our way, and now we felt that big things were in the air.

Hardly had I reached my office than I received a message saying that the Air Officer Commanding, No 5 Group, Air-Vice Marshal Sir Ralph Cochrane, was on his way to talk to the Squadron. This was something that had never happened before and as the crews assembled in the briefing room there was no mistaking their excitement. When Cochrane

Left: Group Captain G. L. Cheshire VC, OM, DSO, DFC.

131

— 'Cocky' as he was familiarly known — arrived, he surprised me by announcing that everyone other than the aircrews themselves was to be sent out of the briefing room, and that while this was happening he and I might as well take a walk along the perimeter track and enjoy the morning sun. The object of the walk, I soon discovered, was to find out whether I could vouch for the ability of every single member of the aircrew to keep an absolutely vital secret for perhaps as long as six weeks. If there was anyone, even one single person, who I thought might constitute a risk then would I please tell him. I pondered the question for a while wondering where I myself stood in such a respect, but he seemed satisfied with my answer when eventually I gave it, and said: 'Well, let's go in and you'll hear what it is all about'. Whatever it was must indeed be important, for as we approached the building I saw that the entire area was surrounded by military police who had arrived from I don't know where. Then, being ever the master of the dramatic announcement, he said: 'Gentlemen, the next time you are airborne operationally it will be D-day'.

There was an audible gasp from the assembled crews as the significance of what we had been told filtered through into our minds. But when Sir Ralph picked up the thread once again and began to outline the role that we were to take, a different atmosphere entered the room, one which I could only describe as a mixture of suspicion, resentment and sheer astonishment. Our task was to carry out a 'spoof' invasion across the Channel using aluminium foil, code-named 'Window', to give the appearance on the German early warning radar sets of a 16 mile wide convoy steaming towards the coast of France at a rate of eight knots.

As if to forestall the inevitable question, 'Why us, when we have been training for six months on something that no one else is equipped to do and which up until now you have told us was of vital importance?' Cocky told us that the spoof was of the highest importance for the success of the invasion; that it had been ruled out as technically impossible by the Fleet Air Arm and Coastal Command; and that only as a last resort had it been handed to Bomber Command who had now passed it on to us. When we had done it we would revert to our intended role.

This we were supposed to have taken as an honour, but the plain fact is that we did not. We were above everything else a special duties Squadron, in some ways the RAF equivalent of the long range desert group, and hitherto our role had been one of lone penetration into occupied and defended territory for the destruction of precision targets without loss of surrounding civilian life. Now it was becoming clear that far from being in the centre of the action of D-day as we had assumed to be our right, we were being assigned to a backroom role, and an extraordinarily tedious and monotonous one at that. Alone, perhaps the navigators took a different view, for the question that was being propounded to us was how could 200mph aircraft simulate an eight knot convoy over a continuous period of four hours, and the navigators were not slow to realise that at last it would be they would call the tune and the pilots who would have to obey. If, that is, the problem could ever be solved.

Cochrane, who could not have failed to sense the disillusionment that his words were occasioning, told us that the reason that he had taken the whole Squadron into his confidence was that although the scientists knew exactly what pattern of flight would have to be followed, no one at any of the Command Headquarters had been able to work out how it could be achieved to the required precision, and that it was to us that he was looking for a solution. He then turned to the subject of security and drove home to us in the most forceful possible terms the consequences to the Allied cause of any careless talk or neglect of duty in this respect. All of us, he said, were responsible for each other: a failure by one single member would be counted a failure of the entire Squadron.

When in due course I was handed a signal which simply said: 'Expect arrival Dr Cockburn 1200 hours', I was perhaps not in the most receptive of moods. This was the electronics specialist — or 'Boffin' as we would have preferred to describe him — whom Cochrane had told us would put us fully in the picture, and who would be responsible for all matters relating to the

technical aspect of the operation. We had lunched together in the mess, which served to let me know and respect him as an individual distinct from the events leading to the night's disaster and thereby to prepare the ground for what was coming. When we had finished what went by the optimistic name of coffee he asked if there was somewhere we could talk without possibility of being overheard, and as the day was warm and sunny I suggested the long stretch of lawn behind the Petwood where no one could come within 50 yards without making himself visible. Dr Cockburn was head of the Telecommunications Research Establishment and, I knew, a leading figure in the sophisticated war of radar measure and counter-measure.

All this was a world infinitely far from my limits of comprehension, and as Cockburn started on his story I hoped that he would not make it necessary for me to disclose my ignorance more than he absolutely had to. Cockburn, however, was in no hurry to come to the technical details behind the operation itself, but preferred to take me slowly through the stages whereby it had been conceived and was now ready to be put to the test.

For Cockburn himself it had begun on a day the previous November when he had been summoned to a planning conference at which he had been told that there would be some top brass. To his great consternation he had suddenly found himself looking at a map which depicted the landing zone for the invasion of Europe and the estimated positions of the Allied and German forces during the three days immediately following D-day. It was information, he said, that he would have given almost anything not to have known. However, like us at our lower level, it was information that he had to have, for his brief

was to explore the various ways in which radar could be used to assist the invasion in general, and in particular to confuse the enemy as to where the main assault was coming. Out of the research that had then followed in TRE there emerged the notion that 'Window' could be used to trick the Germans into thinking that other invasion fleets were crossing the Channel at the same time as the real one. This suggestion had finally been accepted by the planners who decided that one of these 'ghost fleets' should cross the Channel at its narrowest point, where the German High Command was thought to be expecting the invasion, and the other just to the east of Le Havre in the hope that they would tie down all German forces in that area till first light, when the Second Tactical Air Force would destroy all bridges over the Seine and so isolate the beachhead. The first of these two spoofs, known as 'Glimmer', would be carried out by 218 Squadron who would be able to use the newly-issued and highly accurate Gee-H radar navigational system, whereas the other, Operation Taxable, would be our responsibility. We, however, would have to rely upon standard Gee which had never been designed for the kind of accuracy which would now be required; and of course there was a far longer sea crossing to be covered.

Window was by no means a new concept to us, for it had been introduced in 1943 as a countermeasure against the alarmingly accurate German radar-controlled Ack-Ack. It consisted of aluminium foil strips which when dropped from the aircraft reflected some of the radar transmission back to the ground and created a kind of cloud on the radar screen sufficiently dense to make it difficult for the operator to pick out an individual aircraft. But what Cockburn was now saying was that 'Window' of a specially calculated size could be used to create on a ground search radar screen the precise image of a ship at sea. For the suggestion to have been put up to the invasion planners and actually accepted by them must have required some pretty solid supporting evidence, for even assuming that it gave such a response on one of our own early warning sets, what proof was there that it would do the same on enemy equipment, the exact nature and working of which could only be a matter of abstract deduction? But Dr Cockburn was quite ready for this question; he explained that there were basically three types of radar systems with which we had to concern ourselves. The first was *Freya*, the standard early warning radar system that the Germans had perfected and put into operation by the beginning of the war. The second was *Würzburg*, their standard gun laying system, of which there were two forms, the giant one with a range of 40 miles, and the small one with a range of 25 miles. Thirdly there was *Seetakt*, a naval gunlaying system. Of these, it was the small *Würzburg* about which least was known and which was the most difficult to locate. But by a brilliant feat of all arms known as the Bruneval raid a specially trained commando unit had captured the essential elements of a *Würzburg*, and brought them back for study at TRE. The equipment had been installed in full working order at Tantallon Castle on the Firth of Forth and tests done on it had proved that Window did produce on its monitoring screen the exact representation of a ship at sea. Very painstakingly a TRE team had ultimately succeeded in piecing together both a *Freya* and a *Seetakt* set from a ship load of broken parts captured in North Africa and sent home by special request, and experiments with these had given further information about the Window pattern that would be required. The aluminium strips would have to be 6' long with 100 in each bundle and would need to be dropped from a height of 1,000 metres at a rate of 12 bundles a minute. To the long range *Freya*, which would be the first to make a sighting, there would appear a continuous unbroken mass of what could only be interpreted as a vast convoy. All that now remained was to know whether we ourselves, who would not have the help of the ultra-precise Gee-H system, could maintain the necessary flight pattern to the required accuracy over a continuous period of four hours.

TRE had calculated mathematically that in order to create what in effect was a huge radar reflector made up of falling Window, eight aircraft would be needed. These would have to fly line abreast at two mile intervals and keep in perfect formation throughout the entire exercise, though of course they would not be visible to each other. Their flight pattern would consist of a series of oblong circuits, rather on the lines of an Olympic running track, steadily advancing each lap at a rate that would represent a convoy of ships sailing at eight knots. This would mean beginning simultaneously from a pre-determined start-line out to sea off the English coast and flying a straight parallel course for two and a half minutes, which at a flying speed of 200mph — that is to say a little over three miles a minute — would represent a distance of approximately eight miles. At the end of this forward leg each aircraft would begin a slow right-handed turn timed to last one minute and calculated to bring it one mile to its right, now flying a reciprocal course back towards England. At the end of this course it would repeat the slow right-handed turn in such a way as to arrive back over its original track to begin the second circuit. Window would be dropped on each of the two straight legs of the circuit, but not on the turns at either end, so that there would in effect be 16 parallel lines of Window each eight miles long, but to the watching *Freya* these 16 columns would in fact merge so as to make one continuous line.

In order to simulate a steady eight knots forward movement, each circuit would need to begin one mile further forward than the last, and this was to be achieved by the aircraft breaking off the homeward leg after two minutes 20 seconds, in other words 20 seconds shorter than the outward leg. The Window dropped at the beginning of the first leg would still be floating down when the aircraft arrived overhead for the second circuit which would now start forward of the previous ones by one mile. And so it would proceed steadily onwards at a rate of eight knots until after two hours a second section of eight aircraft would arrive overhead and take over for the rest of the operation.

Dr Cockburn concluded his explanation by saying that the spoof could only work if the image on the German radar screens remained constant in shape and in forward movement. If just one aircraft were to miss its turn by a quarter of a mile, or if the Window droppers mistimed their cue at the beginning or end of a leg by eight seconds, then the convoy would behave in a way that wouldn't make sense and suspicion might be aroused. If the worst should happen and the deception be actually detected, then the German High Command would be alerted to the fact that this was a major and deliberate attempt to divert their attention from what now must be the real invasion approaching west of Le Havre; and they would see the urgency of moving their armour across the Seine as soon as possible.

At that point Dr Cockburn stopped his

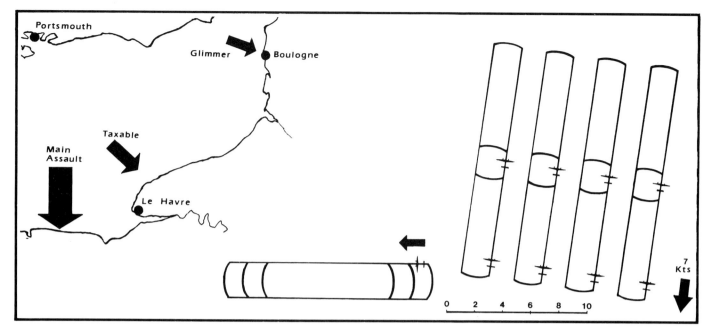

story and looked at me as if to say 'Well, what is your answer?'. My mind however had begun to wander, for I had the feeling of having been catapulted into a strange and unfamiliar world. As members of wartime Bomber Command we lived out our lives in what today must appear remarkably small and watertight compartments. In 617 Squadron our world was more curtailed still, partly for security reasons and partly because of the pressures of the special job that had been entrusted to us. It had taken us a full three months to discover how to bomb a small and obscure target by night with the accuracy required of us, and all our time since then had been devoted to practising and developing the technique itself both over the bombing ranges at Wainfleet and on live targets in occupied France. At the outset we had not known why it was that we had been given this task and why such priority appeared to have been allotted to its fulfilment, but we now knew that Hitler was busily engaged on building in the Pas de Calais area two or possibly three versions of what he considered to be the most lethal and most effective of all his secret weaons, the V-3. This was a huge underground gun operated on a pressure pump system and capable of putting two 500lb shells every minute into London. Because of the attacks that the RAF had mounted upon his V-1 and V-2 sites in northern France, this weapon was being protected by 15 metres of reinforced concrete which no bomb on earth could hope to penetrate, and now that the sites wcre nearing completion fears were being voiced within the War Cabinet that London might have to be evacuated. However, Barnes Wallis, designer of the first airship to cross the Atlantic and more latterly of the skipping bomb that had destroyed the

Dams, had set his mind to the problem posed by the reinforced concrete and was building a deep penetration bomb which he said could cope with it. Aerodynamically shaped and polished by hand in order to achieve increased accuracy and power penetration, these would be capable of blowing up the V-3 from underneath their protective mantles, and were expected off the production line almost any moment. However the fact remained that we ourselves would have to succeed in identifying these well camouflaged underground sites and then drop at least two of these 10,000lb bombs within five metres of the outside of the concrete cover from a height of 5,000 metres. This we felt in our hearts we could only achieve if we continued without interruption of our already heavy training programme, and provided we kept our minds focused on this one objective. As others in different fields will testify, when it comes to the really special occasion there is a psychology to the business of emerging as victor, quite apart from the other more obvious aspects. One needs, so to speak, to prepare oneself mentally, to work oneself up by calculated, progressive stages so that one reaches the peak of one's form and preparedness neither to early nor too late. True, when the time actually comes, one may find that it is not after all quite so difficult, but to bank on this would be to introduce an element of chance in a matter where it had been drummed into us time and again that we simply could not afford to fail. One could not help but wonder whether 'Taxable', even though it should be successful in itself, might not yet prove our undoing when it came to our real task.

The man stretched out on the lawn beside me, picking every now and then at a dasiy as I was, and who was now waiting for me to respond, had been brought up in a different world, one of broad vistas and of great diversity ranging from the nuts and bolts of a specific operation such as he had just oulined to the strategic implications of electronic warfare. Whether he guessed what was going on in my mind I do not know, but what I do know is that he brought me back to earth by saying: 'You are a disappointed man because this is what you have been asked to do, aren't you?'. 'Yes', I acknowledged, 'I am, and the Squadron even more so'. I contemplated trying to explain, but time was passing and it seemed more important that he should come and meet the crews himself. It was they who would have to be won over and convinced even more than I myself, and he, I felt, would be better able to do this than I. So we picked ourselves up, had some tea and drove over to the briefing room.

What was being asked of us was of course first and foremost a navigational problem, and once the navigators knew that it had been dumped on their laps they shut themselves up in their navigation section to see if they could come up with a solution. What they had to resolve was a method of continuously plotting their positions over sea during the intricate flight pattern that was required to an accuracy of less than a quarter of a mile. The instrument upon which they would have to depend was their Gee box which, though in regular use and remarkably accurate for ordinary navigational purposes, had never been devised for precision of this degree. In order to assist them, one of the Gee experts from the Telecommunications Research Establishment, Mr Bellringer, was seconded to the Squadron and upon his arrival was immediately accepted as a member of the 'Navigators Union'. Within four days three possible solutions were produced, each of which was given to one of the three flights of the Squadron to test out in practice. By 8 May it had become clear that one of these was more feasible and effective than the others, and thereafter all three flights began training in this one particular method on an average of three hours per day for way would turn out to be a whole month. But throughout all this period no one forgot that no sooner D-day itself was over than we would be recalled to our real task, and so we continued our training in this as well. The two combined kept us busy, for part of the precision bombing technique called for identifying an obscure aiming point in the light of flares dropped by a section of the Lancasters, then diving through them in the Mosquitos to drop the markers, and this of course meant adding extra night exercises to our already heavy programme. But one evening as dusk was falling — and our spirits a little lower than usual — Les Munro and I

saw a truck covered with tarpaulin driving round the perimeter track towards the far side of the aerodrome. It looked a little different from anything we had seen before and we decided to investigate. On being challenged the driver would merely say that he was carrying spare parts. But if so then he was making for the wrong direction and so I ordered him to lift part of the tarpaulin. Inside was the first consignment of Barnes Wallis' deep penetration masterpiece, Tallboy. So the promise had come true: it was just the fillip we needed.

Throughout this time Cockburn continued to visit us to give us the benefit of his highly expert advice, and also to initiate us into some of the wider issues involved and other D-day measures on which his Department was working. On the Yorkshire coast off Flamborough Head had been installed a Type 11 radar, the nearest British equipment to the German giant Wurzburg, on which we were to do a full scale dress rehearsal as soon as we were ready. Well do I remember my various visits there. Driffield, the scene of my first operational posting just four years ago, was the nearest aerodrome and on the occasion of my first visit I found an American major standing on the tarmac who whisked me very quickly into his car, in which I noticed there was no official driver. Hardly had we started moving than he turned to me and asked: 'How much do you know?'. Slightly mistaking the gist of his question, I promptly answered: 'Everything'. 'Gee,' he replied 'that really is something'.

One of the things Cockburn told us was that whilst 'Window' would present a perfect image on all three forms of German ground based radar it would not work at all against airborne radar, which would almost certainly be sent up to make an independent sighting. To guard against this eventuality a counter-measure system known as 'Moonshine', first used in 1942 to combat *Freya*, was being brought back into service and would be fitted in RAF Rescue Launches which together with a few naval vessels would be accompanying both 'Glimmer' and 'Taxable'. 'Moonshine' acted as a kind of magnifying mirror which reflected back any radar transmissions being beamed at it with greatly increased strength, thus giving the impression of a very much larger force than actually existed. The 'Moonshine' operator in the launches would look out for enemy airborne signals and send them back as greatly amplified echoes to give the appearance of a large mass of ships. In addition the launches would tow a barrage balloon with a nine-foot diameter radar reflector fitted inside it, the echo from which would be as large as that coming from a 10,000 ton ship.

The time for our fullscale dress rehearsal

against Type 11 radar at Flamborough Head had been set at 1 June, and it was arranged that the radar operators would be given no hint of the nature of the exercise that they were being detailed to observe. The news of the naval support that we were going to have over the Channel had undoubtedly boosted our confidence, and when TRE reported that the exercise had been a 100% success with the radar operators saying that they had picked up a very large convoy of ships, in fact the largest they had ever seen in all their lives, we found ourselves dominated by one single thought. How soon would D-day come so that we could get the operation out of our systems and begin to put Tallboy to the test?

Early in the afternoon of Tuesday 5 June, the long awaited and brief coded message was handed to me. I knew now that tonight was the night and that in a few hours time I would be calling the crews into the briefing room for their final orders. This time there would be no pre-flight bacon and eggs as was the invariable custom before taking off on an operation. Just an ordinary supper so that no one would think anything special was happening. After the briefing itself there would be no return to the mess for anyone, just some very hard work for those loading 'Window' into the aircraft, a brief but concentrated session for the navigators, and for the rest, particularly those of the second wave, a tedious wait, killing time.

The briefing itself was a relatively simple affair, for every aspect of our flight pattern procedure was already burned into our minds and it was our habit to keep briefing to the minimum. All that we really needed to know was our exact start and stop line, zero hour for arriving at the start line, our route down England so as to avoid the mass of other aircraft taking off on their individual missions, the weather and any other special instructions for the night. All this having been dis-

posed of in some ten minutes or so, we were then briefed about some of the other things that would be happening that night to protect the invasion proper and to confuse the German High Command as to what was happening. To make the picture clearer for us there was hung on the briefing room wall a large chart depicting the position, approach routes and targets of each of the main elements of the combined assault forces. It was not strictly essential that we be shown this, but to those uninitiated in the broad tapestry of overall planning, such as we were, it was an awe inspiring sight, one well calculated to drive home the utter necessity of not failing in our task. In bold relief were painted the twin approach lanes of the seaborne and airborne forces that would be making respectively for the beach-head and the dropping zone further inland. Everything else that would be taking place that night was designed to protect and cover these most crucial lines of approach. Over each of them powerful home-based transmitters would lay down a total radar and radio jamming blanket so that German ground control, even if it were able to pick out incoming stream of transport and glider-towing aircraft, would not be able to direct their fighters into it. If an enemy fighter did make contact it would purely be by chance.

As for 218 Squadron and ourselves, we likewise would be covered by airborne jammers in order to avoid arousing suspicion, but the jamming would be carried out in such a way as to leave deliberate 'holes' through which the ground radar operators would be able to detect our two 'ghost' convoys. The way it was all put to us as we left the Briefing Room we were made to feel amongst all the innumerable units operating that night we least of all could afford the smallest error. As things were to turn out this did not quite prove true, but it was as well perhaps that we

Below: H. C. 'Nick' Knilans DSO (3rd from L) and his 617 Sqn crew. *H. C. Knilans*

set out for our aircraft convinced that so much would epend on how we carried out our task.

At 2305 the first section of eight aircraft took off with Les Munro, the big dependable New Zealander, in the lead position and I as his second pilot. I had not taken a serious part in the training because of the other responsibilities I had had, and I was happy to leave the control of the aircraft in Les' capable hands and merely to relieve him for a while when he felt tired. In the aircraft there was an unusual silence, each man rehearsing in his mind the task that he would soon have to fulfil and no doubt engaged with his own individual thoughts. It was a night on which strange movements were to be seen on the ground below, and as we approached ever closer to the south coast, the thought was borne in on me that all around us, almost in every single square mile, were individual human beings who were preparing to go into action for the first time in their lives. I found myself trying to picture them and what they would be saying to each other to bolster their morale and to prove to their companions that they were not afraid. For what man is not afraid, at least somewhere in the depths of his being, when he starts out to face gunfire for the first time, particularly gunfire of the kind that could be expected the other side of the Channel?

Zero hour for the eight aircraft to arrive at their individual position on the starting line was 2305hrs, and some 10 minutes previously the navigators had already begun issuing the final changes of course and speed to bring their aircraft on an exactly timed run-in. Each aircraft carried an extra pilot and navigator and three additional crew members for the 'Window' dropping. Originally it had been planned that the second navigator would take over from the first at the half way point, but this had not proved practicable and it was decided instead that one navigator would operate the Gee set while the other would supply him with the data that he needed in order to keep the aircraft correctly positioned on the Gee grid at all times. This he did by sitting rather uncomfortably on the steps beside the wireless operator with a board on his knee which listed the values of the four major co-ordinates prior to the moment of starting and finishing each of the two straight legs. But to guard against a faulty call by the second operator or an error in setting up the co-ordinates on the set itself, the set operator also held a stop watch which he started at the beginning of each straight leg and consulted alternately with the Gee-set signal. It was his responsibility, too, to control the 'Window' dropping process. This he did by means of two electrical switches which operated effectively a green and a red light close to the flare chute down the fuselage. It had been discovered in practice that the illusion of an approaching convoy was heightened by using progressively thicker 'Window' strips the nearer one approached to the French coast. This meant that on each straight leg, both outwards and homewards, two different thicknesses were required, the thicker on the section closer to France and the thinner on the rear section. Then at the beginning of every fourth circuit a further upgrading was required which, with a total of 18 circuits to complete involved six different sizes of 'Window' altogether. The red light at the beginning of the outward leg was a signal to the marshal to commence dropping the thinner 'Window', the green light halfway along the leg signified change to one grade thicker, and green light out meant stop 'Window' altogether during the turns. Then the process was repeated in reverse for the homeward leg. What with the unwieldiness of the bundles, the precise requirement of one bundle every 15 seconds down the flare chute for five minutes out of every seven and such a variety of sizes to be kept in their strict sequence, a high degree of discipline and concentration was required of the 'Window' dropper and the marshal in charge.

Talking on the intercom was kept to an absolute minimum, and in any case was more or less monopolised by the two navigators who were now firmly in charge of the operation, and no doubt feeling that their finest hour had come. For two tedious hours we flew like robots, our heads down and our eyes firmly fixed on the instrument before us. Nowhere was there gunfire to be seen, or searchlights to try and avoid: from the outside we received not a single signal or message to indicate how the operation was going, or even that an operation was taking place at all. Only by faith could we tell that

Below: 'Window' cloud — in this view, over Essen on 11 March 1945.
Imperial War Museum, C.5634

this really was the night before D-day and that we were taking part in a moment of history. Yet we had confidence in Cockburn's vision and in the ability of our navigators to keep us on course, and every now and then our minds would wander to the region of Cap d'Antifer and conjure up a picture of a startled radar operator reporting to his superiors the approach of an immense convoy of ships. We just hoped he was doing his job well. Paradoxical though it may appear, the further we advanced along our course, the greater the strain on our nervous system, like a man building a house of cards who as he approaches the top becomes aware that just one false move and everything will collapse. But with the minute hands coming up to 0200 the second navigator announced that we were about to enter our final circuit, and hardly had he done so than Joe McCarthy's broad American voice came through on VHF to announce that the second flight was approaching their start line. This was the signal for the change-over and we felt in our bones that if only we could get over this hurdle, with fresh crews now at the controls and only two hours to go to dawn all would be well. But this in fact was the most crucial part of the exercise, for if the relieving section did not make a precise positional rendezvous within a maximum time latitude of 90 seconds, all the 'Window' being dropped from the first section would have fallen into the sea and the complete convoy would suddenly vanish off the radar screen. The drill we had worked out was for the eight relieving aircraft to join us at the beginning of the start of our final circuit and to overfly us by a height of 500ft right up to the end of the return leg, at which point we would break off while the second section would descend to 3,000ft during the right handed turn and immediately they had straightened up at the beginning of the outward leg they would start 'Windowing'. One by one they were to confirm that they were correctly positioned using a very brief coded formula. No sooner had they all done so and the change over been successffully completed than a long but gentle sigh was heard down our intercom. It was very different from the usual reaction at the culmination of one of our operations, but somehow it seemed to fit our mood. In any case now that the need to concentrate was gone with not even hostile defences to worry about and only a matter of flying home, debriefing and waiting for news, we felt a little deflated.

For the second section it was a little different. As they entered the final quarter of their slow but steady approach route the sky to the east had grown perceptibly lighter and as they reached their final stop line day was dawning. Ten miles ahead of them the French coast was clearly to be seen. No gunfire was coming from it, nor was there any sign of enemy fighters, so not unnaturally they lingered in the area to see what they could. Underneath them the naval launches were carrying out the final act of the spoof. Behind a thick smoke screen that had appeared along the 16 mile frontage of the 'Window' convoy the launches were emitting with great vigour such sounds as the rattle of ships dropping anchor, landing craft being lowered into the sea, orders being sounded by men with remarkably penetrating voices, even cries for help from the injured, anything in fact that might be expected of an invasion force preparing to beach, and all pre-recorded on gramophone records and played back at high volume through loud speakers. In the Pas de Calais area the shore batteries had opened up on the source of these sounds but by the time the smoke screen had drifted away there was nothing to be seen other than a handful of launches in the far distance heading rapidly for home. In the case of 'Taxable' there was no such reaction, whether because we were too close to what was now manifestly a very real invasion force indeed or whether because the six days of bombing had immobilised the defences we were never to find out. All we were really told was that though there was a moment when TRE had thought that things were going wrong, in fact the 'Window' pattern had as far as anyone could see been on course all the way. Only much later did we learn that by mid-day the German High Command's plotting chart showed three major invasion forces having arrived at the French coast, and that so confused was the general staff by the many reports and counter reports, by so many contradictory sightings, and by the inexplicable failure of their night fighters to make organised contact with the main stream of the incoming aircraft, that they still thought the Normandy beach-head was only a diversion. Much later still we were told that both we and 218 Squadron would in fact have got away with murder, that once a radar operator on the early warning chain had had reported a positive sighting of a large convoy this would have been firmly put on a plotting table, and that under the conditions obtaining that night no amount of contradictory reports even by an aircraft making a visual search of the area would have sufficed to take the plot off the table. But I very much doubt whether anyone in the Squadron would have had it other than it was.

We had come to feel that we were after all a little honoured at having been chosen to do the operation, and all we could hope was that we had made things just that bit easier for the troops on the ground.

A Long Road to Freedom

Ian Smith

The fact that Ian Smith served as an operational fighter pilot in the Desert Air Force in World War 2 is perhaps less well known than some of his postwar activities. Indeed the sterling service of both the Rhodesian and South African Air Forces to the Allied cause tends too often to be conveniently forgotten. Ian Smith was shot down over Italy and escaped through enemy occupied territory as is recounted below.

His story does not tell its sequel which is that by ingenious manoeuvre and typical determination on return to the UK he succeeded in joining a wing of the Tactical Air Force in England and then Europe, where he continued to operate with distinction.

The history of his political career is perhaps too well-known to require further elaboration. His story as told below is certainly typical of the man he is.

Right: The author. *Popperfoto*

140

My main regret about the war was that I was forced to spend too much time on the ground, and too little in the air. After a crash in the Western Desert, I found myself in the 15th Scottish Hospital on the banks of the Nile, opposite the Gezeira Club, strategically well situated, because once I was mobile enough to move around there were many worthwhile sporting events to while away the time. The Sixth South Africa Division had arrived, and it wasn't long before they had organised rugby games against the New Zealanders and others. It was about a year earlier that we (237 Squadron) had moved down from Persia (Paiforce) and on our way through Cairo we had a few games of rugby — we had been keeping our hand in with games against London Scottish and London Irish Regiments, and the Royal Air Force Habbaniya while we were in Persia — the first game was against our own Rhodesians stationed in the Delta, and the second against a team mustered together from all and sundry. We advertised this game as 'Rhodesia vs The World'! We had a great day, both on the field, and afterwards off it.

My spell in hospital, followed by a period of recuperation, and then an air-firing course at Ismailia, took up the best part of a year, and then I made tracks back to my squadron, which was by now stationed in Corsica. We were part of an American Group, and when we were not escorting the American bombers (Mitchells, Bostons and Marauders) on their bombing missions, we spent our time on strafing raids — principally train-busting and attacking heavy motor transport. As German aircraft were conspicuous by their absence, this was the next best thing and provided us with good sport.

One morning I was leading a flight on a strafing trip into the Po Valley. I picked up a railway line and followed it, and, as expected, we came upon a large marshalling yard and went straight in, picking on the most attractive targets of locos and fuel tanks. There were some healthy explosions, and columns of black smoke started billowing up. I then made the mistake against which I had often warned, of going back for a second run — there was no sign of any opposition, but with the element of surprise in our first attack this was normal — it is different once you have stirred the hornets' nest. I had had a long run of successes, leading to over-confidence and complacency, and the target was very inviting. I struck home on another line of tank cars, and, as I pulled up out of my dive, there was a resounding thud which shook my Spitfire. I turned left towards the coast and base, and on the inter-com told my No 2 to follow me, and the rest of the flight to carry on with the mission. Noticing that the oil pressure had gone, I tried to gain as much height as possible. If I could cross the coast and get even a few miles out to sea, there would be a good chance of being picked up by one of our sea rescue craft. However, that was not to be. My temperature gauges were off the clock and I soon felt the heat from the engine. My No 2 — Alan Douglas — told me first of the black smoke pouring out, and then the flames came. There was only one answer — I had often gone through the drill for such an emergency, so there was no equivocation. I jettisoned the canopy, released my harness, and, although I would have liked more height for the operation, I turned the Spit over on to its back, rammed the stick forward — out I came perfectly.

However, that wasn't the end — because of lack of height I to pull my rip cord quickly, and no sooner had the 'chute opened than I landed on the side of the mountain and bounced a few times before coming to a stop alongside a bush. I hastily rolled up the parachute and hid it beneath the bush, and then ran up the hill in order to distance myself as far as possible from the scene. After a few minutes, I saw a thicket of bushes and made for it, thinking it would be a suitable place for refuge. I lay down for a while to regain my breath and survey the scene, and, on reflection, came to the conclusion that this was so obviously the best place in the vicinity to obscure myself, that it would attract attention for that reason — so I moved on a few hundred yards to an inconspicuous bush, similar to many others in the vicinity, and I found that it offered ample cover when I lay down and pulled it around me. I took off my Mae West and laid it down like a blanket — the sun was hot — and then I did another recce and came to the conclusion that I had chosen the right place. I saw a man running and walking a few hundred yards below — he stopped and beckoned towards him, obviously trying to attract my attention — but I lay low, not knowing whether it was a genuine offer of help or a trap. A young boy, with his flock of sheep, moved by about 20 yards away, but did not notice me.

Things were quiet for about an hour. Then a gang of Germans, with a tracker dog, appeared. Fortunately they had not found my parachute, buried a long distance away, and

Below: Spitfire taxying, Naples, 1944.
Imperial War Museum, CNA.1638

local sheep had crossed my tracks. The Germans were obviously frustrated and fired bursts of machine gun fire into the large thicket I had first selected for cover. They then moved on.

With the setting of the sun it grew colder and colder. We had all been told that most of the rural people were friendly and I realised that, as I would have to make contact with someone sooner or later, there was no point in further delay. The young boy with his sheep came back, and I spoke to him. He took me around and down the mountain until we saw a house below us and could hear someone chopping wood. The boy used sign language to tell me to sit and wait. He came back with his brother. They took me to their home and I was given a dinner of minestrone and had a comfortable first night.

Next morning, the mother took me about a half a mile away to a small cave in the mountainside, which was very well obscured by the undergrowth. Her explanation made it clear that this was a precaution against German search — a wise one, because over the next few days the Germans came back repeatedly to question her. She left me with a blanket in what was to be my home for the next few days — she came back twice a day with her basket in which one could see the chestnuts she was collecting, and when she removed these and the cloth which was underneath them, there was food for me. Once the coast was clear, I lived a reasonably normal life, taking into account sensible precautions — the local *Partisani* (resistance movement) had an efficient system of communication if the Germans were moving in the area. I kept fit by walking a lot (collecting chestnuts — *castania* — and mushrooms — *fungi* — after rain), doing my exercises every day, and chopping wood for the fire. My hostess was concerned that I was doing this as compensation for my keep, but after a while I managed to convince her to the contrary — I hope! One of my main preoccupations was learning the Italian language, as I believed this to be important for my return through the lines — something which was constantly in the forefront of my mind.

After about a month, the commandante of one of the local *Partisani* companies arrived — an imposing character sporting a handsome beard, an automatic under his arm, a bandolier full of ammo, and a series of hand grenades around his belt. He had come to enquire after my well-being, if there was anything he could do — his English was adequate for us to be able to understand each other. After a short discussion, it was agreed that I should accompany him back to his headquarters — I obtained from him an undertaking to assist me in returning to the Allied Lines. My rank? I said I was a captain. He said he would promote me to a major forthwith, and from that moment I was introduced to everyone as the *Englasie Majore Pilote*. The quickest and neatest promotion I ever had, and it soon became clear to me that my elevation in rank had the effect of enhancing my Commandante's prestige. I was paraded around like the chief elephant in a circus — after all, none of the other companies in the area could boast an '*Englaise Piloti*' and a '*Majore*' to boot.

It was an interesting change of life, and I enjoyed it — and immediately became a member of the high command and inner war council, planning and participating in raids and ambushes. We lived well on good food and wine which we captured (part of our winnings), a nice suit made from captured material, A Fiat to drive around in, a hair cut from the communal barber.

There were sad times, when some of our boys were killed (infrequently, fortunately). One one occasion, the Germans came into our village with two armoured carriers and a truck load of troops. The senior commandante (Mingo) was killed. He was an engineer who had been in the Italian Army — a fine, intelligent man — I missed the interesting conversations we used to have,

Above: War-Horse. Spitfire of No 2 Sqn, SAAF, No 7 SAAF Wing, over the Sangro River. *via E. Hooton*

and the frequent games of bridge. There were compensating highlights, such as our Victory March into Sasello after our constant harassment had forced the Germans to pull out. Many was the time that members of the company promised that one day they would give me what everyone knew was the Englishman's favourite dish — roast beef! The day of our arrival in Sasello was a cause of great celebration, and the wine flowed freely. I was sound asleep early the next morning when Nino and a few other young officers burst into my room and awakened me, saying: 'Majore, majore, wake up — we goota de roasta beef for you'. One of the locals had produced the goods to celebrate the occasion of our triumphant arrival. In Italy, once there is meat on the table, there must be wine also — so it was quite a day.

Whenever I raised the question of returning to the Allied Lines (I did this approximately on a fortnightly basis), I always met with strong arguments against this: it was important to take more time to improve my command of the language; I looked too much like an *Englaise Officier* — tall, fair and that moustache — if only I would remove it; for me to attempt to go now would be *periculosissime*. For a while I went along with this, but it was beginning to wear a bit thin. I had been with them for three months — certainly three of the most interesting months of my life — but we had witnessed the first fall of snow up in the mountains, and I was not going to allow myself to be hemmed in there for the next six months. I made it clear to my friends that I would be leaving the next week, and when they realised that my decision was final and irrevocable, they philosophically accepted the loss of their 'prize elephant' and gave my every assistance, including letters of introduction for the journey. I decided to go west into France — they concurred. A British corporal who was known in our area as Bill, asked if he could come with me. After about 10 days, three others (French, Austrian and Polish) who were part of a *Partisani* camp asked to join me. Generally on our journey we were given food, shelter and direction, although occasionally people bustled us on — they were afraid of German reprisals. On one occasion, we were taken by a *Partisani* commander to his headquarters in the mountains where he controlled a large area — we were given '5 Star' treatment: beds and excellent food including meat and butter. Next day, a fine looking young doctor in his Alpini uniform accompanied us as our guide, but the following morning he left us and returned, as he was the only doctor in his area and had calls for attention every day. Moreover, he was a marked man by the Germans, and we were now entering a dangerous area. He gave us careful and detailed directions — only two more days needed — and advised me to divide my group in order to be less conspicuous. Bill and I went on and the other three were to follow the next day. That night we were taken in by a Frenchman and his wife in their farmhouse, given a good warm meal and we slept in the barn alongside a fine looking bull.

There was a big German base in the town below and they were doing a lot of patrolling — in case they arrived, the Frenchman could claim no knowledge of our presence in the barn, and we would co-operate. The next morning, his brother — an official in the town — came up to see us (a wonderful effort, as he was disabled with a bad leg). He spoke immaculate English, and was satisfied as to our authenticity. The plan was for us to cross to the other side of the valley that day — across a river, railway and main road — difficult and dangerous, because there was one bridge across, with sentries who halted and interrogated selected people, so it was a question of keeping a cool head and taking our chance — there appeared to be no alternative. We were given careful instructions and a rendezvous the other side for the late afternoon (our host's brother would be there to meet us). I told him of our three friends following, and asked for assistance should they pass by, saying we would wait a couple of days on the other side before the final crossing, which was over the Alps.

Bill and I sat and waited — we didn't say much. I did some exercises, which I hadn't had an opportunity to do for some time. At midday, our hostess gave us some bread and hot milk, and then our host took us along the side of the mountain to a point where we saw the bridge and he gave us our final directions. He bade us goodbye, and I could see that it was an emotional occasion for him — a man of great sincerity and simple strength.

Bill and I moved slowly down and took cover behind a mound alongside the road, a couple of hundred yards from the bridge. I noticed that if people came across singly or in pairs, the sentry seldom stopped them, but if they were in larger groups, he usually stopped them and examined one or two. Bill was beginning to have doubts about the whole plan and suggested that we go back to our hosts of the last night. I reasoned quietly, but firmly, assuring him that there was as much danger in going back now as going on. He still seemed to have his doubts, and so I decided that rather than leaving him to go on brooding, we should move quickly. There was a gap in the people passing below, so I took him by the arm and said: 'Quickly, here's our chance', and he came. I sent him first, saying I would follow about 50 yards after — feeling that if I went first he might turn back. Our luck was in — it worked. We had decided that we wouldn't even look at the sentry, but just walk quietly and non-chalently past. The sentry on the other side was not concerned — we had been told that the only danger was on the entry side.

We went straight to our rendezvous — about an hour's walk — and, as planned, met up with our host's brother and his daughter who had accompanied him on his walk from the village below. We were taken indoors and introduced to a man (who was to be our guide across the mountains) and his wife. We had left the Italian *partisani* and were now in the hands of the French *maquis*.

Our friend, who was the author of that day's successful plan, having assured us that we were in trusted and competent hands, took leave of us, because he had to be home before dark, and his lame leg slowed his movements. His daughter — a fine-looking girl, obviously of courageous character, like her father and uncle — gave me a butterfly brooch which she was wearing on her coat, as a 'Talisman' of good luck for a successful completion of our journey. It was a simple but valued present — something which I have kept and treasured ever since.

The following afternoon, two of the other three arrived safely (the Austrian and the Frenchman) and we had a warm reunion. The young Polish lad didn't make it — at the bridge with the German sentries, his nerve had cracked, and he had decided to go back. We set off mid-morning on the following day for the final lap — we didn't start earlier because the latter part of the climb was out of the forest and up the open side of the mountain, which we couldn't attempt until after dark — it was necessary to cross above the snow line, in order to avoid German camps and patrols.

It was a warm, sunny day, and the walking was pleasant. We reached the end of the forest about 4.00pm and stopped for our meal of wine and bread which we had carried. Just before dark we started to move, as our guide assured us that we were obscured from the German observation posts for the first few kilometres. The climb became progressively steeper, and once we reached the snow line it became much more difficult, although with the snow background we could see surprisingly well. The cold was beginning to bite, because, apart from our guide, we were all clad in light summer clothes. Up the more difficult places we had to help one another, and often we slipped back on the ice. Bill was having more trouble than the rest of us, and when I went back to help him after one of his slides, he said he was too tired and cold and the climb ahead looked so formidable that he wanted to go back — he seemed to think he could find his way down alright. I made it clear in no uncertain way that that was not on, and I put my shoulder behind him and told him to get moving.

We reached the top shortly after midnight, and our guide informed us that we were to wait until dawn, because it was too dangerous to descend in the dark. But our problems were far from over, for the worst was still before us. Sitting for eight hours on a block of ice, on top of the Alps, clad in summer clothes, is an experience which I would not prescribe even for my worst enemy.

The descent was not as difficult as we had thought, and after a few hours' walking we came across an American patrol. We were taken to their canteen for a hot meal, and thence transported to a base camp on the coast. That night we spent in a luxurious hotel in Cannes, and celebrated with a magnificent feast of food and wine.

The next day we parted company. I requested to be sent to London, as it was my wish to be posted to the Western Front, but officialdom decreed that as I had been operating from the Mediterranean area when I was shot down, I was to report back to Naples.

I eventually did arrive in London, and then on to 125 Wing in Germany — but that's another story.